Imperfect Garden

THE LEGACY OF HUMANISM

Imperfect Garden

THE LEGACY OF HUMANISM

by

Tzvetan Todorov

Translated by Carol Cosman

PRINCETON UNIVERSITY PRESS
PRINCETON AND OXFORD

Copyright © 2002 by Princeton University Press

Published by Princeton University Press, 41 William Street, Princeton, New Jersey 08540

In the United Kingdom: Princeton University Press, 3 Market Place, Woodstock, Oxfordshire OX20 1SY

Library of Congress Cataloging-in-Publication Data

Todorov, Tzvetan, 1939–
    [Jardin imparfait. English]
    Imperfect garden : the legacy of humanism / by Tzvetan Todorov ; translated
by Carol Cosman.
        p. cm.
    Includes bibliographical references and index.
    ISBN 0-691-01047-1
    1. Humanism — France — History.   2. Individualism — France — History.   3. Social
values — France — History.   4. Philosophy, French.   I. Title.

B778 .T5613 2002
144'.0944 — dc21   2001036868

British Library Cataloging-in-Publication Data is available

This work was published in conjunction with the French Ministry of Culture — National Center of Books.

This book has been composed in Sabon with Centaur Display

Printed on acid-free paper. ∞

www.pup.princeton.edu

Printed in the United States of America

10 9 8 7 6 5 4 3 2 1

To my philosopher friends, Luc and André

Contents

Prologue
The Hidden Pact 1

Chapter 1
The Interplay of Four Families 9

Chapter 2
The Declaration of Autonomy 47

Chapter 3
Interdependence 80

Chapter 4
Living Alone 94

Chapter 5
The Ways of Love 115

Chapter 6
The Individual:
Plurality and Universality 139

Chapter 7
The Choice of Values 160

Chapter 8
A Morality Made for Humanity 178

Chapter 9
The Need for Enthusiasm 207

Epilogue
The Humanist Wager 226

Bibliography 239

Index 247

Imperfect & Garden

THE LEGACY OF HUMANISM

Prologue

The Hidden Pact

Satan proposed the first pact to Jesus. After forcing him to fast forty days in the desert, he gave him a momentary vision of all the kingdoms on earth. Then he told him: All this is in my power. Yet I am prepared to grant it to you. I ask only one small gesture in return: that you recognize me as your master; if you do this, all is yours. But Jesus replied, I do not want this power, for I wish only to serve God, and his kingdom is not of this world. Jesus thus rejected the pact. His successors, however, accepted it after a while. And from Constantine to Louis XVI, for more than fourteen centuries, they strove to reign over the devil's kingdoms. Somewhat later, a Russian seer claimed that if Jesus returned to earth one day, he would be roundly reproached by the Grand Inquisitor for his rejection: Men are weak, the Inquisitor would have said, faith in God is not enough, God's law is worth more.

The second pact was proposed in the fifteenth century by an emissary of the devil, Mephistopheles, to a proud and ambitious man, a magician, necromancer, and conjuror called Johann (or perhaps Georg) Faust, who had attempted to penetrate the secrets of life and death. Since you are so curious, the devil's emissary said to him, I propose a bargain: You will have access to all knowledge of the world, no mystery will resist you; and you are surely aware that knowledge leads to power. In return, I am not asking you to make a grand declaration of submission: I require only one thing, a little odd, it's true: at the end of twenty-four years (but that is a long time! you might not live to be so old), you will belong entirely to me, body and soul. Unlike Jesus, Faust accepted the terms of the contract. He therefore enjoyed infinite knowledge and garnered unanimous acclaim. But it is said that during the last years of the pact he became disgruntled, lost his interest in secrets, and never left his house; he prayed that the devil would forget him. But the devil does not forget, and the day the contract expired he carried the horrified Faust away, wailing in vain.

The third pact dates from nearly the same era as Faust's, but it has one peculiar feature: its very existence was not revealed at the moment it went into effect. The devil's ruse this time consisted of keeping the other party to the contract, Modern Man, as humanity was then called, in the dark, allowing him to believe that he was gaining new advantages thanks to his own efforts, and that there would be no price to pay. This time, what the devil was offering was not power or knowledge but will. Modern Man would have the possibility of willing freely, of acquiring mastery of his own will and living his life as he wished. The devil hid the price of freedom so that man should develop a taste for it and have no desire to renounce it at a later date — then find himself obliged to clear his debt.

Modern Man — Renaissance Man, Enlightenment Man — took some time to realize the full extent of his possibilities. Some of his representatives asked only for the freedom to organize their affective life to their own taste. They would have the right to choose a life with the people they cared for rather than following the laws of blood or those of the city, or their parents' attachments. They might also freely choose their place of residence: let will and not chance decide the framework of their lives! Later, other representatives of Modern Man found the pleasure of freedom too sweet to be confined to only personal life. They demanded that reason should be liberated too: that it should no longer be obliged to recognize the authority of tradition transmitted by the memory of men. Tradition could continue to rule in civic matters or in dealings with God, but reason should be free to note the true and the false. Thereafter, the only knowledge declared to be certain was knowledge that had been reached by the natural lights of reason. Thus a purely human science was born, quite unlike the omniscience of Doctor Faust.

Having tasted these two freedoms — the freedom to submit exclusively to his own affections, to his own reason — Modern Man was tempted by a new extension of his will. He had yet to assume the vast domain of his public actions. Only an action performed in freedom, on the strength of his will (this is what he would later call his responsibility), was now declared moral; only the political regime chosen by the will of its subjects — now called "democracy" — was judged legitimate. No domain now escaped the intervention of the will, which could enjoy its freedom in every circumstance. During this time — a good two centuries — the devil did not reveal that one day he would demand his due.

In the course of these two centuries, the conquest of freedom was the business of studious thinkers who confined their arguments to the pages of their books. A change took place in the second half of the eighteenth century, when a few men of action, discontented with the state of the world around them, perused the ideas hidden in these books and decided to let them out. They admired the beautiful new principles discovered by their elders and wanted to live in harmony with them rather than subject them to intellectual reflection. The American Revolution and the French Revolution were accompanied not only (in the first case) by a Declaration of Independence, but also by a Declaration of Autonomy never publicly announced, of adherence to the principle according to which no authority is superior to the will of men: the will of the people, the will of individuals.

Now the devil, judging that Modern Man had swallowed the bait, chose this moment to reveal the pact and announce that it was time to start paying for his past bounty. Even before the end of the eighteenth century, and of course repeatedly since, he has continued to present his bill. He did not wish, however, to appear in person but preferred to inspire several dark prophets, whom he charged with revealing to people the total sum of their debt. If you want to keep your liberty, these prophets said to their contemporaries, you will have to pay a triple price, first by separating yourself from your God, then from your neighbor, and finally from yourself.

No more God: You will have no reason to believe that a being exists above you, an entity whose value would be superior to your own life; you will have no more ideals or values — you will be a "materialist." No more neighbor: other men, beside and no longer above you, will continue to exist but they will no longer matter to you. Your circle will shrink: first to your acquaintances, then to your immediate family, and finally to your self; you will be an "individualist." You will then try to cling to your self, but this too will be threatened by dislocation. You will be swept by currents beyond your control; you will believe you are deciding, choosing, and willing freely, when in truth these subterranean forces will do it for you, and you will lose the advantages that had seemed to justify all those sacrifices. This self will be nothing but an anomalous collection of impulses, an infinite dispersal; you will be an alienated, inauthentic being, no longer deserving to be called a "subject."

When modern men (gradually joined by modern women) understood from these dark prophets the announcement of the pact to which they were party, they were divided. They could not agree on how to respond to what seemed to them at times a warning, at times a threat, and at times a curse. After the revelation of the contract, those who aired their opinions in public — scholars, writers, politicians, or philosophers — grouped together into several large families, according to the responses they wanted to make to this pact. These intellectual families still exist in our time, even if overlappings, defections, and adaptions have somewhat muddied the picture.

The first family, the easiest to identify, unites those who think that the devil is right: that the price of freedom truly includes God, society, and the self, that the price is too high and therefore it is better to renounce freedom. More precisely, the members of this family do not advocate a pure and simple return to the old society, because they see quite well that the world around them has changed and that such a return would imply the same exercise of freedom and will that they otherwise condemn. But they regret the previous state of things and try to preserve vestiges of it while opposing the demands of a more radical modernity. This is the family of conservatives: those who would like to live in the new world while appealing to the values of the old.

The other families, reduced here to three, are united in accepting and welcoming the advent of modernity, and for this reason they have sometimes been confused with one another. However, their differences are no less crucial, and their reactions to the devil's challenges have nothing in common. These modern families are the humanists, the individualists, and the proponents of scientism (not necessarily those who practice science).

When the "scientists" hear the claims of the devil, they dismiss them without batting an eye. Don't worry, they reply, there will be no price to pay because there never was any freedom. Or rather, the only freedom is that of knowledge. Thanks to human capacities of observation and reasoning, therefore thanks to purely human science, it is possible to penetrate all the secrets of nature and history. Now, whoever has knowledge has power, as Faust already discovered. Science leads to technology; if we master the laws of the existing world, we can also transform it. As for choosing, and apart from choosing to know, one's freedom is very limited: men are unwittingly led by biological and historical laws, and what they take for their freedom is, more often than not, only their ignorance. Even the values they claim inspire their actions essentially flow from these ineluctable laws of the world. If God, society, and the self participate in human identity, nothing will extract them from it; if they do not, there will be nothing to regret. In either case, the devil will turn away with his hands empty.

The reaction of the individualists, members of the second, resolutely modern family, is quite different. It consists of saying: You believe that our freedom entails the loss of God, society, and the self? But for us this is not a loss, it is a further liberation. Your description of our state is correct, but rather than chilling us (or worse, making us wish to turn back), we shall try to push it even further. Let man affirm himself in his essential solitude, in his freedom from all moral constraint, in his unlimited dispersal! Let him affirm his will to power, let him serve his own interests: the greatest good will emerge for him, and that is all that matters. Instead of mourning we should shout for joy. What you describe as a sickness (or as the painful counterpart of a hidden pact) is in reality the beginning of a celebration.

For scientistic thinkers, there is no price to pay for freedom, for there is no freedom in the usual sense but only a new mastery of nature and history based on knowledge. For the individualists, there is no price to pay because what we have lost merits no regrets, and we shall carry on very well without common values, without encumbering social ties, without a stable and coherent self. The humanists, the last large family, think, on the contrary, that freedom exists and that it is precious, but at the same time they appreciate the benefit of shared values, life with others, and a self that is held responsible for its actions; they want to continue to enjoy freedom, then, without having to pay the price. The humanists take the devil's threats seriously, but they do not concede that a pact was ever concluded, and they throw down a challenge to him in return.

In our part of the world, we are still living today under the sway of the devil's threats. We cherish our freedom but we are afraid of living in a world without ideals or common values, a mass society populated by solitary individuals unfamiliar with love; we secretly — though not always knowingly — dread the loss of our identity. These fears and questionings persist. To come to terms with them, I have chosen to turn to the history of thought. Remembering the dwarf perched on the shoulders of giants, I wanted to defend myself against these threats by calling to my aid the thought of writers from that rather distant period when the unknown pact was concluded; to tell in some fashion the story of the invention of modernity, with its main characters — their adventures, conflicts, and alliances. I believe, moreover, that one of the modern intellectual families, the humanists, might be more helpful than the others in thinking about our present condition and overcoming its difficulties. And so this book is devoted to them.

The term *humanist* has several meanings, but we can say in a first approximation that it refers to the doctrines according to which man is the point of departure and the point of reference for human actions. These are "anthropocentric" doctrines, just as others are theocentric, and still others put nature or tradition in this central place. The term *humanist* figures, perhaps for the first time in French, in a passage by Montaigne in which he uses it to characterize his own practice, in contrast to that of the theologians. Though he grants the theologians their right to respect, and certainly to existence, he prefers to separate the two domains and reserve a new field for the "humanists," which consists of strictly human activities or "fantasies," of "purely human" writings, those concerning subjects that are "matters of opinion, not matters of faith," treated in "a lay not clerical manner" (*Essays*, I, 56, 234).*
The specificity of human affairs (in contrast to those that relate to God) is therefore the point of departure for humanist doctrine, even if it is not confined to that; its other ingredients will emerge in the course of the present investigation. This initial choice does not mean, as we shall also see, that man is granted unconditional esteem: Montaigne himself never forgets that human life is meant to remain an "unfinished" or "imperfect" garden (I, 20, 62).

To conduct this investigation to advantage, I have imposed limits on myself in time and space. I deal exclusively with humanists in the French tradition (an arbitrary limitation but a necessary one). Furthermore, the texts I have read do not belong to the contemporary period. The thought of the authors who founded the doctrine has not been radically revised in the course of 150 years; moreover, it seems to me richer and subtler than the "humanist" vulgate, which can be glimpsed in the common discourse of our day. Humanism is the ideology under-

---

* Wherever possible, material quoted from other sources is from the standard English translations of the works, which are listed in the bibliography. All other quotations are by the translator of the present volume.

pinning modern democratic states; but this very omnipresence makes it invisible or insipid. Because of this, although everyone today is more or less a "humanist," the doctrine in its original form can still surprise and enlighten us. It seems to me that these classic authors had in a sense given a rejoinder to the "dark prophets" even before the prophecy had been formulated, while not limiting themselves, of course, to this response alone.

The humanist thought that I examine flourished during three strong periods: the Renaissance, the century of the Enlightenment, and the aftermath of the Revolution. Three authors embody these periods: Montaigne, who produced the first coherent version of the doctrine; Rousseau, in whom it reached its full flowering; and Benjamin Constant, who understood how to think about the new world that emerged from the revolutionary upheaval. I will turn to them to seek tools for thought that can serve us again today.

This book, in its way, participates in the history of thought. I say specifically thought and not philosophy, since its field is wider, closer to practice, and less technical than the other. The intellectual families that I identify are "ideological" rather than philosophical: each of them is an aggregate of political and moral ideas, of anthropological and psychological hypotheses, that participate in philosophy but are not limited to it. By choosing to study thought in itself, I am already committing myself to the humanist family, since thought would not deserve to be examined separately if it were not free but only the mechanical product of a cultural community, a social class, a historical moment, or the biological necessities of the species.

Yet I must specify that what chiefly interests me is not to reconstruct the thought of Montaigne, Rousseau, Constant, and several others yet again; but while trying to read these authors attentively, to use them to build a model of humanist thought that is sometimes called an "ideal type." My object of knowledge is not "the Renaissance" or "the Enlightenment" or "Romanticism," but modern thought in its diversity, with humanism at its center, as it has manifested itself in each of these epochs. In other words, my project is typological rather than historical, even if I am convinced that the only useful typologies are those that help us to know history. For the same reason, I have renounced at the outset any concern with an exhaustive approach and opt most of the time not for the first formulation of a thought but rather for what I judge to be the most powerful or eloquent.

These qualifications are even more necessary since the establishment of humanist doctrine is not — or not always — part of the conscious project of these authors. It is by meditating on various subjects, sometimes quite far removed from mine, such as the self or the world, the spirit of the law or political principles, that they establish as though in passing the tenets and nuances of this new thought. They imply humanism more than they state it outright. I am therefore led to divert their arguments from their original goal while trying not to betray them.

The use to which I mean to put these authors of the past is responsible for the way I read them — a dialogue with history rather than a history in the strict sense. I aspire to understand their thought and to convey its meaning more than to explain it by tracing its causes or reconstituting its original context. This desire to go downstream rather than upstream, and to stay in the realm of ideas, does not imply that I would consider the opposite choice illegitimate; it is simply not part of my present project.

Is there something anachronistic about bringing texts of the past to bear on a present discussion? Perhaps in this case it is a "paradox of the critic," indeed of any historian just beginning his or her activity, since this critic, this historian, is always addressing his contemporaries and not those of his author. The commentators' habitual squinting condemns them to tack continually from one dialogue to the other, from author to reader; the balance they attempt is a gamble. Moreover, the thinkers of the past aimed both at their contemporaries, with whom they shared the same historical context, and at future readers, representatives of humanity as a whole; they addressed themselves both to the present and to eternity. So at the risk of displeasing pure historians as well as pure ideologues, I persist in believing that the past can help us to think about the present.

By relying in this way on the history of thought in order to advance my own reflections, I am pursuing (and perhaps, personally, completing) an inquiry begun in 1979 that led to my publication, in 1989, of *On Human Diversity*, a work in which other humanist themes were already evoked, notably that of universality; these two books are therefore, in certain respects, complementary.

Chapter 1

The Interplay of Four Families

$\mathcal{A}$ revolution took place in the mind of Europeans — a slow revolution, since it took several centuries — which led to the establishment of the modern world. To grasp it in its most general sense, we can describe it as the passage from a world whose structure and laws were preexisting and immutable givens for every member of society, to a world that could discover its own nature and define its norms itself. The members of the old society gradually learned their assigned place in the universe, and wisdom led them to accept it. The inhabitant of contemporary society does not reject everything passed down by tradition but wants to know the world on her own, and demands that whole swathes of existence should be governed by the principles she chooses. The elements of her life are no longer all *givens* in advance; some of them are *chosen*.

Before this revolution, an act was declared just and praiseworthy because it conformed either to nature (that of the universe as well as that of man) or to divine will. These two justifications can sometimes conflict and sometimes be reconciled (this is sometimes described as the rivalry between Athens and Jerusalem); but both require that human beings should submit to an authority external to them: nature, like God, is not accessible except through common wisdom or religion — a tradition accepted and transmitted by society without one's consent. The universe one inhabits, including its human laws, is based on an elsewhere upon which this particular person has no purchase. It was revolutionary to claim that the best justification of an act, one that makes it most legitimate, issues from man himself: from his will, from his reason, from his feelings. The center of gravity shifts, here, from cosmos to

9

anthropos, from the objective world to the subjective will; the human being no longer bows to an order that is external to him but wishes to establish this order himself. The movement is therefore double: a disenchantment of the world and a sacralization of man; values, removed from one, will be entrusted to the other. The new principle, whose consequences may still affect us, is responsible for the present face of our politics and our law, our arts and our sciences. This principle also presides over the modern nation-states, and if we accept them, we cannot deny the principle without becoming incoherent. On the other hand, we can do so in the name of a return to the supremacy of religion (as in theocratic fundamentalism) or to the primacy of a natural order that reserves no special place for man (as in certain ecological utopias).

Today we readily agree to describe this passage from the Ancients to the Moderns, which began in the Renaissance, in more or less similar terms. Consensus disappears, however, the moment we begin to analyze its effects. My working thesis is as follows: Modernity itself is not homogeneous; the criticism to which it has been subjected has revealed several tendencies within it that constitute the framework of social thought in which we are living today. For this reason, I find it disconcerting to use a single word to designate these reactions, such as *modernity*, or *individualism*, or *liberalism*, or *rationality*, or *subjectivity*, or "*Western*," especially since the amalgam imposed by such terms is often used to polemical purpose. I call each of these major tendencies a *family*, both because the various representatives of one family each have their own peculiarities, and because alliances between members of distinct families are always possible. These families are four in number, and they were clearly outlined by the second half of the eighteenth century. Condorcet, Sade, Constant, and Bonald were all born in the middle of the century, between 1740 and 1767; and they embody these four distinct families, which appear quite distinctly in the aftermath of the Revolution, when those who reject it begin to challenge the mode of thought that made it possible. This does not mean, of course, that our families do not have their roots in a much earlier tradition.

It is always awkward to regroup the thought of individual authors under generic labels. No one likes words ending in *ism*, and for good reason: every regrouping has something violent and arbitrary about it (I myself hesitated until the last moment to decide whether it was fairer to speak of three, four, or five major modern families); someone can always challenge you with intermediate or hybrid cases. Every authentic thinker has his or her individuality, and it is a simplification to amalgamate them with others; every work itself is unique and deserves to be considered separately. Only disciples and epigones properly correspond to labels; the original thinkers always participate in more than one intellectual family — witness Montaigne or Rousseau. I am not unaware of the disadvantages of this procedure. I have decided, however, to use it because I also see its advantages. First, we must have at hand a common language in order to speak of the past (proper names are not enough); then, my acquaintance with the texts has convinced me, although it is impossible for me to prove it, that certain affinities, certain differences are more important than others and therefore justify this or that regrouping. Finally, the amalgam of distinct families seems to me to be one of the chief obstacles to the lucid analysis of our current situation. That is why I would now like to evoke them in greater detail.

To begin with, we must recall the principal reproaches addressed to modernity as a whole; these will allow us, paradoxically, to identify the first modern family.

The Conservatives

In the wake of the French Revolution, voices were clearly heard condemning the earlier revolution, the revolution in thought. Its partisans had, of course, been challenged before; but this purely ideological debate remained limited to a particular author or an isolated theme. Once ideas were transformed into actions and institutions, they provoked a reaction of much greater intensity and unremitting resistance. Yes, the opposition maintained, it is possible to see individuals, like collectivities, as self-governing, but this freedom is too dangerous and its benefits insufficient to compensate for the havoc they wreak. It would be preferable to return to the earlier situation, with less freedom but without the new disadvantages.

We might say, then, that whatever the nuances in their different formulations, the advocates of this general argument always proceed from a position of *conservation*. At the same time, this position does not lead us back to the world of the Ancients, pure and simple: this return has become impossible in reality, and only the most extreme reactionaries reject the modern world as a whole. The usual conservatives also constitute a modern family, one that accepts a minimum of modernity, one for whom all the other modern families tend to merge and to deserve equal condemnation. The conservatives are those who think that modern men have sold their souls to the devil, and that they ought to regret it, indeed that they should attempt to buy it back. But this critique is not the way they define themselves. Their positive stance is to value and seek to preserve the existing order against revolutionaries and reformers on all sides — against reactionaries as well as progressives (the project of a "conservative revolution" is to them a contradiction in terms). What already exists deserves to exist; changes have, on the whole, more drawbacks than advantages. The conservatives privilege if not immobility, at least gradualism.

In finding a spokesman for this family, we have an abundance of choices, since conservative warnings have never ceased, from the Revolution until our day. To illustrate its variety, I have decided to keep two of its representatives from among the earliest, chosen by design for being as different from one another as possible. One is a theocrat, the other a democrat; yet the substance of their reproaches is very much the same.

The first is Viscount Louis de Bonald, declared enemy of the Revolution, who attacked it, beginning in 1796, in his treatise *Théorie du pouvoir politique et religieux*, and who would develop his criticisms over the next three or four decades.

Bonald begins with what he considers a disastrous effect — revolutionary reality in France — and works his way back to its causes, which he finds in philosophy (Revolution, he assures us, is the freakish child of Philosophy and Atheism), the philosophy of Descartes and Rousseau, itself heir to the Reformation.

Where did the Revolution come from? "From that doctrine which substituted the reason of each for the religion of all, and the calculations of personal interest for the love of the Supreme Being and his fellow men" (*Théorie*, I, 494–95). Thought bears a heavy responsibility: before manifesting itself in action, freedom was in men's minds. It acted like a corrosive agent in two directions, which Bonald always associates: love of God and love of men, elevation above the self and attachment beyond the self; "religion," it is readily said, comes from the verb *relier* (to bind, to tie). "Each" is substituted for "all": this is the fault of Luther and Calvin, followed on this point by the Savoyard Vicar, who claims that the conscience of the individual can be the ultimate judge of good and evil. And reason has replaced religion: the guilty party here is

Descartes, at least as far as knowledge of the world is concerned. Consequently, we have come under the rule of personal interest, meaning what does not go beyond the individual (he is alone) and also what serves him (he is selfish). In short, modern man, contrived by Calvin, Descartes, and Rousseau, and put into the world by the Revolution, knows nothing external to himself. Neither above himself (a superior being), nor beyond himself (his fellow men), he is condemned to remain shut inside himself.

The price of freedom is therefore double. On the one hand, modern man is destined to become an "individualist," in the current sense of the term: to be preoccupied only with himself, to ignore the ties that bind him to other men. It was the philosophers of the social contract, above all Rousseau, who believed that this transformation was necessary; it was the revolutionaries who wanted to impose it. "The philosophy of the last century [that is, the eighteenth century] saw only man and the universe, and never society. On the one hand, it has — if I may use this familiar expression — *made mincemeat* of states and families, in which it saw neither fathers nor mothers nor children, nor masters nor servants, nor powers, nor ministers, nor subjects, but only men, that is to say *individuals*, each with their rights, and not *persons* bound together by relationships. . . . On the other, it has proposed to our affections only the human race" (*Mélanges*, II, 246–47). Such an extension makes any real attachment impossible. The very idea of a contract, the attempt to base everything on the will of consenting individuals, brings with it an "individualistic" conception of humanity, which is deeply disconcerting: "The author of *The Social Contract* saw only the individual in society" (*Législation primitive*, I, 123).

On the other hand, this same modern man is condemned to be nothing but a "materialist," in the still common sense of the word, that is, a being who has no ideals, who cherishes no value above his personal interest, who can have no moral code. For the only possible basis of morality is religion, the faith in a power infinitely superior to that of men and capable of sanctioning their acts in this world below. "*If God does not exist*," writes Bonald, "men can legitimate nothing for each other, and all *duty* ceases between beings, where the *power* over all beings ceases" (Rousseau, *Legislation Primitive*, II, 142). If God is dead, then all is permitted: this highly problematic linkage, made familiar to us by Dostoevsky, is already present in Bonald.

Faced by what he judges to be the individualism of all modern families, the conservative privileges the social: individual human beings acquire their identity only through the groups, institutions, and customs in which they participate. That is why their duties (which flow from their membership in these larger bodies) prevail over their rights as simple individuals, members of the human race. Man is made by his community; he owes it his allegiance.

This demand for submission to the collectivity has the potential to conflict with the universal appeal of religion. Modern conservatives evade this conflict by making a clean separation between politics and morality. Moral conservatism affirms absolute values based on the will of God or on the natural order (among conservatives the connection with religion is frequent but optional). Yet this moral order does not determine the political order, as in the case of theocracies (and as Bonald recommends; in this respect he is more revolutionary than conservative). The political order is dictated by national interest, and it can differ from one country to the next, even if the two share an affiliation with the same religion. Within the country, conservatism does not seek to submit everything to a single principle, nor to control the individual's whole life; it is satisfied with assuring the rule of law: it is not absolutism, and even less totalitarianism. In the international sphere, political conservatism values above all the defense of the status quo; it is not animated by a proselytizing spirit nor does it engage in crusades, any more than it spearheads imperialistic wars or seeks to impose its values everywhere (the French conservatives of the nineteenth century were opposed to the colonial wars). We might say that for a conservative like Joseph de Maistre, man does not exist, only members of various societies: the French, the Germans, the Russians; on the other hand, God exists (in the singular), and not as a so-called plurality, to say nothing of a war of the gods. This very separation is bound up with the opposition between morality and politics.

From either perspective, the individual must submit to common values, to the group to which he belongs. Man is radically bad and weak: Bonald is in agreement here with the Augustinian tradition, hence with the Jansenists, but also with Luther and Calvin, whom he denounces. Other conservative Christians, even if they do not share such a dark vision of humanity, nonetheless believe in original sin. Consequently, only a force greater than man's can constrain him to behave virtuously. Rather than futile revolt, our goal should be to place ourselves in harmony with the higher order. This is why the very idea of choice is prohibited: one might run the risk of choosing in the name of one's personal interest, whereas if something happens that we haven't willed, this is the sign that it has been decided by God. Anyone who would like to arrange his fate by putting himself in God's place is imitating Satan. Obedience, not autonomy, is the cardinal virtue.

Attempts to base a morality outside of religion are doomed to failure (Bonald has only contempt for the doctrine of the rights of man, which he hopes to see replaced by a defense of the rights of God). How could men, who are wicked, find the strength in themselves to repress this wickedness? "Atheism places the supreme power over men in the very men it must contain, and dreams that a dike will be the child of a flood" (I, 61). What madness! In all logic, Bonald thinks that men will become good only through constraint; for their own good, liberty must be eliminated rather than cultivated. He dreams, therefore, of a theocratic state whose final ends are defined by the Church, which retains ultimate power.

Yet, even a mind as extreme as Bonald's does not truly belong to the Ancients. Witness his taste for rational constructions, for comprehensive plans for the future and authentic theocracy—a thousand times removed from the actual society of the Old Regime, which was an accumulation of heteroclite traditions and customs. One cannot imagine Edmund Burke, the exemplary conservative, writing a work whose title begins *Theory of the* . . . This incompatibility is so strong that one even hesitates to consider Bonald a conservative—he is, in some respects, a "philosophe" lost among the reactionaries. If conservatives so cherish traditions, it is because they consider them the repository of collective wisdom, unarguably superior to individual reason; indeed, this is why the autonomy of the individual, the freedom he has acquired in league with the devil, must be prohibited. Men are not only morally imperfect, they are intellectually weak; traditions, on the other hand, contain a wisdom that individuals cannot explain but ought to respect. Contrary to what the rationalists believe, it is judgment that errs and prejudice that is wise, because it is shared. The old have experience, the young have only reason: the advantage goes to the first. An intuitive knowledge is accumulated in the bosom of traditions over the course of years, which no reason will ever be able to reduce to principles and rules. That is indeed why real conservatives, unlike Bonald, do not write systematic treatises but content themselves with commenting on current events or recounting their experience.

Bonald *chose* to be conservative—and for that very reason he was not entirely conservative after all. His thought is, as a result, particularly anachronistic, and though he remained an influential politician under the Restoration, his conservative utopia would never see the light of day. That is why his prophecies readily take on the tone of curses: if the world does not want to set itself on the right course, let it beware of what awaits it! On the other hand, future conservatives would find in his writings, as in those of his contemporary Joseph de Maistre, a source of continual inspiration.

The Broken Chain

The second author I would like to evoke here, Alexis de Tocqueville, flourished after the July Revolution of 1830. To illustrate conservative thought, I have not chosen a man who is known for his stubborn commitment to liberty and his defense, however thwarted, of democracy simply out of a taste for paradox or provocation. I wanted to show that philosophical and political positions far removed from each other can adopt visions of the modern world that are, in the end, quite similar. Tocqueville is, more precisely, both a conservative and a humanist; and his singular position resides in this paradoxical conjunction.

His point of departure is entirely different from Bonald's. First, he does not believe in the possibility of turning back. Viewing things from a historical perspective, he asserts that the advent of modernity is irreversible, that the French have left the aristocratic age behind and have entered the democratic age. The inhabitants of this new age are animated, in his view, by three passions. The first is the passion for liberty, the right to decide one's fate; unlike Bonald, Tocqueville himself cherishes this passion above all things. This cannot be explained according to him, because of a higher goal that might thus be achieved, but finds its justification in the intransitive pleasure experienced by its practitioner. "It is the pleasure of being able to speak, act, and breathe without constraint, under the government of God and the laws alone. Whoever seeks for anything from freedom is made for slavery" (*The Old Regime and the Revolution*, III, 3, p. 217). The object of the second passion is equality, and Tocqueville's judgment of this subject is much more mixed. Finally, the third is the passion for well-being, for which he feels no particular admiration.

What Tocqueville dreads, then, is not what terrified Bonald. Bonald regretted the erosion of authority, the only means of instituting the general welfare; Tocqueville fears for the future of liberty. The source of the threat, however, is the same: it is the modern society born of the Revolution. And the idea of a hidden pact, of the price to be paid for what has been gained, is there too. Modern man will have to pay for his choice of equality and well-being by accepting the taints of individualism and materialism.

Tocqueville must be one of the first authors to use this new word, *individualism*, to designate, he says, something equally new belonging to democratic societies, namely, the preference for private life led in the bosom of one's family and friends, and a lack of interest in the global society in which one lives. "Our ancestors lacked the word 'individualism,' which we have created for our own use, because in their era there were, in fact, no individuals who did not belong to a group and who could regard themselves absolutely alone" (II, 9, pp. 162–63). The chief reason for this evolution is not, according to him, free will but the principle of equality. Traditional society, which depends on a hierarchy, makes relations between people necessary. "Aristocracy had made a chain of all the members of the community, from the peasant to the king" (*Democracy in America*, II, 2, 2, p. 99). Modern or democratic society gives everyone the same status; as a result, its inhabitants no longer have need of one another to constitute their identity. "Democracy breaks that chain and severs every link of it": we are not far here from the "mincemeat" society dreaded by Bonald. Individuals no longer really live together. "Each of them, living apart, is as a stranger to the fate of all the rest . . . , he exists only in himself and for himself alone" (II, 4, 6, p. 318). This absence of specifically social relations is only partially compensated for by a more intense private life, on the one hand, and by a certain feeling of belonging to universal humanity on the other ("every individual's duties to the species are much clearer": in this, too, Tocqueville follows Bonald).

The tendency to desocialization, Tocqueville suggests, may be further reinforced. No longer counting on a place designated by society and confirmed by several generations of ancestors, the individual begins as self-contained and is accustomed to thinking of himself as isolated. After reducing society exclusively to his close relations, he no longer even thinks of them; democracy "throws him back forever upon himself alone and threatens in the end to confine him entirely within the solitude of his own heart" (II, 2, 2, p. 99). At first attacking public life alone, the individualist spirit ends by corrupting social life as a whole.

The other great threat that weighs on democratic society comes from the fact that men become obsessed with thinking about the satisfaction of their material interests. For this very reason, they discard spiritual values. "While man takes delight in this honest and lawful pursuit of his own well-being," Tocqueville writes, "it is to be apprehended that in the end he may lose the use of his sublimest faculties, and that while he is busied in improving all around him, he may at length degrade himself" (II, 2, 15, p. 145). This fear is more than a hypothesis: observing American mores, Tocqueville sees the powerful love of wealth everywhere, since the rich now occupy the summit of the hierarchy, reserved in aristocratic societies for men of honor. "Democracy encourages a taste for physical gratification," he explains. "This taste, if it becomes excessive, soon disposes men to believe that all is matter only; and materialism, in its turn, hurries them on with a mad impatience to these same delights" (II, 2, 15, p. 145). Materialism is the natural bent of men in democracy.

It is at this point that Tocqueville once again diverges from Bonald: it is to protect liberty and not to annul it that he warns us of the dangers concealed by the other features of life in democracy. For he has discovered that specifically democratic conditions of life can empty the freedoms so laboriously acquired of their contents. Modern man, launched on the search for material satisfactions, requires the state to guarantee his security, his property, his well-being (he turns it into what we call a welfare state). But by always demanding more of the state, he continues to shrink the domain of actions for which he is himself responsible. "Thus it everyday renders the exercise of the free agency of man less useful and less frequent; it circumscribes the will within a narrower range and gradually robs a man of all the uses of himself" (II, 4, 6, pp. 318–19).

The outcome of this process is a democratic (or egalitarian) despotism that is highly adapted to the restriction of our interests to private life alone: "Despotism, rather than struggling against this tendency, makes it irresistible, because it takes away from citizens all common feeling, all common needs, all need for communication, all occasion for common action. It walls them up inside their private lives" (*The Old Regime and the Revolution*, preface, p. 87). Power is, of course, the expression of popular will rather than the legacy of tradition; but this power is at the same time out of reach for the isolated individual. He votes, to be sure, and can therefore repudiate his rulers; but immediately after elections, he is again delivered up to them, bound hand and foot, so that "This rare and brief exercise of their free choice, however important it may be, will not prevent them from gradually losing the faculties of thinking, feeling and acting for themselves, and thus gradually falling below the level of humanity" (*Democracy in America*, II, 4, 6, pp. 320–21).

The use of liberty, for Tocqueville, is therefore a distinctive feature not only of modern society, but even of the human race; yet democracy, appealed to as it is, can annul its own effects. (Is it really so easy to fall back again into being an animal like other animals? Tocqueville is no stranger to a certain amount of catastrophizing.) And it is not just political freedom that is in question: in an even more insidious way, democratic society also annuls the freedom of taste and feeling by augmenting the uniformity of individuals and their inclination to conform, already stigmatized by Rousseau. Modern man is constantly changing his taste; but these changes are similar for everyone. Within a society, men increasingly resemble one another; communication between peoples causes whole societies to resemble one another as well. "When I survey," Tocqueville writes, "this countless multitude of beings, shaped in each other's likeness, amid whom nothing rises and nothing falls, the sight of such universal uniformity saddens and chills me and I am tempted to regret that state of society which has ceased to be" (II, 4, 8, p. 332). If all desires are similar, can they still be considered free?

Tocqueville is tempted by the return to aristocratic society, but only in a manner of speaking; in reality, he never gives way to this temptation. His vision of the modern world is conservative, but his political project remains democratic. What he wants to do through his work is to make modern man conscious of the dangers that threaten him and to seek remedies for them. Associations of citizens, freely formed, can attenuate the effects of individualism; a private practice of traditional religion can usefully counterbalance the drawbacks of materialism. There is indeed a price to pay for liberty, but it is worth negotiating.

Finally, the modern revolution has a third consequence, beyond the dissolution of society and morality, which is bemoaned by conservatives: the dislocation of the self as such. Here we are leaving the political framework and entering into the realm of individual analysis. For this reason, we will not find formulations as systematic as in the first two cases: this reproach was uttered by poets and novelists, not by social theorists. The individual who prided himself on thinking, feeling, and willing according to his own lights would no longer even be the same person: the abandonment of his predetermined traditional place has opened him up to all sorts of influences and mutations; rather than an autonomous subject, he has become an inauthentic and alienated individual, moved by many contradictory and changeable forces. Thus, taking still further the shift Tocqueville thought he observed, the individual has abandoned not only his close relations so as to focus only on himself, but also himself so as to know only his own ingredients, the various drives that move him. The ultimate result of individualism, then, would be the disappearance of the individual.

The Scientists

I have identified the conservative family in terms of its reaction to the advent of modernity. Modernity affirms the freedom of the subject, individual or collective, along with other causes of his action. The conservative reaction says: the price of this freedom is too steep; we would do better to renounce the transaction so as not to have to pay. On this level, the position of the conservatives is clear. The picture becomes complicated when we turn to the three other major families, which all accept the principle of modernity but draw different conclusions from it.

Scientistic thought involves several theses. First, the scientists adhere to a deterministic vision of the world. This vision becomes manifest in France in the wake of the materialism of the Enlightenment, among the Encyclopedists, from Diderot to Condorcet; it penetrated the nineteenth century and its doctrine is found again in Auguste Comte, Ernest Renan, and Hippolyte Taine. But it has much earlier antecedents, as do all the other modern families, in Greek philosophy and the Christian religion. In fact, concerned only with our convenience, we give these general labels a narrow meaning, when in reality each of them covers as great a diversity as the label "modernity." The conservative family, as I said in passing, can already claim this double heritage, Christian and pagan, by privileging the reference to God or nature, the teaching of the Church, or the laws of the city.

Determinist doctrine is similar. It shares with Greek tradition the conviction of a universal order that man can know; it stands against this tradition in the modalities of this knowledge (Galileo and Descartes would not have flourished in ancient Greece), as well as in its results (the world of homogeneous matter comes to replace the hierarchical universe of the Ancients). In the Christian tradition, determinism resembles one of the two major parties that are in conflict throughout its history: the party that favors divine grace to the detriment of human freedom; this resemblance consists specifically in the refusal to admit the existence of freedom. Saint Paul uses the metaphor of clay in the potter's hands (Rom. 9:21): If man is the material and God the craftsman, can we still speak of freedom and can we expect salvation to come from a place other than grace, the call, or faith? Saint Augustine eventually denounced the heresy of Pelagius, who imagined that human works are adequate to assure our salvation. Luther and Calvin later rebelled against papist practices, the possibility left to men to pay for their sins through a simple act of will. The Jansenists and Pascal then fought the Jesuits (in vain), who tried to spare a place for human initiative. According to the doctrines of grace, the will is nothing because all power rests in God; according to the scientists, it is because nature (or history) has already decided everything for us. The verdict of blood, as people said then, or that of society replaced divine will. Man is powerless because his fate is in God's hands, Pascal says; because he is guided unwittingly by his race, his heredity, and his place in history, Taine would correct.

The forces that drive individuals can be different in nature; the crucial thing is that their reign is absolute. The nineteenth century witnessed the successive rise to power of three great forms of causality, which would be the subjects of three distinct sciences. The first, developing at the very moment of the conservative challenge, was social and historical in its inspiration: men believe they are free, when in reality they are the product of historical circumstances, social conditions, and economic structures. A second form of determinism, biological causality, was added in the second half of the century: the fate of men is decided by their blood (or by the form and volume of their skull, or their size — or any other physical characteristic), and therefore by their heredity. At the end of the century a third form of causality was affirmed that is purely psychic and individual: the behavior of the individual is dictated to him not, as he naively believed, by his conscience and his will but by forces acting inside him unconsciously that are themselves the product of his personal history — in psychoanalysis, the configuration formed around him by his nearest relations in early childhood.

These three determinisms sometimes struggle with one another for supremacy and sometimes combine. Every generation favors its form of causality, which the following generation discards and tries to replace. These forms of thought are, moreover, always present among us: we have not stopped talking about the laws of history or unconscious drives; and if we no longer believe in the destiny of blood, we are much more certain about the decisive role played by our genes. Racial thought reappears in our times as well. The only thing these three causalities — social, biological, and psychic — have in common is the fact that they consider the freedom of the individual to be essentially an illusion.

Causality is not only omnipresent, it is also the same everywhere: scientism is a universalism. There are still, however, significant differences: if the laws (of nature or history) are everywhere the same, the facts they govern are not. Races are different, as are historical epochs, but all are strictly obedient to the forces that determine them and provoke equally predictable consequences.

To this first scientistic thesis bearing on the structure of the universe, a second is added: the inexorable linking of causes and effects can be thoroughly known, and modern science is the royal road to this knowledge. In this respect, scientistic doctrine is opposed to the passive acceptance of the world as it is. It also diverges — and this rupture is decisive — from the fatalism of the Ancients. Not satisfied with describing what exists but searching for the mechanism that produced it, scientism can envisage that another reality, better adapted to our needs, might emerge from the same laws. Freedom, formerly reduced to zero, is here reborn; but it can exist only thanks to the mediation of science. He who has penetrated the secret of plants can produce new ones, more fertile and nourishing; he who has understood natural selection can institute artificial selection. We need not be satisfied with existing means of communication, we need not accept that rivers flow in one direction to no purpose, we will prolong the span of human life. Knowledge of existing conditions leads to technology, which allows the manufacture of improved existing conditions. There is a temptation to extend the same principle to human societies: since we know their mechanisms, why not engineer perfect societies?

However, when we speak of the production of something new, we are also speaking of an ideal that stands behind our production. What is a *better* vegetable or animal species, how do we judge that one countryside is *superior* to another, by what criteria do we decide that a certain political regime would be *preferable* to the one that already exists? The scientists' answer would be (and this is their third thesis): Values follow from the nature of things, they are an effect of the natural and historical laws that govern the world, so again, it is up to science to make those values known to us. Scientism, in effect, involves basing an ethics and a politics on what is believed to be the results of science. In other words, science, or what is perceived as such, ceases to be a simple knowledge of the existing world and becomes a generator of values, similar to religion; it can therefore direct political and moral action. "To know the truth in order to conform the order of society to it, such is the unique source of public happiness," writes Condorcet (*Vie de Turgot*, p. 203). This order is a reconstruction adopted because of a particular strategy; historically, it is the desire to improve the lives of men who will open the doors to "scientific" knowledge.

Scientism does not eliminate the will but decides that since the results of science are valid for everyone, this will must be something shared, not individual. In practice, the individual must submit to the collectivity, which "knows" better than he does. The autonomy of the will is maintained, but it is the will of the group, not the person. The followers of scientism act as if there were a continuity between the constraints that man endures at the hands of nature and those that society inflicts on him, effacing the boundary between two kinds of freedom: freedom that is opposed to necessity and freedom that resists constraint. Postulating the absence of the one, they conclude the desirable absence (for the individual) of the other.

Having discovered the objective laws of the real, the partisans of this doctrine decide that they can enlist these laws to run the world as they think best. And this direction, claimed to be imposed by the world itself, becomes a motive for progress: one is acting for the benefit of nature, humanity, a certain society, not of the individuals being addressed. This is already evident among the foremost representatives of the family in the nineteenth century who are "activists," even as they adhere to determinist theses: Darwin recommends eugenics, Marx social revolution. The scientific scholar is tempted to become a demiurge.

In the twentieth century and now in the twenty-first, scientism has flourished in two very different political contexts, which have influenced it to such a degree that we may well hesitate to recognize their offspring as part of the same family. The first variant of scientism was put into practice by totalitarian regimes. The rulers of the countries in which these regimes prospered believed, or encouraged the belief, that the evolution of the world obeyed strict laws of a social or biological nature. But far from viewing this as a reason for passive resignation, they judged that, with truth on their side, they could pursue their goal with even more assurance. Everything is necessary, of course, but one has the freedom to accelerate necessity in order to follow the direction of history or the direction of life. The scientism found at the basis of the totalitarian project brings together two extremes: a systematic determinism and a boundless voluntarism. The world is entirely homogeneous, entirely determined, entirely knowable, on the one hand; but on the other, man is an infinitely malleable material, whose observable characteristics are not serious obstacles to the chosen project. Everything is *given* and at the same time everything can be chosen: the paradoxical union of these two assertions comes by way of a third, according to which everything is knowable. And it is this union that makes totalitarianism dangerous: determinism alone can lead to resignation, voluntarism alone can be contested by a rival.

We have moved, here, from the old utopias, dreams of an ideal society meant as criticism of real societies, to modern utopianism, the attempt to establish heaven on earth, here and now. And we have seen the brutal consequences. Since class enemies are destined (by the laws of history revealed by science) to disappear, one can eliminate them with impunity. Since inferior races are both harmful and fated to perish in the struggle for survival, according to the laws of evolution established by science, the extermination of these races is a benefit to humanity, a way of giving destiny a hand. Likewise for less macabre aspects of these societies, from industrialization to the organization of daily life: everything is decided by an iron will, unhindered by any hesitation since it claims to rely on the verities of scientific knowledge.

Controlling society in its entirety, its rulers may be animated by an ideal that is not altogether foreign to that of the conservatives: they are trying to impose greater social cohesion and a submission to common values. This was true of the "socialism" inaugurated by the October Revolution in Russia: victory of the collective over the individual of submission over freedom. In this respect they remind us of the thinking of counterrevolutionaries like Bonald, for example, in France, who tried to reestablish the Old Regime's way of life by force. In a similar fashion, the so-called conservative revolutions of the twentieth century, fascism or Pétain's "national revolution," sought to recover values dear to the conservatives.

We might be surprised by this proximity of conservatives and revolutionaries. We are usually aware of the differences between them: the first claim stability, the second change; the first locate their ideals in the past, the second in the future; the first take revealed religion as their reference point, the second the nation or class. Yet Bonald and Claude de Saint-Simon (to name one of the first French representatives of the scientistic and utopian tendencies) offer the same objections to the thought embodied by Benjamin Constant, defender of democracy. The preeminence of the "social" over the "individual," the accent on collective membership (in a race, a class, a nation) are features common to socialist revolutionaries and conservative traditionalists; and similarly, the demand for a public moral order. This explains in part the facility with which a good number of people have been able, in more recent times, to shift from "the extreme right" to "the extreme left," or vice versa.

The second branch of scientistic ideology emerges within the framework of the Western democracies. Its elements—everything is determined, everything is knowable, everything can be improved—intervene in numerous aspects of public life: the neglect of the ends that political or moral actions are supposed to pursue (or the disappearance, pure and simple, of such actions); the conviction that these ends flow automatically from the processes described by science; the desire to submit action to knowledge. Economists, sociologists, and psychologists observe society and individuals, and believe they can identify the laws governing their behavior, the direction of their evolution; politicians and moralists (the "intellectuals") then urge the population to conform to these laws. The expert replaces the sage as purveyor of final aims, and a thing becomes good simply because it is frequent. Freedom of choice is preserved, remarks Victor Goldschmidt, but it is exercised by "a technocratic collective," and not by autonomous subjects (*Ecrits*, I, 242). This ideological proximity does not, however, prevent democratic regimes from opposing totalitarian societies: the practice of those States that ensure the freedom of individuals prevents persuasion from becoming coercion, and insubordination from being punished by imprisonment or death.

The Individualists

The scientists' point of departure is an epistemological postulate: the universe is entirely determined and knowable. The next family defines itself within the same modern framework, but bases itself on another anthropological hypothesis: that the individual human being is a self-sufficient entity. This is why I am giving it the name *individualist*, a term I use here in a much narrower sense than when it was made to designate all of modernity (I am following the usage of Alain Renaut). If we return to our starting point, the revelation of the pact and the unforeseen consequences of freedom, the individualist reaction consists not in denying the existence of freedom, as the scientists do, nor in regretting its consequences, as the conservatives do, but in recognizing the truth of the proposition while reversing the value judgment attached to it: instead of deploring it, the individualists rejoice in it. Those things the conservatives decried as threatening or wounding — individualism, materialism, fragmentation of the self — they proclaim loud and clear. If they have one regret, it is that man is not even freer of those fictions consisting of morality, communal life, and the coherent self.

Like the preceding families, the family of individualists has its roots deep in a distant past. The Stoic tradition presents man as a self-sufficient being, or at least as able to aspire to this ideal. Skeptical wisdom shows the relativity of all our judgments and the impossibility of justifying a moral position other than by our habits and interests. In the Augustinian tradition, within the heart of Christianity, one always insists on recalling that weakness is inherent in human nature, therefore also that man is a solitary being, aggressive and amoral. Individualism finds another of its ingredients in William of Occam. If nothing exists outside individual bodies, if abstractions are merely phantoms, the social entity is no longer a necessity: each being is complete in himself. The relations he establishes with other beings around him do not alter him, he does not form a new entity with them. "In order for a thing to exist, it must be so through its own self and no other" (*Lagarde*, V, 174). Occam, who transposes to the life of the city certain principles of monastic life in which the individual stands alone before God, conceives of man as independent of his peers, compelled therefore to attain goodness on his own. "To be a person is to have no need of any other competing reality to subsist" (VI, 42).

This heritage of traditional ideas nourished an image of man that crystallized in France in the seventeenth century, in the thought of La Rochefoucauld. The human being is fundamentally solitary and egotistical; all his actions are motivated by his self-regard and personal interest. But we dare not show our true face to others, for fear that they might punish us; therefore we disguise our egotistical actions as disinterested and generous gestures. The role of the moralist consists, then, of pulling off this virtuous mask and revealing our true nature. "We cannot love anything except in terms of ourselves" (*Maxims*, 81). "Our friendship is really based on interest alone" (85). By deceiving others, we end up believing in our own fictions, and we imagine that life in society is indispensable to us. Yet "social life would not last long if men were not taken in by each other" (87). Pascal, who participates in the same Augustinian tradition, will say much the same thing: "Human relations are only based on mutual deception" (*Pensées*, B. 100, L. 978). But La Rochefoucauld, like Pascal, regrets this solitude and egotism, and seeks to mask if not eliminate them — La Rochefoucauld with courtesy and the acquisition of what he calls honesty, Pascal with grace.

This conception of man was taken up again in the eighteenth century by those same men who would establish the scientistic family, the materialist-encyclopedists; and it was gradually freed of the negative judgment it prompted in La Rochefoucauld and Pascal. Man is a self-interested, self-sufficient, solitary being? Fine, Helvetius would say, we must take him as he is rather than rebel futilely against nature; we must bring the ideal and the real closer together. Yet Helvetius is not yet openly individualistic, since for him the common interest, that of the group, must prevail over personal interest.

The first straightforward "individualist" in the French tradition is simultaneously the most extreme: that is Sade. He first observes, in keeping with his predecessors, that man, in the image of other animals, is a purely egotistical being who knows only its own interests. That is the general law of nature: "Nature, the mother of us all, speaks to us only of ourselves, nothing is as egotistical as her voice" (*Philosophie dans le boudoir*, III, 123). Social life is imposed on men from the outside; it is not necessary to them. "Are we not all born in utter isolation? I say more: all enemies of one another, all in a perpetual and reciprocal state of war?" (V, 173). Like La Rochefoucauld, Sade believes that our virtues are merely the homage rendered by vice to convention. "Charity is rather a vice of pride than a true virtue of the soul" (III, 57). "It is always only for oneself that we must love others; to love them for themselves is merely delusion" (V, 178).

And what is, is good: we must in all things and everywhere submit to "nature." There is no more question of joining together "to be" and "ought to be," being and duty, as in Diderot or Helvetius, but of the disappearance of the second term to the advantage of the first. "Any human law that would contradict those of nature would deserve nothing but contempt" (III, 77). Happily, nature has given us pleasure to allow us to know precisely what is in our interest; and it is here that the experience of the individual is irrefutable. The relativity of values, which in Helvetius stopped at the group, now reaches the individual: what is good *for me* is good. The individual does not have to consider social conventions. "We can surrender in peace to all our desires, as peculiar as they may appear to the fools who, offended and alarmed by everything, stupidly take social institutions for the divine laws of nature" (96). The individual is sufficient to himself; he should therefore be concerned only with his pleasure. "Our tastes, our temperaments alone must be respected" (61). "No limit to your pleasures but that of your powers and your will" (66). The movement of liberation, which is in the process of being accomplished with the French Revolution, must be pursued on the personal level: the individual will emancipate himself from all social constraint. Common laws are merely a hindrance to sexual pleasure. If the body plays such a large role in Sade's imaginary world, this is precisely because it belongs exclusively to the individual. "Your body is yours, and yours alone; you are the only one in the world who has the right to enjoy it and to give enjoyment with it as you see fit" (68).

We know that Sade himself derived more specific consequences from this doctrine: having discovered that the pain of others gives him more pleasure than their joy, he recommends situations in which the subject can make this other human being suffer or, taken to an extreme, put him to death. "We are not concerned with knowing whether our actions will please or displease the object that serves us, we are concerned only with igniting our nerve endings by the most violent shock possible" (121). But this sadistic variant is not indispensable to the doctrine; its substance is its individualistic anthropology and its hedonistic morality, if we can call it that.

In the nineteenth century, Sade was the black sheep of the individualist family, and his existence was best ignored. Hedonism was practiced much more than proclaimed. Utilitarianism, which is the individualist doctrine's philosophical form, claimed a direct line from Helvetius or, further back, from Epicurus. Moreover, egotism was repressed by utilitarianism, since its declared objective was the happiness of all members of the community (of "the greatest number"), not of the individual.

This quantitative extension would not, however, transform the initial anthropological hypothesis: individuals are the atoms of society, which is formed by their juxtaposition and addition, rather than being an internal characteristic of these individuals.

The appearance of the very word *individualism*, signaled by Tocqueville, illustrates the wide dissemination of the doctrine. The individualist family has other members as well, such as aestheticism, to which I will return; and individualism is equally manifest in the demand for the blossoming of the self or of an authentic personal existence, which is familiar to all of us. I shall not go into detail about these subdivisions, since they are marginal to my purpose. Our concern here is only the place of the individualists within the ranks of the other families: theirs is a doctrine that welcomes from earlier constraints with satisfaction the liberation of the individual and wishes to push that liberation still further, even if this means emancipating oneself from social ties or common values — a sacrifice made all the easier as the individual, according to this doctrine, is a self-sufficient being.

The Humanist Family

These three major reactions to the revelation of the pact have been identified; one is still missing, however, which has the greatest importance for me and to which I will devote the rest of this book. That is the reaction of the *humanists*, who deny that there ever was a pact, known or unknown — in other words, they deny any necessary relationship between, on the one hand, the acquisition of the right to self-government and, on the other, the dissolution of society, morality, or the subject. We will do well enough by avoiding a few mistakes, by sidestepping a few traps, and there will be no price to pay, the humanists say. They want, say their adversaries, to have their cake and eat it too: to keep their precious newfound freedom without being compelled to renounce the social bond, the recognition of values, or the identity of the self.

The word *humanist* has at least three quite distinct, if significantly related, meanings. The oldest, imposed by the Renaissance, corresponds to people who devote themselves to the study of the humanities, in particular to history and the literature of Greek and Latin antiquity; hence they valorize this study or its subject. The most recent is a purely affective meaning: "humanists" are those who behave humanely toward others or who tell us that we must treat human beings decently; in short, they are philanthropists. But I am using the word in neither its historical nor its moral sense; I am using it to designate a doctrine that grants the human being a particular role. Just what is this role? It consists, first of all, of initiating one's own acts (or some portion of them), of being free to accomplish them or not — therefore of being able to act at one's will. The distinctive feature of modernity is constitutive of humanism: man *also* (and not only nature or God) decides his fate. In addition, it implies that the ultimate end of these acts is a human being, not suprahuman entities (God, goodness, justice) or infrahuman ones (pleasures, money, power). Humanism, finally, marks out the space in which the agents of these acts evolve: the space of all human beings, and of them alone.

To denote these three characteristics of the humanist family, I will often resort to briefer formulas, such as the *autonomy of the I*, the *finality of the you*, and the *universality of the they*. I use an opposition here familiar to theorists of language between the personal (I, you) and the impersonal (the "third person"), on the one hand; and between *ego* and *alter* on the other — for it is clear that the man who is the end (the goal) of my actions is not myself but an other (humanism is not an egotism). What guarantees the unity of these three features is the very centrality granted to the human race, embodied by each of its members: it is at once the source, the goal, and the framework of its actions. When during the period of the Renaissance we shift from a geocentric to a heliocentric worldview, and our Earth is expelled from the center of the universe, on the level of human affairs we move from theocentric (or from a pagan "cosmocentric") to anthropocentric. Every human being, whatever his other characteristics, is recognized as responsible for what he or she does and deserves to be treated as an end in him- or herself. *I* must be the source of my action, *you* must be its goal, *they* all belong to the same human race. These three characteristics (which Kant called the three "formulas of one and the same law" (*Fondements*, II, 303) are not always found together; a particular author may retain only one or two of them, and mingle them with other sources. But only the uniting of the three constitutes humanist thought, properly speaking.

This thought is at once an anthropology (it tells how men are: a race apart whose members are sociable and partially undetermined — and who for this reason are led to exercise their freedom), a morality (it tells how they should be: cherishing human beings for themselves and according the same dignity to all), and a politics (it privileges regimes in which subjects can exercise their autonomy and enjoy the same rights).

It is conceivable that the motto of the French Revolution — Liberty, equality, fraternity — refers, if only approximately, to this triple humanist demand: liberty designates the autonomy of the subject, equality the unity of the human race; as for fraternity, is treating others as if they were our brothers not tantamount to making them the goal of our affections and our acts? In turn, modern democratic States adopt these same three principles, after transposing them from the individual to the collective level. This collective wields a sovereign power, an expression of popular will; the well-being of its subjects is the ultimate goal of its action; the universality of the law for all citizens is the basic rule of its functioning. Here we see the deep affinity between humanist thought and democratic politics.

Liberal democracy as it has been progressively constituted for two hundred years is the concrete political regime that corresponds most closely to the principles of humanism, because it adopts the ideas of collective autonomy (the sovereignty of the people), individual autonomy (the liberty of the individual), and universality (the equality of rights for all citizens). Nonetheless, humanism and democracy do not coincide: first, because real democracies are far from perfect embodiments of humanist principles (one can endlessly criticize democratic reality in the name of its own ideal), then because the affinity between humanism and democracy is not a relationship of mutual implication exclusive of any other. The fact is, the conservative, scientist, and individualist families prosper equally well within democracies; and in turn democratic societies are not threatened by the presence of these other families in their midst. Heirs to the spirit of religious tolerance, democracies accept a certain pluralism of values: different ideologies can contribute to the pursuit of the same end, the common good. There is no simple correspondence between ideological families and political regimes.

However, whereas humanist thought is central to liberal democracy, the other modern ideologies adapt themselves to democracy but have different centrifugal tendencies that make them diverge from it. The individualists are tempted by anarchistic and libertarian aspirations; they prefer that the common rule, embodied in laws and in the apparatus of the state, be as weak and as limited as possible. The conservatives, who do not believe in the strength and soundness of the individual will, favor authoritarian regimes. A state founded on scientistic principles may veer toward totalitarianism: if one masters the whole range of biological and historical processes, one can dispense with consulting the will of individuals. Conservatives and the adherents of scientism can at the extreme be recognized in the same type of ideocratic regime, where contradictory ideological justifications are given — science here, theology there, utopia on the one side, tradition on the other. Only the humanist family is free of these centrifugal tendencies.

If we turn toward morality, a new distinction arises. Political humanism with its corollaries (universal suffrage, protection of the individual, etc.) is obviously a minimal humanism, which might be qualified as *passive*. The rejection of the arbitrary prerogatives of royalist rule, of the individual's subjection to slavery or forced indoctrination — these are necessary elements of humanist practice, but they still tell us nothing about its positive values. *Active* humanism, however, is based on the finality of the *you*, on the acceptance of the particular human being (other than self) as the ultimate goal of our actions. Here, even the term *morality* is no longer adequate, or it must be given a broader meaning, since humanists favor not moral injunctions but the value of human attachments, friendship, and love. In turn, such a "morality" intervenes in "politics": the affairs of the country are no longer conducted in the same manner if we decide to take it into account.

As for the humanist doctrine's anthropology, it is relatively meager. Apart from the biological identity of the species, it is reduced to a single feature, sociability; but its consequences are numerous. The most important, in our view, is the existence of a consciousness of self, which animals never achieve; whereas the human child begins to acquire it quite early, from the time he manages to intercept the gaze of the adult leaning over him: *you* look at me, therefore *I* exist. This consciousness of self, inseparable from that of others, will in turn have decisive effects. On the one hand, an increasing complexity of the intersubjective relationship, whose emblem will be human language; on the other, a splitting of the self, equally basic to humanity: the individual is at once a living being like others *and* the consciousness of that being, which allows him to detach himself from it, indeed to stand against it. Such is the basis of human liberty (and of the demand for autonomy that will be its political translation). Man is characterized by this biological trait, the capacity to separate himself from his own being. Sociability and liberty are intrinsically bound together, and they make up part of the very definition of the species.

Family Quarrels

In order to complete our picture of humanist doctrine with a little more precision, we should now locate the humanists in relation to the other modern families and identify their response to the devil's claims. The humanists renounce neither values (but these are human, not divine), nor society (which takes multiple forms), nor the responsibility of the subject (however plural it may be). Unlike the individualists, the humanists — Montesquieu, Rousseau, Constant — confirm the fundamental sociability of mankind (man without society is not man, contrary to Occam's contention). Men are not atoms that would have been united, after the fact, within society; their interaction is fundamental to the very identity of the species (the *you* is posed simultaneously with the *I*), and the irreducible individual presupposes intersubjectivity. Against the proponents of scientism, the humanists maintain not only the autonomy of values (these do not flow from facts) but also the possibility of freedom: the human being is not the plaything of forces from which he cannot hope to escape.

There is a kind of symmetry in the opposition between the humanists and the members of these two other families. The individualists believe in personal autonomy but neglect the social membership of individuals. The proponents of scientism accept the autonomy of man but attribute it to the species and the group rather than to the individual: for them, personal autonomy has no real meaning. On their side, the humanists think that the individual can achieve autonomy, that is, act by reason of his own will and in accord with the laws that he himself accepts, without necessarily conceiving this to be outside the human community. The humanists are also distinguished from the conservatives both because they do not deplore the freedom of individuals and because the values to which they adhere are purely human. For this combination of reasons, the humanist response seems to me the most satisfying if not the only worthwhile response to the devil's challenge.

The usual criticism addressed to the humanist doctrine comes from the scientistic and conservative families, and it consists of saying that the humanists ignore, willingly or not, the power of determinations that govern human actions — whether biological, social, or cultural. The humanists' response is deployed on two fronts. On the first, the plurality and complexity of causal series are such that they finally result in indeterminacy: our species is characterized by its plasticity, its capacity to adapt itself to all circumstances, to change. "Man, that flexible being," said Montesquieu (*The Spirit of the Laws*, preface, p. xliv). In the eyes of the humanists, man is a potentiality rather than an essence: he can become this or that, act one way or another; he does not do it *out of necessity*. But in addition, and this is essential, even in the presence of the clearest determinations, human beings always have the possibility of opposition, therefore of standing aside from themselves; without that, they are no longer, or not yet, fully human.

We might illustrate the interaction between necessity and freedom by this simple example. Human beings are programmed to speak by their biological nature; neither the parents of a child nor that child herself are at liberty to deprive her of the capacity to speak (except by tampering with her brain). These parents and this child live in a society that uses a particular language: the cultural determination is added to biological causality. Now, as an adult, the child can decide to speak her mother tongue or refuse to speak it and use another language. This rupture in the rule of nature, as in that of culture, is sufficient to introduce the idea of human liberty, and with it all of modernity.

When they are questioned by the representatives of the other families, the humanists therefore do not entirely reject the idea of determinism governing the fate of societies or that of the individual; they do not claim that the human subject is completely free, that he can choose everything in his life and that he alone is master of his fate. But they contend that freedom, choice, and the exercise of the will are options that are equally open to him; that they deserve to be valued more than the situations in which the subject acts by necessity or under constraint; indeed, that certain people manage to multiply these occasions for freedom while others never, as it were, enjoy them. The humanists do not claim that human beings are entirely ruled by their reason or their conscience. They are not unaware of the power of what were formerly called the passions and what we call the unconscious or instinct, nor of the constraints exercised on the individual by biological givens, economic necessities, or cultural traditions. They simply contend that the individual can *also* oppose these constraints and act from his will; and this is what they see as specifically human.

Therefore they value voluntary action, yet without the need to believe in men's unlimited malleability or in their omnipotence: the place of the given is also irreducible. Humanists do not think, as Sartre does, that man alone makes his own laws: first because man is multiple and this multiplicity can be problematic; then because men today are made also from the past, and this past is in turn shaped by men over whom one has no power; finally and above all, because men must take into account the constraints over which they have no control — constraints imposed by their bodies, the physical characteristics of the countries they inhabit, Earth's place in the universe.

The humanists can even keep company for some distance with members of the family of scientists, but ultimately they go their separate ways. Tocqueville, a humanist here, ends *Democracy in America* with this conclusion: "Providence has not created mankind entirely independent or utterly enslaved. It is true that around every man a fatal circle is traced beyond which he cannot pass; but within the wide verge of that circle he is powerful and free; as it is with man, so with communities" (II, 4, 8). Nature itself is familiar with chance and not only with necessity; history even more so; finally, man can oppose the dictates of nature and history. Natural and historical causality in no way exclude autonomy and voluntary action. In writing these lines, Tocqueville is behaving like a faithful disciple of his liberal predecessors, Montesquieu and Constant.

Humanism is not a monism: it understands human beings and their societies as the result of the interaction of several mutually limiting principles, rather than as the effect of a single cause. The *given* restrains the territory of the chosen, but the will in turn opens a breach in the reign of necessity. This pluralistic choice repeats itself in the area of values, yet without leading to relativism. The paths toward the good are multiple, as becomes evident from the plurality of cultures (this pluralism is therefore a consequence of universalism: one cannot start from the hypothesis that everyone, save us, is mistaken). At the same time, plurality does not degenerate into a war of the gods: just as the spirit of religious tolerance allowed that there are several approaches to the same God, the humanist framework implies that even if values are multiple, it is possible to debate values by means of human dialogue, therefore within a common framework. The gods may be many, but humanity is one.

The same moderation (to use Montesquieu's term) characterizes the humanist attitude toward knowledge. Contrary to the conservatives, who postulate that the effort of men to know the world is condemned to semifailure in advance, contrary to the scientists, who believe they already understand the truth about the laws governing the world, the humanists contend that knowledge is limited by fact but not by right. No curse weighs on the world that would make it forever unintelligible, and the capacities of human reason are theoretically unlimited. But in practice, the complexities of matter and mind are such that we know only a small part of them: pride ill-becomes reason, Montaigne observed. That is why a considerable place must be left, next to science, for other forms of comprehension and expression, which allow access to the truth by ways that cannot be made perfectly transparent. Symbol is no less necessary than sign, myth no less than discourse, art no less than science. Humanism locates itself beyond the dichotomy of rationalism and irrationalism; it accepts that knowledge sometimes follows paths that elude rational analysis.

This is perhaps what also explains the humanists' complex relations with religion. On the one hand they separate themselves from it: they want the individual to be able to choose freely whether to believe or not; they want societies to be governed by the will of the people and not by divine right. They also think that man, and not only God, is worthy of being an end in himself. But on the other hand, and even leaving aside the historic affiliation between humanism and Christianity, one cannot help noticing that all the great French humanists, from Montaigne to Constant, described themselves as religious persons and Christians; and this cannot be construed as simply a convenient submission to the laws of the times. Rather, humanism, which is not in itself a religion, is nonetheless not a form of atheism. It separates the management of human affairs from any theological basis or justification; but it does not demand an elimination of the religious dimension of experience. It provides a somewhat vague place for it, outside of politics and science: religion remains a possible response to each person's inquiries into his place in the universe or the meaning of his life.

"Pride" and "Naivete"

We must insist on the irreducible character of the initial human *given* (which does not at all contradict the recognition of freedom as a basic element of the human), for humanism is commonly confused with what may now seem to us its prideful perversion, belief in the omnipotence of man. In this respect, the humanists stand apart from Pelagius and the Pelagians, who nonetheless figure among their precursors. For Pelagius, man is entirely free and therefore responsible for his fate; one can ask him to be perfect, since he is his own master. His nature is good (original sin does not exist), all his imperfections are therefore his own fault, his sins are also willful and cannot be excused. The temptation is great, then, to move from the possible to the obligatory: we demand perfection by providing him with examples to follow (Christ, the Saints) and punishments to dread (the fires of hell).

Similarly, one of the most famous formulas connected to the origin of humanism, Descartes's promise to "make ourselves [like] the lords and masters of nature" (*Discourse on the Method*, pt. VI, *Philosophical Writings*, I, pp. 142–43), refers less to humanist doctrine itself than to this prideful perversion: Humanists affirm that man is not nature's slave, not that nature must become his slave. This Cartesian promise, which is located in the tradition of Ficino or of Francis Bacon, belongs rather to the tradition of the scientistic family. Humanists do not claim the omnipotence of man but deny the omnipotence of God or nature; they claim that alongside the *given* there is a place, and a considerable place, for the chosen. Nor are we to conclude that the possibility of intervening in our fate leads inevitably to an infatuation with utopias, the desire to build paradise on earth—which, as we know from the experience of the twentieth century, is more likely to resemble hell. The utopian temptation is more closely related to scientism than to humanism; it rests on the conviction that total mastery of historical processes is possible—which contradicts the hypothesis of liberty. By affirming the role of liberty in man, the humanists know that he can use it in the service of good—but also of evil. The construction of a city in which evil would be excluded plays no part in the humanist project.

The same uncertainty also characterizes the human race, precisely, in its relation to good and evil. Is man good or bad? If one adopts the second hypothesis, one finds oneself in the company of Saint Augustine and a long line of Christian thinkers who derive from him. If one adheres to the first, one sides with the defenders of the "noble savage," of the enemies of education and civilization (not to speak of the extreme position of Sade and his emulators, who make "good" synonymous with—actually, superfluous to—"natural"). The humanist refuses to incline in favor of goodness for simple empirical reasons: should he proudly perceive himself an exception to the rule, he need only take note of his country's history, or observe his friends and relations, to renounce the idea that man is thoroughly good. But the humanist also refuses the Jansenist or Protestant position, which makes man another Satan. If he thought, like Bérulle, that "we possess nothing in our own right but error and sin" (*Opuscules de piété*, LXXXV, 1, 403), why would he place even the slightest responsibility for his salvation on his own shoulders? Human nature is imperfect, in Montaigne's words: such is the working hypothesis of the humanists. Man is neither good nor bad; he can become one or the other, or (more often) both.

This point must be emphasized, for it is the source of another frequent confusion, which attributes to the humanists an entirely positive vision of man. In reality, this is a new perversion of the doctrine, not prideful, this time, but *naive*. Whenever we hear about the "grandeur" of man or his "nobility," the need to "venerate" him as a god or to "respect" him for his intrinsic qualities, we are dealing with this "naive" vision. Of course we can insist that man must be treated as a noble being or that all men must be respected, but these would be moral imperatives, not anthropological hypotheses. In this regard, man in the abstract is merely uncertainty and potentiality—which does not prevent some men from being positively good and others downright evil. A clear boundary therefore separates the humanist family from its neighbors who worship man. To imagine that man is entirely good or omnipotent is an illusion, in the humanists' view: neither man's power nor his goodness should be overestimated.

On the other hand, what characterizes the humanists is a certain faith in education. Since, on the one hand, man is partially undetermined and moreover capable of liberty, and on the other, good and evil exist, one can become engaged in that process which leads from neutrality to good, and is called education. Lacking this, certain positive inclinations may be repressed and disappear, while negative inclinations may prosper. Evil is also learned. Montesquieu wrote: "Where does that ferocity come from which we find in the inhabitants of our colonies if not from that continual practice of punishments on an unfortunate part of the human race?" (*Grandeur*, XV, 463). It is not accidental that so many of the great humanists, Montaigne, Montesquieu, Rousseau, and many others evinced, a particular interest in the subject of education. While the conservatives recommend the pure maintenance and faithful transmission of traditions, the scientists lean toward training that mechanically produces the desired results, and the individualists are happy with searching for anything that contributes to the flowering and maximal satisfaction of each person, the humanists would like to have common principles of education that allow men to acquire a greater autonomy, give a human finality to their acts, and recognize the same dignity in all members of their species.

Natural or Artificial

The ultimate reason for these differences between humanists and other modern families lies perhaps in the status respectively granted to values. Let us recall the terms of the classic argument: two major options confront each other historically, as early as the Greek Sophists, according to which values are either based in nature or emerge from human law alone. The two options have always been envisaged, but we can say in a first approximation that the Ancients prefer to think of values as given (by nature, by God), while the Moderns, and in particular the individualists, most often believed that they were, above all, chosen. When Hobbes declares: "it is Authority, not Truth, that makes the Law" (*Leviathan*, XXVI, p. 202) — and this is only one of a thousand formulations, but a particularly influential one — he becomes the spokesman for the purely voluntarist hypothesis concerning the origin of values. If values have no natural justification, they are "artificial" and can arise only from human will; if certain values are more imperative than others, that is because their partisans possess a stronger will.

As one might have expected, these radical declarations provoke a dismissive reaction, the demand to return in some fashion to the earlier situation — to the wisdom of the Greeks or the faith of the Christians — or at least a solution of compromise between the requirements of our will and those of tradition. This "naturalist" or religious reaction belongs to the conservatives. As for the scientists, their choice is naturalist from the outset: they want to discover values in the world (for example, to deduce them from the instinct for self-preservation), not to see them introduced by voluntary decision. Their deductions turn out, however, to be illusory, hence we are generally dealing, in their case too, with an act of will — no less pure but less open.

Yet these two positions, highly present in the contemporary debate, do not exhaust the field of possibilities, as their respective defenders would have it, certain that criticism of the adversary will irresistibly convince all those with any hesitations. Values can be artificial without becoming arbitrary. This has always been the humanists' claim. They refuse to consider man a being in which fact and value are inseparable, as the Ancients would have done; but neither do they accept the choice of many other Moderns who declare that values are the result of a purely arbitrary choice, the product of will alone. They refuse to allow themselves to be trapped into seeing naturalism or relativism as the only alternatives. It is clear, on the one hand, that the three humanist values — autonomy of the *I*, finality of the *you*, universality of the *they* — have not always been admitted. Other societies have vaunted the virtues of submission, required the veneration of one God, or affirmed that *ours* are always preferable to *theirs*. And yet the subject of modern societies does not feel that his choice is really arbitrary: humanist values, unlike their opposites, possess the force of self-evidence. The quasi-unanimous condemnation of racism, claimed today even by parties of the extreme right, is not perceived as the simple effect of our customs or of an overpowering will. What accounts for this feeling of self-evidence? The answer to this question is not clear, and yet the feeling itself is difficult to deny.

The humanists have therefore sought to establish a meaningful relationship between their values and what they have recognized as the very identity of the human race. The universality of the *they* seems, then, to be the counterpart of the membership of all human beings, and they alone, in the same living species. The finality of the *you* accords with the affirmation of the fundamental sociability of men, of their need for one another, not only for their survival and reproduction, but also for their constitution as conscious and communicative beings: the enjoyment of others is the result of this necessary relationship. The autonomy of the *I* corresponds to the human capacity to remove oneself from any determination. Membership in the same species, sociability, or the existence of a consciousness of self are not values in themselves; but humanist values conform to these characteristics of the species. They bear witness in turn, then, to the doctrine's anthropocentrism.

This correspondence between morality, politics, and anthropology is highly present in humanist texts.

In *The Spirit of the Laws*, Montesquieu is first concerned with establishing a scale of beings, not according to their greater or lesser intelligence or rationality, but according to their degree of submission to the laws of their species. Men are not cut off, in this respect, from the rest of living nature; they simply possess this characteristic to a degree unknown elsewhere. At the bottom of the scale are plants, which strictly obey the laws of their nature or divine will (which is the same thing for

Montesquieu). Above them come the animals who know feeling, since they can prefer one individual to another; they are already in a non-determined state. "They do not invariably follows their natural laws" (I, i, p. 5). Man is inscribed at the summit of this hierarchy, since he is the most complex being; but in addition, there is one difference between him and the other species that is no longer one of degree but one of kind: he can, in full knowledge of biological and social laws, act despite them or against them. "Man, as a physical being, is governed by invariable laws like other bodies. As an intelligent being, he constantly violates the laws God has established and changes those he himself establishes" (I, i, p. 5). From a genealogical perspective, liberation in relation to natural constraints is progressive, from plants to man; but structurally, the difference is radical: the human race is the only one that knows how to reject the laws that govern it.

Or, according to a paradoxical formula that nonetheless accurately represents Montesquieu's position: "particular intelligent beings" — that is, men — stray from natural or positive laws not only because they can err, but also because "it is in their nature to act by themselves" (I, i, p. 4). Their nature — that is, their identity — consists in this capacity to oppose the laws of their biological nature. And if political liberty (autonomy) is a value for Montesquieu, that is also because it suits the nature of beings with a capacity to will. In a parallel way, it is human sociability that is at the basis of justice, in his view. "Justice is not dependent on human laws. . . . [I]t is based on the existence and sociability of reasonable beings, and not on the dispositions or particular wills of those beings" (*Traité des devoirs*, 181). The Law corresponds to the identity of the human species, and not only to its will. This is also what Constant means when he states: "To wish to subtract nature entirely in a system of legislation, is to deprive laws of their support, their foundation and their limit all at the same time" (*Principles of Politics*, in *Political Writings*, ed. Fontana, XVIII).

Rousseau sees the chief difference between men and animals in the possibility men have to oppose the biological constraints characteristic of their species. "A pigeon would die of hunger near a bowl filled with the best meats, and a cat on heaps of fruit or wheat, although both might very well nourish themselves with the food they disdain if they were wise enough to try it" (*Discourse on the Origin of Inequality*, I, 141). Man, however, knows how to change customs and go against his natural instincts; therefore it is not by chance that autonomy becomes his ideal. Tocqueville also thinks that the desire for liberty, hence the pulling away from natural givens, is part of the identity of the species; if it were merely a matter of choice and interest, as we have seen, this desire could not have persisted from the beginning. "There is an instinctive, irrepressible and seemingly involuntary instinct for it [liberty], which is born at the invisible source of all passions" (*L'Ancien Régime*, vol. II, 345). The taste for liberty is an instinct that man does not choose freely.

Humanism is neither a "naturalism" nor an "artificialism"; it defends its values neither because they are embodied in the natural order, nor because the will of the most powerful has decreed it. It is not the "authority" invoked by Hobbes that makes us prefer the right to choose between *yes* or *no* to submission. Likewise for the finality of the *you*, that is, the fact that I prefer to see the human individual as the goal of my action rather than to be satisfied with his exploitation as, say, an agent of economic progress; and for the universality of the *they*, the respect due to all men considered worthier than the preference for "ours" over "theirs." If the humanist is against slavery, the manipulation and objectification of individuals or the extermination of part of humanity, it is not only because such is his goodwill, in which he might be joined by the pure voluntarist; but also because these values of freedom, respect for others, and the equal dignity of all impose themselves on him with the force of self-evidence, and seem to him more suitable to the human species then others.

It is clear, however, that other values might claim a similar "suitability" and yet are not part of the humanists' set of values. Why not? Egotism, the preference for one's own, or the comfort found in submission to the strong are no less "natural" than their opposites. To rationalize their feeling of self-evidence, the humanists are then led to refer to a discriminatory criterion, which is universality itself. One can wish that all human beings were autonomous, that they were all treated as ends in themselves, or provided with the same dignity; one cannot say as much of principles like the survival of the fittest, submission, or the instrumentalization of others. Human universality does double duty in the humanist doctrine, both as one value among others and as the means of legitimizing values.

Humanism in History

Although it is dangerous in the history of thought to use formulas like "for the first time," I believe I can claim that the various ingredients of the humanist doctrine are found united for the first time in France in the writing of Montaigne. Let me simply indicate here, before going into further detail, that the autonomy of the *I* is implied by his preference for actions that flow from "our voluntary choice and liberty" (*Essays*, I, 27, p. 134); the finality of the *you* by his declaration that the practice of friendship is more necessary and sweeter to man than "the elements of water and fire" (III, 9, 750); the universality of the *they* in his adherence to this principle: "I consider all men my compatriots, and embrace a Pole as I do a Frenchman, setting this national bond after the universal and common one" (III, 9, p. 743). We shall take up the later evolution of the doctrine in the following pages.

As with the other modern doctrines, however, one can find elements of humanism in Greek thought as well as in the Christian religion. The Greek city aspired to govern itself, which is a form of autonomy, and the democracy that it practiced implied that one might prefer voluntary decision to the law transmitted by tradition. Greek literature and painting bear witness to the fact that the individual can become the intransitive aim of other individuals' aspirations; and the Greeks knew and respected "philanthropy," or the universal love of mankind.

Humanism also has its roots in certain Christian principles: Christ's words are addressed to all people without distinction; in addition, humanism takes up the tradition attributed to the name Pelagius, for whom the salvation of men is in their own hands; they are therefore free to save themselves or be damned. This tradition was extended along different lines by Occam, who clearly separates divine and human affairs, and sees in liberty the distinctive feature of our actions. For him, "the very dignity of the human person derives from the faculty that makes him capable at any moment of doing the act that pleases him, as it pleases him" (*Lagarde*, VI, 46). It continues in the thought of Erasmus, who, in contrast to Luther, wants to locate liberty next to grace; similarly with Arminius or with Molina and the Jesuits, whom the Jansenists would pursue with their wrath in the seventeenth century. In other aspects of its doctrine, Protestantism prepares for the advent of the modern individual. Indeed, we can see all the *heretics* as precursors of humanism, since they are, etymologically, "those who choose," as opposed to those who submit to prevailing doctrine, in other words, the *orthodox*.

The presence of these traditions in European history sometimes gives the impression that we are always engaged in the same debate, in which only the labels change, or the actors rather than the roles. This is especially true of the conflict already evoked between grace and freedom in the Christian religion, and of the conflict in the nineteenth and twentieth centuries between freedom and natural or historical necessity, as revealed by science. To justify the free intervention of men, the humanists of different eras in turn had been forced to enlist the same arguments: men are not entirely bad, Erasmus asserts against Luther; they are not moved by self-interest alone, Constant retorts to Helvetius. And the solutions of compromise between the two extremes also bear a close resemblance: the genetic disposition of man allows him to adapt to any situation and to invent a framework for a new life, contemporary biologists will say; "God has created free will," said Erasmus (*Le Libre arbitre*, 844), and Montaigne: "Nature has put us into the world free and unfettered" (*Essays*, III, 9, 743).

We must not focus exclusively on this revelation of continuities, however. When we study the history of thought, we see that it almost never comes down to single combat between two great coherent and mutually exclusive theses, as we like to imagine, but instead resembles a long rivalry, sometimes specific and sometimes confused, between several major families. The humanists, in particular, are constantly led to engage in separate debates, which prompts them to use arguments that at first sight appear contradictory.

I shall return later to some of their controversies with the other major families. It is enough here to indicate that they are quite conscious of these conflicts themselves. Thus, when Tocqueville writes: "The former abandon freedom because they think it dangerous; the latter, because they hold it to be impossible" (*Democracy in America*, II, 4, 7, p. 329), he is formulating the opposition between conservatives and scientists. Before him, Constant felt compelled to battle both the conservatives à la Bonald (his political adversaries, the ultras, partisans of a Restoration to the bitter end) and the scientists à la Saint-Simon, descendants of Helvetius and of Enlightenment materialism. Against Bonald he asserts the right to autonomy; against the prevailing individualism he rejects the idea that man is a being engaged in the solitary pursuit of his own interest. This intermediary position surely explains why his master work *De la religion* was generally rejected: Constant was too much of a devout for the individualists, not religious enough for the conservatives.

Rousseau insists at length on the need to take a stand simultaneously against two quite distinct adversaries. As the *Lettre à Beaumont* summarizes, the Savoyard vicar's profession of faith is composed of two parts. The first "is meant to combat modern materialism, to establish the existence of God and natural religion with all the force of which the author is capable" (996). The second part, in contrast, "proposes doubts and difficulties concerning revelations in general" (996–97). The *Confessions* relate that it is in this spirit of double opposition, to the traditional Christians and to the "philosophers," that the characters of Julie and Wolmar were conceived (IX, 435–36). The *Dialogues* reprise the double combat conducted in *Emile*: here too, Rousseau distances himself as much from the "philosophers" as from the faithful. And long before him, Erasmus was already quite conscious that his position placed him between two extremes; no doubt recalling Aristotle, he defended that position by saying: "This is not an unhappy navigation that stays the course between two contrary evils" (*La Diatribe*, 874). Humanism and democracy can therefore be attacked by the conservatives for their radicalism, while they are reproached by the scientists and the individualists for their excessive timidity. These contradictory reproaches explain why humanist discourse itself sometimes seems incoherent.

It is all the more urgent to identify the plurality of voices that constitute the debate, since each family is inclined, with polemic intentions, to reduce all the other families to a single voice, generally the one that seems most easily attacked, and to regard the others as simple opportunistic camouflage. This last role is attributed, more specifically, to humanism precisely because of its central position: for the conservatives, it is merely a mask for individualism ("Nietzsche fulfills Descartes"); for the individualists, it is a barely attenuated form of scientism ("totalitarianism is an effect of humanism"); as for the scientists, they can describe it as a form of conservatism ("the moral order comes back"). Certain ideological stances could be defined as the simple refusal to recognize this or that boundary.

It must be admitted, at the same time, that more or less stable alliances can indeed be made. Humanists and individualists make common cause in celebrating liberty, which scientists and conservatives condemn (from this point of view, I repeat, Tocqueville is a humanist). Humanists and conservatives defend the necessity of common values, which scientists and individualists reject for opposite reasons (all is necessity — all is freedom). Humanists and scientists make common cause in declaring that rational knowledge of the world is possible, something that conservatives and individualists cast in doubt. Within a single work, different doctrines can collaborate or combat one another. Indeed, certain schools of contemporary thought must be described (in our view) as hybrids, offspring of the crossbreeding of several families. This multiple affiliation does not mean that these schools lack coherence: seen from a historical perspective, all thought is hybrid (our four major families as well), exactly like communities themselves.

It will be clear by now that familial regrouping is a risky and thankless task; I have already explained why nonetheless it seemed to me unavoidable. From now on, I will stick by and large to the humanist family. This unique perspective prohibits me from any claim to an even-handed clarification of the other families: I shall systematically privilege one of the voices in the dialogue of the past.

The way I have identified the devil's challenge concerning a hidden pact explains the order of chapters in this book. In chapter 2, I try to understand the actual meaning of the humanist claim for a freedom characteristic of modern man; to this end, I examine the writings of the great French humanists, from Montaigne to Constant, following which I describe the humanists' parries to the devil's threats, or the reasons for their refusal to pay a price for freedom. Chapters 3 through 5 are devoted to the dangers that menace life in society; I deal here with the humanists' conceptions of society and solitude, of love and friendship. Chapter 6 describes the dispersal of the self and is based on the autobiographical practices of Montaigne and Rousseau. Chapters 7 through 9 analyze the question of values in a world in which God is no longer their source nor their guarantee. The epilogue, finally, returns to the present historical context in order to situate within it the responses provided by the humanist thought of the past.

Chapter 2

The Declaration of Autonomy

*J*ust what does the freedom of modern men consist of? To find out, I will examine how a series of French thinkers between the sixteenth and the nineteenth centuries have answered this question. But first, more detailed information on terminology: I shall use the word *autonomy* here to designate one's choice to feel, to reason, and to will for oneself. The word is not employed by the French humanists but by Kant, in writings that systematize the contribution of earlier thinkers and at the same time transform it. For Kant, autonomy consists not only of governing oneself but also of obeying only the law that we ourselves have prescribed. He speaks in the same sense of *dignity*: to preserve one's dignity is to act in conformity only with those principles and maxims accepted by the subject. The French humanists themselves use the term *liberty* instead — an essentially political liberty, with an extended meaning that involves not the right to do as we like, but to do *also* as we like; a meaning that involves not ignoring laws, but submitting to the laws one has chosen. *Liberty* — or freedom — has the advantage over *autonomy* in belonging to ordinary language; its disadvantage is that the word lends itself to a thousand contradictory uses and suggests the radical absence of any norm or determination. I will therefore avail myself of *autonomy* not in the specifically Kantian sense, but in the more general sense, meaning action that finds its source in the subject himself.

Autonomy is, unquestionably, a conquest of modernity — its first political value. Between Montaigne and Constant, its field has continually widened and its definition has become more detailed. Nonetheless, its history does not form a linear progression. What are the high points in this declaration of autonomy?

Montaigne

Montaigne, the pivotal figure between the old and the new, who read all the Ancients and whom all the Moderns would read, is an inevitable point of departure for anyone who studies the history of thought in France.

Montaigne illustrates, first, a form of affective autonomy: he wants to be able to live with those he loves, not with those whom custom imposes on him. In a traditional society, your place in space and in the social order is decided in advance; the country where you are born is your natural setting and will remain a lifelong attachment. Montaigne declares that he prefers what he chooses himself to what is imposed on him, the chosen to the given. He writes: "I am scarcely infatuated with the sweetness of my native air. Brand new acquaintances that are wholly my own choice seem to me to be well worth those other common chance acquaintances of the neighborhood. Friendships purely of our own acquisition usually surpass those to which community of climate or of blood binds us" (*Essays*, III, 9, 743). Men are not rooted plants; they are at liberty to change the setting of their lives. We have already seen that Montaigne believes we have a nature, but one that is paradoxical, since it leaves us free.

Friendships, which reflect our choice, are worthier than relations imposed by blood ties alone. Montaigne is not content to reiterate the precept of the Bible, according to which man must leave his family of origin and found a new one, preferring his wife to his parents (Gen. 2:24); he states that as far as he, personally, is concerned, his children are less dear to him than his friends — always in the name of the same principle according to which what is chosen is worth more than what is imposed. Unkind remarks about his daughter are not absent; he prefers even his intellectual descendants, his books, to the children of his flesh. How do we explain these judgments? The asymmetry in the love we bear our parents, on the one hand, and our children on the other, is revealing. Why do we prefer the second to the first? This love is not the result of choice, Montaigne explains, but of instinct, the preservation of the species. We love our children whatever they are, good or bad, likable or detestable. In so doing, we are hardly different from animals. No such feeling, on the other hand, attracts us to our parents, once we have become adults ourselves. If our love for our children were governed by judgment, we would prefer them grown rather than small (we would then be able to judge with full knowledge of the facts), and would love them only if they deserved it: "For if they are raging beasts, such as our age produces in profusion, we must hate them and shun them as such" (*Essays*, II, 8, 284). One can question the pertinence of this analysis of relations between parents and children; nonetheless, for Montaigne, the good consists not in submitting oneself to nature (it is bestial), but in tearing oneself away from it.

Similarly with other blood ties: they have not been chosen, and in this respect they are imperfect. "He is my son, he is my kinsman, but he is an unsociable man, a knave, or a fool. And then, the more there are friendships which law and natural obligation impose on us, the less of our choice and free will there is" (I, 28, 137). The accumulation of terms — choice, freedom, will, literally, voluntary freedom — effectively reveals the importance Montaigne attaches to that category which challenges human laws (constraints) as much as natural ones (necessity). The fact that we tend to cleave to our blood relations is proof that we have not left the "animal" condition, that we have not achieved a separate "humanity."

Montaigne also voices another suspicion toward our attachment to our children. Those who place all their hopes and ambitions in their children are concerned more with the line than with the individual, and forget to grant themselves the requisite attention. "I have never thought," Montaigne declares, on the other hand, "that to be without children was a want that should make life less complete and less contented": one must live in the present rather than in the future, and in the self rather than in others. "I am content to be in Fortune's grip by the circumstances strictly necessary to my existence" (III, 9, 764): children play no part in it, and with respect to these in no way indispensable attachments, freedom is a good. This is a new demand to be judged for what one is, taken individually, rather than for what one represents within a family or a social group; it ranks with the claim to obey the choice of one's affections. This could be formulated by men in the sixteenth century; women would have to wait until the twentieth.

This right to manage one's personal life is not the only form of autonomy Montaigne demands. The activity of the mind itself must be freed from the grip of tradition in order to rely solely on its own forces. That is the reason why Montaigne prefers to educate "understanding and conscience" rather than "to fill our memory" (I, 25, 100). A parrot can repeat what the Ancients have to say; human beings must judge and act on their own. Montaigne does not think very highly of those who "have a full enough memory but an entirely hollow judgment" (102), and prefers to have, according to the now famous formula, "a well-made rather than a well-filled head," and a mind that knows how "to choose . . . and discern . . . by itself" (I, 26, 110). For this reason, he also deprecates books, though finding them preferable to children. In books, or at least in traditional books, one finds knowledge, something that issues from yet other books. Now, this knowledge, the work of memory, should not be an aim in itself: the aim of living is to live. Montaigne ends with something close to a eulogy to the uneducated. He has only scorn for those who put all their pride in citing an ancient author, in parading their bookish knowledge: this is not learning but pedantry; he prefers those who exercise their judgment, even if they are ignorant of the past.

Does this mean that Montaigne is "against" memory, as some of his formulations might suggest? Not exactly. He is opposed to the tyranny of memory, in which the fragment of the past—the knowledge of the Ancients—is transmitted intact from generation to generation, always prompting the same pious attitude. The *Essays* are, after all, a work of memory as well, since in them their author seeks to define his own identity and the results of his experience; but memory, here, is in the service of a larger goal: meditation on the human condition. If literal and repetitive memory is devalued, exemplary and instrumental memory, which leads to wisdom, is held in high esteem.

By staking out this position, Montaigne expresses a choice familiar to modern man: against scholastic knowledge and the submission to tradition, in favor of the autonomy of reason and judgment. "Among the liberal arts, let us begin with the art that liberates us" (I, 26, 117). This demand concerns not only knowledge of the world, but also the judgment of good and evil: it is worthier to seek reasons for it by oneself rather than to follow the authority of others. "To found the reward for virtuous actions on the approval of others is to choose too uncertain and shaky a foundation," writes Montaigne (III, 2, 612). "I have my own laws and court to judge me, and address myself to them more than anywhere else" (III, 2, 613). This claim is conceivable only because

Montaigne was earlier engaged in displaying the power of customs, therefore in renouncing any natural foundation for laws: custom is a second nature, which in turn is merely an even older custom. Since nature is silent, reason must speak.

It is important to observe at this point that the reorientation of human action toward strictly human reference points is not accompanied in Montaigne by any systematic eulogy to man, by any boundless confidence in his capacities (Montaigne is not a "naive" humanist). On the contrary, he hastens to show how human reason is weak, how men's pride has little justification. "The most vulnerable and frail of all creatures is man" (II, 12, 330). "There is no beast in the world so much to be feared by man as man" (II, 19, 509). Montaigne has so little esteem for the human race that any negative description of humanity seems to him surrounded by an aura of truth. "Likewise, this is generally true of me, that of all the opinions antiquity has held of man as a whole, the ones I embrace most willingly and adhere to most firmly are those that despise, humiliate, and nullify us most. Philosophy seems to me never to have such an easy game as when she combats our vanity and presumption" (II, 17, 412). It is therefore not because men are good or intelligent that one must let them conduct their own affairs (they are not); it is because no one else can do it for them. Reason is weak and fallible; it is nonetheless preferable to blind submission to tradition. Men are neither entirely good nor entirely bad: "good and evil are . . . consubstantial with our life" (III, 13, 835), which is why Montaigne meditates on education. Memory can be useful but it gives me a borrowed knowledge; reason is weak but it is mine: it is therefore the better of the two.

What exactly is the scope of this new liberty? Here Montaigne's opinions vary a little, perhaps due to a certain prudence in their formulation. Sometimes, professing humility, he seriously restrains its limits, claiming that he has chosen to submit to the public (and notably religious) authorities "not only my actions and my writings, but even my thoughts" (I, 56, 229). But his usual attitude is otherwise, and consists precisely in contrasting thoughts to actions, the first entirely free, the second subject to the authorities of the day. "We owe subjection and obedience equally to all kings, for that concerns their office; but we do not owe esteem any more than affection, except to their virtue" (I, 3, 9). Reason, like feeling, escapes the obligation to submit; if the king is not virtuous — and I myself will be the judge of whether he is or not — I will neither love him nor respect him. "The wise man should withdraw his soul within, out of the crowd, and keep it in freedom and in power to judge things freely; but, as for externals, he should wholly follow the accepted fashions and forms" (I, 23, 86). Inner freedom, external submission: the division seems clear and clean. Other formulas confirm it: "Will and desires are a law unto themselves; actions must receive their law from public regulation" (III, 1, 603). "My reason is not trained to bend and bow, it is my knees" (III, 8, 714).

Sometimes, however, Montaigne opens up larger perspectives. It must be recalled here that one hundred years before the *Essays*, a work appeared in Italy that is often perceived as one of the manifestos of the new humanist spirit, *De la dignité de l'homme* (The dignity of man), by Pico della Mirandola. Pico was not the first to profess this spirit, or even to practice this kind of oration to the glory of man, seeking to contain Augustinian pessimism. Yet his eloquence prevails over that of his predecessors. At the beginning of this brief text, he brushes aside the various traditional justifications of human grandeur (the acuity of the senses or our intelligence, reason, or virtue) in order to retain, finally, a single true feature of man's superiority over the animals: these have a nature that determines their conduct, while man has none but must choose freely what he will become.

To take up the terms introduced previously, Pico disavows "naive" humanism (man is not obviously better than other species), but his formulas belong to the "proud" humanists: man *can* become anything, unlike other species. In this new version of the myth of Prometheas, as Protagoras tells it in Plato, God speaks to man in these terms: "If we have given you, Adam, neither a determined place nor an aspect that is your own, nor any particular gift, this is because the place, the aspect, the gifts that you yourself have wished for are already yours, you possess them according to your desires, to your idea. For the other animals, their defined nature is held in check by the laws that we have prescribed: as for you, no restriction holds you in check, it is your own judgment to which I have entrusted you, that will permit you to define your nature. . . . If we have made you neither celestial nor terrestrial, neither mortal nor immortal, that is because, endowed as it were with the arbitrating and honorific power of modeling and fashioning yourself on your own, you give yourself the form that would have been your preference" (7–9).

If Pico so strongly affirms the dignity of man, that is because he is leaning on a venerable tradition: the human being is a microcosm, therefore containing in himself all the complexity of the macrocosm. Man is made in God's image and so participates in the infinite. Nonetheless, his formulations are powerful: Man (or at least man before the Fall) is a chameleon who can become mineral or vegetable, human or angelic. One sees that Pico's formulations allow us to imagine an extreme version of autonomy, according to which men are wholly free, wholly undetermined, without any positive nature (nothing is given, everything is chosen). In this respect he embodies a version of "proud" humanism. And, although he glimpses the possibility of making "disastrous use of free choice" (15), he still regards this presence of freedom as a reason to admire and magnify man.

Montaigne may have been unacquainted with Pico's text and does not, like him, sing man's praises; yet he comes close when he takes up a distinction established by Plutarch between man and the animals. His version is less extreme than Pico's. "The young of bears and dogs show their natural inclination, but men, plunging headlong into certain habits, opinions, and laws, easily change or disguise themselves" (*Essays*, I, 26, 109). In his text (*Sur les délais de la justice divine*), Plutarch compared the "forthrightness" of animals (their young immediately reveal their hereditary characters) to human hypocrisy. Montaigne significantly reorients the direction of his source: for him, the opposition is not only between forthrightness and hypocrisy, but also between sustaining the "natural" and the possibility of change. The facility to change does not mean that before its intervention men were nothingness, as Pico would have it; rather, their identity consists in diverse and modifiable mores and choices (but always human ones: man cannot share the fate of a stone without ceasing to be man). Montaigne therefore glimpses the possibility of surmounting the dichotomy between nature and culture: the nature of men is precisely their capacity to have a culture, a history, an individual identity; their nature consists of not being entirely determined by nature. If individual man were not free, his history would be of no interest in itself, and Montaigne would not have written the *Essays*: the very existence of this book, devoted to the search for the self, is an indication that for him, the individual is not a simple plaything in the hands of Providence.

Building on the skepticism of the Ancients, Montaigne takes the decisive step that marks the advent of modernity: the good is not defined by God or given in nature; it is the product of human will: "Our duty has no rule but an accidental one" (II, 12, 436). Here, law prevails over nature, values are the effect of customs. But we must not mistake the meaning of this categorical formulation for Montaigne: the fortuitous itself is not fortuitous; its possibility constitutes the nature of man. As for custom, second nature, it can seem as unshakable as the first. Rather than deduce from this arbitrariness the possibility of recomposing laws as we see fit, as the Moderns do, Montaigne concludes — in this respect closer to the Ancients — that we are at liberty to understand this order as independent of our personal will, and to accept the place reserved for us in it; this is the purpose of reason. Submission to these laws in itself (fortuitous but naturalized) might then be lived in freedom: we will obey them, not because, like the beasts, we would not know how to do otherwise, but because we would have understood them and we would have *chosen* obedience. "Since it has pleased God to give us some capacity for reason, so that we should not be like the animals, slavishly subjected to the common laws, but should apply ourselves to them by judgment and voluntary liberty" (II, 8, 279). Here, the defining feature of man no longer seems to be reason but freedom; reason itself is a means of liberation.

If the laws of each nation are arbitrary instead of imposed by nature or God, is it not tempting to submit them to human judgment, if not to base them on it, at least to evaluate them? Montaigne seems to demand a radical freedom when he writes: "For a slave I must be only to reason" (III, 1, 603). But this phrase is immediately completed by a restriction: except insofar as the laws of the city are concerned. Montaigne makes a claim for autonomy, but a limited autonomy: he wants to act freely within the framework of the law, to choose his path, but only where his private life is concerned. The search for the best form of government in order to create the ideal city seems to him a vain exercise, for concrete men do not act like undetermined natures but like beings equipped with culture and history. One must know how to reconcile the chosen with the given: Montaigne isn't in the least a "proud" humanist, and when it comes to the social order, he looks like a conservative. "Not in theory, but in truth, the best and most excellent government for each nation is the one under which it has preserved its existence. . . . Change lends shape to injustice and tyranny" (III, 9, 731). We shall return to this theme.

Descartes

Where affective choices governing private life are concerned, Descartes follows the teaching of Montaigne; what is more, he puts it into practice. Montaigne declares that in principle one should be able to adopt the country that suits one best, and so Descartes, for this reason, emigrates to the Netherlands. The possibility of choosing is part of the human condition: "human beings are not like trees, which are never seen to grow so well when they are transplanted in soil less rich than the soil where they had been sown" (to Brasset, 23 April 1649, in *Oeuvres*, III, p. 375): therefore, what distinguishes them is the freedom to choose. One has the right to reside in the place where one *feels* at home, rather than submitting to the accident of one's birth. Even more than Montaigne, Descartes sees an advantage in not growing too attached to any country, homeland of origin or of choice. "Staying as I am, one foot in one country and the other in another, I find my condition very happy, in that it is free" (to Elizabeth, June–July 1648). The individual is more strongly self-affirming when he does not belong to a country; the uprooting from his native ground (and customs imposed by habit) procures an advantage. Descartes was able, then, like his elder, to prefer freely chosen friends to the neighbors whom circumstances may have placed beside him. "In any case nothing could possibly happen that might prevent me from preferring the happiness of living in the place where Your Highness lives, if I had the chance to do so, to that of living in my own country" (to Elizabeth, 31 January 1648, III, p. 329).

On the other hand, though always in accord with Montaigne, Descartes declares that he submits entirely to the prevailing authorities insofar as his actions are concerned. His first moral rule, he says, is to "obey the laws and customs of my country" (*Discourse on the Method*, pt. III, I, p. 122). It is not that these laws or mores are necessarily good or reasonable; but if I have chosen to stay in one country rather than go elsewhere, I *must* "be guided by those with whom I should have to live." One conforms to mores because they are what they are: this is a pure argument from authority. Descartes illustrates this aptitude to submission by the choice not to publish his *Traité du monde*, following the Church's condemnation of Galileo. Having learned that Galileo's opinions provoked the discontent "of persons to whom I defer," and thereby whose authority has complete power over his actions, he decides to keep his writings to himself: the act of the authorities "was enough to make me change my previous decision to publish my views" (*Discourse on the Method*, pt. VI, I, p. 142). We may think that Descartes is more fainthearted than Montaigne, who agreed to his book's examination by the services of the Pope but did not follow their recommendations; we may also speculate on how much this prudent decision delayed the evolution of science (we know today that it amounted to nothing: his physics was wrong!). Yet the principle is the same: outward submission, inner freedom. Descartes bent his knees, not his reason.

From the point of view of reason, however, of knowledge and judgment, Descartes is much more radical than Montaigne: only the autonomous exercise of reason deserves respect. Montaigne prefers a mind well-made to one well-filled; Descartes makes this difference the very principle of his method. While keeping in mind that his public actions remain in submission to the powers that be, he does not refrain from specifying: "Since I now wished to devote myself solely to the search for truth, I thought it necessary to do the very opposite" (pt. IV, I, pp. 126–27); only his reason has authority over his thoughts (pt. VI, I, p. 142). Because of this, memory is treated even less respectfully than it was in Montaigne: "There is no need for memory in any of the sciences," he declares preemptorily on the verge of his career (in *Cogitationes privatae*, 230), freeing it for the theologians to claim it for themselves. Descartes's famous method, then, consists first of all of systematically doubting all knowledge that comes from the outside, transmitted by tradition; and once this work of housecleaning is accomplished, of putting in place a different knowledge, certain and no longer only possible, for which the subject himself is responsible. Henceforth, only autonomous knowledge — in contrast to knowledge sustained by the authority of tradition — will have the right to respect. All of modern science will rush into the breach thus opened by Descartes.

It might be said that Descartes's contribution to the problematic of autonomy is characterized by two movements: the first consists of establishing a clean separation between the domains of thought and action. We cannot renounce our freedom in the first sphere (man is endowed with a free will), while prudence leads us to suspend our freedom in the second. Freedom in the metaphysical sense is inalienable; political freedom depends on the circumstances. One of the domains (which includes knowledge of the world) demands autonomy; the other allows one to renounce it. The same principles, therefore, are not applicable everywhere; the territory of existence is not homogeneous: this, too, permits Descartes to reconcile theology and philosophy. Divine revelation, he writes in the *Principles of Philosophy*, produces an "incomparably more certain" outcome than imperfect human reason; yet it teaches us nothing about a great part of the world, about the "truths into which theology does not delve": here is where reason recovers all its rights (*Principles of Philosophy*, pt. I, 76, in *Philosophical Writings*, I, p. 221). Again, one submits to "divine Providence," whose "eternal decree" is "infallible and immutable"; yet beside it "things" also exist that depend on "our free will" (*The Passions of the Soul*, 146).

Descartes's second contribution resides in the fact that the demand for autonomy in the sphere of the mind is radical. Indeed, where the activity of knowledge is concerned, Descartes breaks with the prudence of Montaigne, who subjected tradition to reason, but without entirely repudiating it; Descartes sets off on the path of "proud" humanism. The best knowledge now preserves nothing of tradition transmitted by memory. Yet, at the same time, the quality of this knowledge is regarded as enviable. The domain of human knowledge has certain limits; but within these, the Cartesian method is sovereign. "In order to arrive at the highest knowledge of which the human mind is capable there is no need to look for any principles other than those I have provided" (*Principles of Philosophy*, preface, I, p. 184). The "fruits" of these principles include not only the legitimate satisfaction one draws from the victory over ignorance, but also a perceptible amelioration of our behavior: "The truths they contain, being very clear and very certain, will strip all subin short, one might thus "reach the highest level of wisdom" (p. 188).

The intensity of the second Cartesian postulate promises to threaten the separation affirmed in the first. Will and reason enjoy such prestige, in Descartes's own eyes, that the decision to subtract an important part of human existence will sooner or later seem arbitrary. "I see only one thing in us which could give us good reason for esteeming ourselves," writes Descartes, "namely, the exercise of our free will and the control we have over our volitions. For we can reasonably be praised or blamed only for actions that depend upon this free will. It renders us in a certain way like God by making us masters of ourselves" (*The Passions of the Soul*, 152, I, p. 384). But if we regard "the supreme perfection of man" (*Principles of Philosophy*, pt. I, 37, I, p. 205) as the free use of the will, why withhold it from the public world? We note at the same time how the judgment of value (freedom is what is best in us, what is most human) tends to inflate Descartes's anthropology with an assumed "pride," namely, that thanks to our will, we are masters in our own house. "There is no soul so weak that it cannot, if well-directed, acquire an absolute power over its passions" (*The Passions of the Soul*, 50, I, p. 348). Yet fact does not follow value, any more than the reverse: we can value freedom more than anything and nonetheless admit that our passions, our unconscious, or our membership in a culture cannot always accept being guided by will, even an enlightened will, but continue to influence our actions.

However, the comparisons Descartes himself had at his disposal cause him to take several additional precautions. The second chapter of the *Discourse on the Method* opens with a famous parallel that is meant to make us feel intuitively the superiority of the work of reason over the work of tradition. Would we not all prefer, Descartes asks, a town built according to the plans of a single architect to a town whose layout is the result of numerous generations of inhabitants and builders? On the one hand, then, "the will of several men using reason"; on the other, "old walls built for different purposes," "crooked and irregular streets" (pt. II, I, p. 116).

Descartes would have rarely had occasion to observe entirely new cities; we, who do it much more frequently, would tend to make the opposite judgment — and not because, being too modern, we feel an obligatory nostalgia for all that is old, but because tradition, here, is like an alluvial deposit left by the will and reason of men belonging to earlier generations, something superior to the individual reason of the contemporary engineer (this is the conservative criticism of individualist pride). The relevant opposition here is not between freedom and submission but between several forms of freedom, or of will, or of reason. In other words, it is not because they escape the mastery of a *single* consciousness that a work or a behavior is "unreasonable" and deserves to be condemned; conversely, the boundless ambition of a single person easily leads to error, for to err is human, even if one is very knowledgeable.

In principle, as soon as it is a question of public actions, of laws and institutions, of the whole social order, Descartes falls back on conservative positions close to those of Montaigne: The inconveniences of existing laws are often corrected by usage, he will say, so that change in itself is harmful. The comparison he chooses here is much more convincing than the new towns: the main roads "that wind through mountains," established in the course of past centuries, are more convenient than the solution that would consist of "trying to take a more direct route by clambering over rocks and descending to the foot of precipices" (*Discourse on the Method*, pt. II, I, p. 118). Tradition is more reasonable than innovation because the reason of several is stronger than that of a single person; it would be disconcerting to present this opposition as one of tradition and reason. But this new comparison suggests that along with the chosen, a large place is assigned to the given: even if our present reason does not understand its justification, we must assume its existence on principle.

The barriers that Descartes erects between the private world, where the freedom of reason reigns, and the public world, obedient to traditions, seem, in truth, quite fragile. "These large bodies are too difficult to raise up once overthrown . . . and their fall cannot but be a hard one," he writes, speaking of public institutions (p. 118), as if this observation were sufficient reason for everyone to renounce all activism. But those who believe in the omnipotence of reason and will in the domain of the mind are not stopped by so little: You don't make an omelet without breaking eggs, they tell themselves. As for reconstruction, difficulty is not a reason to renounce it since the result, the work of the social engineer, will be so much more beautiful than what went before! What Descartes might have countered was not a voluntary limitation of the field controlled by reason, but the plurality of its social forms and the fallibility of individual reason. To admit that none among us could master the totality of the processes that constitute the life of human societies does not mean that we renounce the autonomy of reason, but only the pride of the individual.

"It would be unreasonable for an individual to plan to reform a state by changing it from the foundations up and overturning it in order to set it up again" (p. 117). Doesn't this look like the rough sketch of a portrait of some future revolutionary, a Robespierre, for example, who would not hesitate to overturn everything to build it anew? Why abstain from throwing oneself into this revolution when it is driven by the sole principle in man that deserves praise? Why hesitate to become like God in everything, not only in one's intellectual activities, but also in the public world, to build not only rational towns but also societies and individuals, becoming their "single architect" (p. 116)? Men of letters would come to agree with this argument on the eve of the French Revolution; as Tocqueville says, in this era "they all think that it would be good to substitute basic and simple principles, derived from reason and natural law, for the complicated and traditional customs which ruled the society of their times" (*The Old Regime and the Revolution*, III, 1, p. 196).

Descartes's proposition would combine moderation and radicalism. "My plan has never gone beyond trying to reform my own thoughts and construct them upon a foundation which is all my own" (*Discourse on the Method*, pt. II, I, p. 118). The small extension of the domain of action (only my thoughts) does not, however, offer sufficient resistance to the ambition of mastery: "all my own"; quantity will cede to quality, unshared domination will be generalized, sweeping away all the barriers meant to contain it. But the slippery slope was already being prepared in the text of Descartes himself, who counted on the increase of knowledge to ameliorate conduct. In this respect, the partisans of the Enlightenment would be his heirs, and not until Rousseau would this principle be stated: knowledge does not itself lead to wisdom. Descartes is not a defender of scientism, but the total power he attributes to the will and the reason of the individual paves the way for the theoretical justifications the scientists will use to support their policies.

A "proud" humanist, Descartes cannot, however, be accused of "naivete": it is not because man is free that he is good. In the *Fourth Meditation*, Descartes set about showing that knowledge of the true and the good does not diminish my freedom but, on the contrary, augments it because my choices are now more clarified; human freedom is therefore compatible with divine omnipotence. And when Hobbes reminds him of the Calvinist objection, which would counsel abandoning freedom in favor of grace, he is content with turning back to our common experience, the capacity we all have to exercise our will (liberty is nothing else), meaning that since the good is chosen and not imposed, evil might have been chosen instead. This is a traditional argument that is found, for example, in Erasmus.

Descartes goes a little further: it is precisely the choice of evil that would attest most clearly to the existence of our freedom. "A greater freedom consists . . . in a greater use of the positive power which we have of following the worse although we see the better." We might even imagine that we do evil expressly to prove our autonomy. "It is always possible for us to hold back from pursuing a clearly known good, or from admitting a clearly perceived truth, provided we consider it a good thing to demonstrate the freedom of our will by so doing" (to P. Mesland, 9 February 1645, III, p. 245). But if the chief perfection of man resides in the exercise of this same free will, is it not evident, too, that nothing is more human than evil and that there are excellent reasons for its abundant presence on this earth? While conscious of the moral imperfections of men, Descartes does not subscribe to the thesis of definitive intellectual imperfection; his humility, in this case, clashes with his pride. He himself has no trouble entertaining these two attitudes, and the revolution of the mind that he promotes never reconciles him to a revolution of action. His successors and disciples, however, will not be as prudent.

Montesquieu

An admirer of Montaigne and Descartes, Montesquieu was perceived by his contemporaries and most of his subsequent readers as a defender of the idea that human behavior is the product of the geographical and historical conditions of the country in which men live. After all, his main work, *The Spirit of the Laws*, the fruit of a quarter century of observation, analysis, and meditation, is the greatest synthesis achieved until that time of knowledge about people's mores in relation to their laws, and thereby a point of departure for the modern social sciences. If this were the substance of Montesquieu's thought, he would not have his place in the family of humanists but would belong to that of the partisans of scientism instead. But is it?

In Montesquieu's work itself, there is no lack of programmatic declarations that would seem to justify such an interpretation. Summing up his *Considerations on the Causes of the Greatness of the Romans*, he writes: "It is not fortune that rules the world," not chance, then, or accident. "There are general causes, be they moral or physical, that act in every monarchy, raise it up, sustain it, or hurl it down; all accidents are subject to these causes. . . . [I]n a word, the chief allure brings with it all particular accidents" (*Complete Works*, XVIII, 472). This precept will be put to work in *The Spirit of the Laws*, in particular in parts 3 to 5, which examine in detail this action of "physical or moral causes": climate (bk. XIV), geography (XVIII), the forms of trade and modalities of labor (XX–XXII), the nature of the population (XXIII), religion (XXIV and XXV).

Unquestionably, Montesquieu grants great importance to the context in which every action is produced. Moreover, he also aspires to penetrate the design of God the Creator, or to recover, beyond human institutions, the true "nature of things." It looks as if a certain continuity could be established in his work between the Ancients' notion of "nature" (harmony of the cosmos, the will of God) and that of the Moderns (physical and moral laws), between the fatalism of believers and determinism of atheists. But if, from this point of view, Montesquieu's thought has a certain ambiguity, it is nonetheless systematic in its refusal to grant an unlimited extension to this causality. More precisely, it does not follow from the fact that everything is the effect of a cause, that nothing can be changed; philosophical determinism does not exclude political will.

In the theological debate that pits Augustinians against Pelagians — those who think that salvation depends on predestination and divine grace, and those who hold that human works are, on the contrary, decisive — Montesquieu would be on the side of the Pelagians. Saint Paul said that man lay in the hands of God like inert clay in the potter's hands; but if so, would Montesquieu exclaim with Erasmus, "What is the purpose of man?" Man must have been meant for some purpose. Yet what distinguishes man from the rest of creation is a higher degree of indeterminacy; therefore, he serves God's design by becoming responsible for his own acts. Even in the absence of predestination and grace, man is not definitively lost: he can save himself by his own efforts. "Sometimes God grants man [predestination], by which he is infallibly saved, but without which he does not lack the power to be saved" (*Mes pensées*, 674).

It would be a serious misunderstanding, then, simply to imagine that Montesquieu adopts a stance of resignation. Yet his first readers already engaged in this misunderstanding, which can perhaps be explained by the fact that liberty is a principle posed once and for all and which, by definition, does not enhance knowledge, whereas determinations can be observed, registered, and analyzed. These are the primary subjects of *The Spirit of the Laws,* and that is why Montesquieu has long been seen as a pure determinist — the result of a confusion of epistemological constraint and ontological hypothesis. Montesquieu was consequently forced to combat this misunderstanding by insisting that "my purpose is not to show that the will is powerless."

The reason Montesquieu treats the margin of indeterminism in the movement of history lies, in the first instance, in the very plurality of determinisms: every cause has multiple effects; every effect can issue from numerous causes. "Although every effect depends on a general cause, so many other particular causes are mingled in it that every effect has, in a way, a separate cause," he writes in the *Essay on Taste* (p. 851); or : "The majority of effects . . . occur by ways so singular, and depend on reasons so imperceptible or so distant that they cannot be foreseen" (*Traité des devoirs*, 182). The world is not irrational but it can be impenetrable; it is overdetermined rather than indeterminate — but in the end this comes down to the same thing. So laws suffer exceptions. This is why Montesquieu is at the opposite pole from scientistic utopianism: he does not believe that the laws of society can become perfectly transparent, or that it is possible to base a politics on the science that brings us knowledge of those laws.

That is not all. Montesquieu, as we have seen, distinguishes between physical causes (climate, geographical conditions) and moral causes (religion, forms of trade and labor, mores); yet if he insists on the power of the first, this is so we shall be better prepared, if need be, to redirect them. Even if "the empire of climate is the first of all empires" (*The Spirit of the Laws*, XIX, 14, p. 316), it is possible to "conquer the laziness that comes from the climate" (XIV, 7, p. 237). And Montesquieu declares: "bad legislators are those who have favored the vices of the climate and good ones are those who have opposed them" (XIV, 5, p. 236). Despotism is most frequent in countries with a large territory and extremes of climate; moderate governments prosper in temperate climates, much to our surprise; the republic is favored by small territory, monarchy by an average one. But one should not count too much on this: "if . . . despotism became established at a certain time, neither mores nor climate would hold firm" (VIII, 8, p. 118). In other words, moral causes are more powerful than physical causes. Montesquieu was irritated by the incomprehension of his readers on this point, and was anxious to say so openly in the *Explications* addressed to the Sorbonne in the wake of criticism concerning his work: "The book of *L'Esprit des lois* forms a perpetual triumph of morality over climate, or rather in general over physical causes" (824).

Montesquieu had broached this question directly in a text that was contemporary with *The Spirit of the Laws* but remained unpublished: *Essai sur les causes qui peuvent affecter les esprits et les caractères*, in which, after reviewing "physical causes" and "moral causes," he concluded: "Moral causes form more the general character of a nation and decide more the quality of its spirit than physical causes" (493). Now, if man can already redirect physical causes by transforming the natural framework in which he lives, how much more do moral causes allow his will to intervene! This intervention has a name: education. Montesquieu distinguishes two major forms of education: "particular" education, specific to each individual (studies, travels, encounters); and "general" education, which one receives through laws, religion, customs, or even the desire to imitate the great of this world. By all these means, it is therefore possible to surmount the determining force of conditions that preexist voluntary intervention. These are not to be ignored, but they are only preliminary givens: it is men who, in the final analysis, make their laws and their lives. The determinism of "moral and physical causes" does not deprive them of their freedom to act and does not relieve them of the responsibility for their actions. Montesquieu concludes: "We fashion for ourselves the spirit that pleases us, and we are its true artisans" (*Essai sur les causes*, 494).

If so many things depend on the will, what is the point of spending so much time studying causes that do not depend on it? For Montesquieu, the best action is one taken with full knowledge of the facts. To surmount the action of climate, we must begin by familiarizing ourselves with it. To palliate the inconveniences generated by a certain form of trade, we must study it first. Furthermore, the most efficacious action is not one that launches a frontal assault on negative influences but one that chooses an indirect way and modifies their conditions first. Education will effectively transform the spirit of the nation and will achieve the desired aim more quickly than a law that would confront it directly; that is why we must know this spirit.

At the beginning of the preface to *The Spirit of the Laws*, Montesquieu announces: "I began by examining men, and I believed that, amidst the infinite diversity of laws and mores, they were not led by their fancies alone" (p. xliii). One tends to read this as an understatement, and to interpret it to mean "they never are." Yet it must be taken literally. Human actions are not purely arbitrary; they are conditioned by a thousand factors that can be known (that is the subject of this present book); but they are nonetheless not entirely determined. Fancy — that is to say, also, will — plays its part. His "not alone" is difficult for any monistic mind to accept; yet this is what distinguishes Montesquieu's position as a humanist stripped of all pride. The arbitrary element in human action is, in his view, irreducible. What can be said, on the other hand, in favor of the determinist option is that this arbitrary element diminishes as one moves away from the individual and approaches generalizations in time or space: large numbers of people obey laws better than individuals do. "These causes become less arbitrary to the extent that they have a more general effect. Thus we know what gives a nation a certain character better than what gives an individual a certain spirit, what modifies a sex better than what affects a man, what shapes the genius of societies that have embraced one sort of life better than what shapes a single person" (*Essai sur les causes*, 485).

This interpretation of the human condition is found at the basis of Montesquieu's analysis of political regimes. Beyond the varied forms these reveal, one large category structures their field that pits despotic regimes against moderate ones. The difference between the two consists (we shall return to this) of the first leaving all power concentrated in the same hands, while the second allows a certain balance of powers. Now, Montesquieu's analysis is certainly not neutral: he stigmatizes and caricatures despotism and praises moderation. The division of power between several authorities is a good because it allows the individual a greater chance of acting in accordance with his will — which best corresponds to the nature of man.

Since human beings, more than other living creatures, must by rights act for themselves, one consequence follows for their institutions: those alone are good that do not hinder this autonomy of action. The political freedom more or less guaranteed by states is not to be confused with the human being's freedom in principle, that is, with his relative indeterminacy. Nonetheless, the second motivates the first. "Every man, considered to have a free soul, should be governed by himself," writes Montesquieu (*The Spirit of the Laws*, XI, 6, p. 159). Opposed to Hobbes elsewhere, he comes around here to another of his fundamental theses, namely, that man is characterized by his preference for liberty: "Hardly anyone is so naturally stupid that he does not think it better to rule himself than to let others rule him," wrote Hobbes (*On the Citizen*, III, p. 49). Good political regimes are those that preserve this margin of freedom for individuals. But Montesquieu does not extend the demand for autonomy to the regimes themselves, any more than Hobbes does. In some regimes — the republic, for example — the people want to govern themselves: "Yet another fundamental law in democracy is that the people alone should make laws" (II, 2, p. 14) But in the monarchy, which is also a legitimate regime since it ensures the freedom of the individual, the demand for the sovereignty of the people would not make any sense. One should not, therefore, extrapolate from the individual to the state.

Rousseau

A century after Descartes, Rousseau no longer felt the need to demand the autonomy of reason with regard to knowledge of the world. By the time of the *Encyclopédie*, this was taken for granted; empirical observation and logical argumentation had replaced the docile transmission of scholastic knowledge. On the other hand, Rousseau was no more a revolutionary than Montaigne or Descartes: he considered that the actions of individuals must remain subject to the prevailing laws, even if those laws leave something to be desired in terms of justice. This point should be emphasized, for we know that Rousseau did not shrink from reflecting on "the principles of political right" (this is the subtitle of *The Social Contract*), an activity that Montaigne and Descartes considered futile, and that thirty years later revolutionaries would transform, according to his doctrine, into a program for action. For Rousseau, however, "nothing in the world is more different" than the meditation on principles, on the one hand, and concrete social practice, on the other (*Emile*, V, p. 458). The one deals in abstractions, the other treats the behavior of men in the grip of passions; between them there is a breach in continuity. In practice, Rousseau — like Descartes — chose exile if necessary, but never revolt.

At the same time, Rousseau takes up and amplifies the principle that Descartes formulated in *The Passions of the Soul*: only the act freely accomplished can be virtuous. "Moral freedom," Rousseau grants, ". . . alone makes man truly a master of himself" (*Social Contract* I, 8, p. 142). He explains himself at greater length on this subject in *Emile*, in which he makes liberty the Savoyard vicar's "third article of faith" (IV, p. 281). As far as human actions are concerned, "it is not the word *liberty* that means nothing, it is the word *necessity*" (586). Man is free in his actions, whatever the forces that weigh on him; he "acts by himself," and for this reason can do good or evil. This would not be the case if his acts were dictated to him exclusively by Providence or his nature. Like Montaigne, like Montesquieu, Rousseau sees in this liberty — and therefore in the possibility of doing good and evil — the decisive difference between men and animals. "Nature alone does everything in the operations of a Beast, whereas man contributes to operations by being a free agent. The former chooses or rejects by instinct and the latter by an act of freedom. . . . Nature commands every animal, and the Beast obeys. Man feels the same impetus, but he realizes that he is free to acquiesce or resist" (*Inequality*, I, pp. 25–26).

It will be noted here that Rousseau does not adhere to the "proud" version of humanist doctrine. Man "concurs with" the direction of his fate; he does not order it all alone: human action is the result of two forces, nature and freedom. Man does not entirely escape the commandments of nature, yet he has a margin of maneuverability that animals lack: he can also resist. Like the other species, he has a nature, but his is less constraining. And in all his reflections Rousseau will seek to articulate the given and the chosen: love of self and pity are in the nature of man, although they are equally the source of virtues, which depend on the will.

Rousseau's chief contribution to the humanist doctrine of autonomy is, however, to be found elsewhere: in his extension of that doctrine from the private world, where Montaigne and Descartes had confined it, to the public world; or rather from the individual subject to a collective subject (the people). Rousseau's attachment to political freedom is not, in itself, a true innovation. The Greeks' idea of political freedom already held that an individual's public life is governed by laws that he himself instates rather than by orders from elsewhere to which he submits. In addition, democracy is opposed to tyranny, in which power depends on the arbitrary will of the leader: in democracy it results from the common will of all citizens. Theseus, in Euripides' *The Suppliant*, can say: "The city is not ruled by a single man but is free. The people rule, and offices are held by yearly turns" (403–6). By recovering the idea of political autonomy, then, Rousseau rejoins Greek political thought (which left fewer traces in the forms of autonomy claimed by Montaigne and Descartes); Rousseau's "general will" is closely bound to what Benjamin Constant would call the "liberty of the Ancients." Yet Rousseau gives it a form that touches the hearts of the Moderns.

Rousseau's formulas are radical. What confers legitimacy on a political regime, an institution, or a law? Their simple existence obviously does not suffice, just as the notoriety of an opinion alone does not in Descartes's view prove its truth. Facts do not allow the deduction of right. What does the presence of a social convention signify? That in the course of an earlier conflict, it prevailed over rival laws, rules, and institutions. Tradition—history—consecrates the triumph of might, not right. That is why Rousseau begins his inquiry by resolutely setting aside all the "lessons of history," all the "reasons" we think we find in it. "Let us therefore begin by setting all the facts aside," he writes brutally at the beginning of *Discourse on the Origins of Inequality* (19); and from the first pages of *The Social Contract*, he attacks Grotius, who was, in his view, wrong to cite examples drawn from history as an argument. "His most persistent mode of reasoning is to establish right by fact. One could use a more consistent method, but not one more favorable to Tyrants" (I, 2, p. 132).

The only legitimate government of a country is the one chosen by the free will of the people of that country; this is the famous general will. Insofar as each person has accepted the social contract of a common life regulated by laws, he participates in this general will. It is the law that "teaches him to act according to the maxims of his own judgment" (*Economie politique*, 248): his judgment, not another's. The individual chooses to act according to his own will, and this action consists of forming a general will that dictates the laws applicable to all. At the same time, the freedom of his will gives legitimacy to the law. We see here how the argument shifts from the autonomy of the individual to that of the political regime: since "man is born free and master of himself" (*Social Contract*, IV, 2, p. 200), only the regime to which he adheres freely is free (and therefore legitimate). Hence that formula whose revolutionary potential will be exploited thirty years later: "Every legitimate government is republican" (II, 6, p. 153). In other words, only the republic is legitimate.

However, on this level as well Rousseau does not spill over into "proud" humanism. The general will alone confers legitimacy; this does not mean that concrete laws must be the product of that will exclusively. Rousseau remains close to Montesquieu here, who saw good laws as the outcome of a long interaction between what is given—geographical and climatic conditions, history, forms of religion or trade—and what is chosen or inspired by an ideal of moderation, which allowed Montesquieu to condemn tyrannies of every stripe. In turn, Rousseau imagines neither man nor society as a tabula rasa on which one might, as a function of one's will alone, build new constructions. He knows that no one can remove himself from his history or his culture. He writes, "Each people must be assigned a particular system of institutions that is the best, not perhaps in itself, but for the State for which it is destined. . . . Apart from the maxims common to all, each people contains within itself some cause that organizes it in a particular manner and renders its legislation appropriate for it alone" (*Social Contract* II, 11, p. 163). The art of governing does not consist of reasoning in the abstract, but of judiciously transforming general principles in accord with the circumstances of time and place; he addresses himself to real men, not to saints or sages. Simply, what was central for Montesquieu will be marginal for Rousseau, and vice versa.

Finally, we must pause at another aspect of autonomy. I should be able to act in accord with my preferences and my tastes, instead of obeying chance conventions or nature, said Montaigne and Descartes; for example, to live with my friends rather than with my cousins. However, Montaigne himself already noticed that this purely personal autonomy turns out to be much more difficult than one imagines, for everyone suffers the pressure of common opinion: he thinks he is behaving on his own; in reality he is merely conforming to a mode, to a dictate from elsewhere. "We defraud ourselves of our own advantages to make appearances conform with public opinion. We do not care so much what we are in ourselves and in reality, as what we are in the public mind" (*Essays*, III, 9, p. 729).

The moralists of the seventeenth century concur: man believes he is choosing; in reality he submits to trends and tastes that are alien to him. He believes he is acting for himself, while others dictate his behavior. Pascal writes: "We are not satisfied with the life we have in ourselves and our own being. We want to lead an imaginary life in the eyes of others, and so we try to make an impression" (*Pensées*, bk. 147, line 806) Appearance prevails over being, yet appearance is imposed on us by others: our autonomy is therefore illusory. La Rochefoucauld would say much the same thing: people "believe that they must imitate what they see done by others. . . . Everyone wants to be another, and to be no longer what he is" (*Reflexions diverses*, III). We claim to desire and to judge on our own, but this pretense, much of the time, merely conceals an illusion. "We forget ourselves, and we are imperceptibly estranged from ourselves"; we lack an adequately sensitive ear to hear our own thoughts and feelings. What we hear instead, and submit to, are the customs, trends, and tastes that we read in the gaze of others.

Rousseau grants, as we shall see, a still more important place to this consideration for the gaze that others turn on us; but he also interrogates himself on the ways to be free of it. It is not enough to say, It is my will, for our desires do not obey the will but unconscious forces within us; we do not freely choose the beings we love. Rousseau therefore suggests acting on those unconscious forces by a method adapted (to this purpose), which in *Emile* he calls "negative education." This consists, in the first instance, of encouraging the child to get to know his own tastes by protecting him from the value-laden speech that surrounds him (I will return to this). For this reason, the child sees few adults outside his teacher and reads hardly any books (with the single revealing exception of *Robinson Crusoe*: the hero of this novel lives on his island isolated from the judgments of others). The purpose of the operation is to turn him not into a savage, but into an autonomous being—even in his tastes and preferences. "It suffices that, enclosed in a social whirlpool, he not let himself get carried away by either the passions or the opinions of men, that he see with his eyes, that he feel with his heart, that no authority govern him beyond that of his own reason" (*Emile*, IV, p. 255).

This "natural man" would yet be no stranger to society. What Emile will have learned to avoid, in fact, is not sociability but servile submission to current opinions and absurd conventions, the habit of conducting himself according to the norms of the day even if they are constantly changing, the concern with the crowd's judgment of him (the "what will people say?"). Like an ancient "cynic" philosopher, the person educated like Emile will act "without concern for the arbitrary judgments whose only law is fashion or prejudice" (670). Saint-Preux already said: "The main objection to large cities is that there men become other than what they are, and society imparts to them, as it were, a being other than their own." Women in particular, "derive from the way others look at them the only existence that matters to them" (*The New Héloïse*, II, 21, p. 223).

Already described by La Rochefoucauld, this drift is associated by Rousseau more particularly with urban life and, we might add, with modern society. But social man is not confused with worldly man. "The man of the world is whole in his mask. Almost never being in himself, he is always alien and ill at ease when forced to go back there. What he is, is nothing, what he appears to be is everything for him" (*Emile*, IV, 230). Being and appearance are equally social, but the individual who clings only to appearance has renounced his autonomy. Rousseau rediscovers here another of La Rochefoucauld's ideas (shared by the Stoics):

one must know how to accept oneself, to escape alienation (in the literal sense of submission to others), this would be the result of an aspiration to the good. "[I]f in these parallels he just once prefers to be someone other than himself — were this other to be Socrates, were it Cato — everything has failed. He who begins to become alien to himself does not take long to forget himself entirely" (243). Rousseau suggests that submission to one's own nature reduces the risk that the individual will submit to the model of others. Once trained in this way, the individual will be able to preserve the autonomy of his feelings and desires: liberty might then be lived in harmony with nature, rather than in opposition to it.

Constant

With Rousseau, the notion of autonomy is no longer limited in scope: it intervenes in knowledge and in action, in public life and in private life; and yet it is not absolute but limited. The humanists do not misjudge the power of the given, either of physical nature or of social custom. They think, however, that *liberation* is always possible. Human life is an imperfect garden; autonomy is a plant that must be tended to flourish. Freedom (greater or lesser) is the result of a process, therefore a goal inscribed in us, that can moreover become the horizon of political institutions. The autonomy of the *I* is, of course, partial, but it is omnipresent; based on the relative indeterminacy of the human being, it allows him to direct his own public and private life. As the primary constitutive element in the humanist doctrine, its affirmation marks a point of no return. However, this conjunction between principles and action, conceived by Rousseau, has not yet entered the realm of practice. That would be accomplished in the wake of the French Revolution: the ideas of Rousseau and his predecessors are transformed into a political program, passing from words to acts. Yet the very victory of autonomy here will give rise elsewhere to an unforeseen danger. The credit for its discovery belongs to Benjamin Constant.

First, it must be said that Constant was particularly sensitive to the power of historical conditioning: he knew how much the past weighs on the present, how much context influences individual action. "A century is the necessary result of those that preceded it. A century can only be what it is" (*Littérature du 18e siècle*, 528). Without necessarily being conscious of it, individuals participate in the spirit of their times. "Human things have a progressive course, independent of men, and which they obey without knowing it. Even their will is included in this, because they can never want anything but what is in their interest, and their interest depends on coexisting circumstances" (*Du polythéisme romain*, XIV, 3; II, 168). The best attitude therefore seems to be the acceptance of this determination. "If the human race follows an invariable course, one must submit to it. Resignation alone will spare men senseless struggles and dreadful misfortunes" (*Pensées detachées*, 603).

Yet it would be a mistake to take Constant for a determinist. And it is precisely because he is aware of the power of the causal series that his arguments against total determinism work. Indeed, taking up Montesquieu's idea, Constant is careful to specify that even when historical conditions determine the general movement, they leave a large margin of freedom for individuals. "Everything is moral in individuals, but everything is physical in the masses. . . . Each person is free individually, because he is involved, individually, only with himself, or with forces equal to his own. But as soon as he enters into a whole, he ceases to be free" (*Littérature du 18e siècle*, 528). The individual acts according to his will; his acts can therefore be judged on the moral level (it goes without saying that this is the individual "in principle," not the concrete person caught in a network of dependencies, subjected to his superiors, who is never "involved only with himself"). But as members of a whole — a people, an epoch — individuals are swept along by a movement that engulfs them: an invisible force then leads them toward its own goal.

Concerning political action, Constant does not add the requirement of a new autonomy alongside those already formulated; and how could he? He confirms the demands of his predecessors. For him it goes without saying that individuals have the right to make free use of their reason to know the world or to formulate judgments. He also adheres to Rousseau's principle according to which political power is the emanation of the general will: the people are sovereign. "In short there are only two sorts of power in the world: one, illegitimate, is force; the other, legitimate, is the general will" (*Principles of Politics*, I, p. 175). He discovers, however, that the primary form of autonomy, the one that allowed Montaigne and Descartes to organize their lives to suit themselves as long as no laws were broken, is now threatened; and he will try to build a protective wall around it.

Where does this new evil come from? From the very generalization of the idea of freedom.

The autonomy granted to society as a whole, the political sovereignty of the people, can pose a challenge not only to an illegitimate power but also to the autonomy of the individuals who constitute that people (as Hobbes already understood). In the old society, where a demand for collective autonomy did not challenge the powers that be, individual freedom alone was at stake: the freedom of feelings, reason, and will. That the people in turn should become autonomous is a victory for freedom; but it does not guarantee that individuals remain free. Instead of being an extension of individual autonomy, the autonomy of the group may lead to its negation. This harm must therefore be prevented before it is too late, and individuals must be protected against a possible encroachment of power that would be no less painful because the power itself is autonomous.

Constant was the first in France to draw larger theoretical conclusions from the revolutionary experience. The men of 1789 believed they had done well to replace the monarchy with the republic, royal sovereignty with that of the nation. Then came the Terror, which provoked their fear, if not their destruction. Why this perversion of such a fine initial project? It was because, as Sieyès noted on the eve of 9 Thermidor, the worm was already in the apple. In a sense, the Revolution of 1789 did not go far enough: it was satisfied with replacing one actor with another and maintaining the same script. It was no longer the king who reigned but the "people"; yet power was no less absolute. By leaving no space outside its control, it transformed every adversary into an enemy and any divergence into a reason for a fight to the death. The Terror was the direct consequence of that absolutism: 1793 was nascent in 1789. The revolutionaries believed they were breaking totally with the Old Regime, when in reality they were prolonging one of its most sinister features: absolutism. They should have gone one step farther and changed not only the actor but the play; it was no longer enough to appeal to national sovereignty alone; they should have limited it as well by resorting to another principle.

Constant's warning is formulated in a critique of Rousseau's thought, a critique that does not take up the principle of collective autonomy (which the two authors share) but the absence of clear limits between this new power of the people and that of the individuals who constitute the people. Constant cannot accept what Rousseau calls "the total alienation of each associate with all his rights, to the whole community" (*Social Contract*, I, 6, p. 53). That the source of power is legitimate is no guarantee against abuses. The reason for Rousseau's error, Constant thinks, lies in the abstract nature of his system: he forgot that in practice, the general will is placed in the hands of several individuals only, and that this fact allows for all forms of abuse. "By giving ourselves entirely, we do not enter a condition equal for all, because some derive exclusive advantage from the sacrifice of the rest" (*Principles of Politics*, I, p. 178).

Constant corrects this error of Rousseau's by adding to the first principle of sovereignty a second principle, inspired by Montesquieu (*The Social Contract* and *The Spirit of the Laws* are named in the first line of *Principles of Politics*, and the plural "principles" is clearly significant here).

For Rousseau, as we have seen, power is illegitimate if it is not instituted by the general will of the people. Montesquieu sees things quite differently: it is not its origin that makes a power legitimate, nor its structure (whether it is exercised by one, several, or many), but the way it functions. In his eyes, power is legitimate when it is limited. One can limit it either by laws or by another power. Montesquieu, then, wants government to be subjected to existing laws, without concerning himself with how they have been instituted or by whom. When he observes particular societies, he notes that certain peoples live under laws that they have given themselves, others according to laws they have not chosen; thus in a monarchy, the laws are granted by the sovereign, who may have received them from his ancestors. However, both republic and monarchy obey laws; they are, in Montesquieu's eyes, equally "moderate" regimes, and therefore legitimate. The same goal, which is to place limits on power, can be achieved by other means: by arranging things in such a way that the executive, legislative, and judicial powers are not concentrated in the same hands, so that one might counterbalance the other. It hardly matters, then, where power comes from; its "moderation" is what counts. In the contrary case, we are dealing with a despotic regime, since it unites all powers in a single one; it is the absence of any protective counterpower that makes despotism so disastrous.

Like Montesquieu, then, Constant adds that power is to be condemned if it is not exercised within certain limits. "When this authority is extended to objects outside its sphere, it becomes illegitimate" (*Principles of Politics*, II, 1). Yet Montesquieu's formulation no longer satisfies him.

There is no point in respecting laws if those same laws do not respect the rights of the individual (for Constant, the unjust law is a much more palpable reality than it is for Montesquieu). And it is futile to distribute power between distinct branches of government (the legislative, the executive, the judicial): if together they deprive me of a protected territory, I cannot approve of such a regime. "What matters to me is not that my personal rights may be violated by some power, without the approbation of some other; but that this violation should be forbidden to all powers. It is not enough that executive agents need to invoke the authorization of the legislator, the legislator must not be able to authorize their action except in a determined sphere" (II, 3). What counts, in this case, is neither the precise extent of this sphere nor how it is delimited, but the very fact of its existence.

Montesquieu says: All power must not be allocated to *the same body*. Constant replies: Power must not *all* be allocated. Montesquieu is careful to arrange things such that power checks power. Constant asks: "How can power be limited other than by power?" (II, 4), and answers: by the establishment of a territory where no social power, legitimate or illegitimate, shared or unified, has any right—the territory of the individual. And he concludes: "Liberty is none other than what individuals have the right to do and what society does not have the right to prevent" (I, 3). The existence of every human being is shared between two spheres, one public, the other private; one over which society exercises its control, the other which the individual manages himself. The territory of the individual is not subjugated to social sovereignty, whatever its form (he will choose his gods, his friends, his work, indeed his country himself). "Liberty" is the name given to the boundary separating these two spheres, to the barrier beyond which any intervention by society is illegitimate.

This requirement was already there at the source of liberal thought, which demanded freedom of religious conscience; Montesquieu had the merit to introduce it into politics. Constant generalizes it and formulates its consequence: a single criterion is no longer sufficient to describe the best political regime; the autonomy of the individual is not assured because the people have become autonomous; the two forms of liberty are not necessarily allied. The democratic regime must refer to two elementary principles: the autonomy of the people and the autonomy of the individual, the general will and individual freedom.

It is the freedom of individuals in relation to the state and society that

Constant designates as the "liberty of the Moderns." He notes, in effect, that it has not always been claimed in this form, which had its beginnings only in the sixteenth century and came into its own in the eighteenth. Even when Montaigne or Descartes demand the right to live where they wish or to love whom they wish, they do not require the judicial establishment of a territory over which the public force has no right of surveillance. Yet this tacit tolerance may no longer suffice. It is not that the old society allowed more freedom to the individual but that it was, in this respect, less systematic. What was described by Montaigne and Descartes as a personal practice must, according to Constant, be protected by the law as an inalienable right.

Constant does not invent a new form of autonomy; he is concerned only with ensuring the (public) protection of one of its forms: that of private life. The criticism he addresses to popular sovereignty is an internal warning: He cautions against a possible abuse of what is a fundamentally positive principle. His point of view may be judged too biased. Does the strengthening of the state necessarily operate to the detriment of the individual? Can't harm come, rather, from other individuals? Can't society with its institutions play the role of a protective shield? Doesn't the individual require, for his full flowering, that society ensure not only his invulnerability but also his well-being? Must liberty itself be subtracted from the action of the state, or is it guaranteed by action of the state? Constant does not imagine the modern "welfare state."

The state can be protective or oppressive; Constant is sensitive to the second aspect and ignores the first. For him, the choice presents itself differently. If, as Hobbes does, one decides that the greatest danger of all is civil war, insecurity, the threat of death, one must pray for an absolute power that guarantees order, even if that implies the loss of individual freedoms. If one thinks, as Montesquieu does, that the worst calamity is the loss of liberty, power is best limited.

Constant chose Montesquieu against Hobbes and, resolutely committing himself to the path of liberalism forged by Locke, he corrects the first democratic principle (the sovereignty of the people) by the second (the freedom of the individual); in a democratic state, the sovereignty of the people is no longer unlimited. What was an abstract question for Locke becomes the basis of an ample development for Constant (the *Principes de politique* of 1806), and will later serve him as the rule for his public action. Constant thus sketches out, just after the Revolution, the only framework in which a politics in accord with humanist principles can be situated.

The meeting of these two sides — "republican" on the one side and "liberal" on the other — is what distinguishes modern democracies. The common good and the happiness of each are democracy's equally legitimate ends, which, even if they spring from the same source, cannot always be pursued simultaneously: their field of application does not coincide. Tocqueville says it in his own way: "Our contemporaries are constantly excited by two conflicting passions: they want to be led, and they wish to remain free. As they cannot destroy either the one or the other of these contrary propensities, they strive to satisfy them both at once" (*Democracy in America*, II, 4, 6, p. 319). The republican and liberal sides of modern states will undoubtedly never manage to form anything but an unstable equilibrium, each moderating the other's excess.

Inscribing the principle of individual autonomy on the same level as collective autonomy, Constant is not satisfied with putting the two separate requirements together; he also transforms the relationship between morality and politics. This relationship had already been overturned in the Renaissance. In the earlier Christian perspective, morality (and its underlying theology) dominated politics, which was of necessity its illustration. No one wondered whether the Crusades served the country's interest; it was enough that they contributed to the glory of God. In the Renaissance, the novelty was the radical dissociation of the theological from the political: what is good for one is not always, or very often, good for the other.

It was Machiavelli who engineered this break: civic *virtu* has nothing to do with Christian virtues, and strong states are not built by practicing charity with their enemies. Christianity is suitable for moral edification, but it produces poor citizens. Machiavelli's formulation, then, corresponds to the reality of modern states; even if his ideas were officially condemned and refuted, they found ample echo. Montaigne would think, in his turn, that what is "useful" in politics is not to be confused with what morality qualifies as "honest"; immorality is necessary to politics, just as poison can be to health. "The public welfare requires that a man betray and lie and massacre" (*Essays*, III, 1, 600). Rousseau would set in opposition — mostly without hope of reconciliation — "man" and "citizen," therefore also morality and politics. In *The Social Con-*

tract, he would judge that Christianity makes poor citizens, since Jesus declared that all men are brothers, not only fellow citizens.

In the twentieth century, we have been witness to a new attempt to reconstruct the relations between morality and politics: in totalitarian regimes, politics dictates the rules of morality. The state defines political imperatives but also the moral aims of its citizens; since nothing escapes its reach, the moral autonomy of individuals has no place.

Benjamin Constant, who meditated on the absolutism of monarchy, revolutionary terror, and Napoleonic tyranny, had a presentiment of this totalitarian danger, and to conjure it away he proposed another kind of articulation between morality and politics: no longer the submission of one to the other, nor their definitive separation, but the introduction of individual autonomy as a legitimate principle within politics itself. Constant's "second principle," the right of the individual to an inviolable territory, ensures the independence of morality from any other imperative; at the same time, it introduces into political life a moral principle that acts on it without dominating it. Constant imagined, in effect, the situation of civil disobedience in an instance when laws would dictate behaviors running counter to one's judgment of one's moral obligations (for example, the duty of hospitality, or the duty not to engage in denunciation). Individuals have rights independent of the laws in force and prior to them, which we call the rights of man. These rights do not decide the politics of states, but they pose limits that this politics must not violate; at the same time they constitute a ground from which one can evaluate existing laws and institutions. Constant once again recovers the essentially *moderate* spirit of humanism, which allows divergent principles to be mutually limiting, rather than ignoring one another or engaging in mortal combat.

Humanism is above all a thought that informs all human actions, not a particular institution. However, institutions allow thought to operate freely or, on the contrary, silence it. Montesquieu and Rousseau did not think only about the place and role of man in the world; they reflected on the concrete social forms that would ensure the maintenance of that place and that role. The separation of powers and the general will point toward those institutions favorable to the flowering of a life in harmony with the humanist project. But it is with Constant that humanism leads to a political structure, the structure of liberal democracy. Constant was not only a philosopher and a writer; he was also a political man actively engaged in the construction and improvement of institutions corresponding to his ideal. Rousseau dreamed of the constitutions of Poland and Corsica, but his speculations did not lead to concrete actions; Constant, on the other hand, sought to influence the politics of his country directly. This contact with practice makes his reflections closer to the real situation in which modern men find themselves, and pushed him to articulate clearly his two principles of politics. The democratic subject submits to the laws of his country, and in this sense he renounces his natural liberty. But he elects his legislative representatives, and can recall them if they do not satisfy him. In addition, he has the right to preserve his personal territory from all intrusion and to reject the law if he judges it unjust. He can conduct himself as a moral citizen.

Chapter 3

Interdependence

$\mathcal{M}$odern men see individual freedom as a good; but don't we pay for it in the end? The most immediate danger, which was perceived at the time of the Revolution and still threatens us today, concerns our relations with other human beings. Wishing to be free, don't we risk cutting ourselves off from our community of origin, and worse, risk that community's dissolution? Is solitude the necessary counterpart of our autonomy — and what would be more terrifying than to be condemned to solitude in the midst of others? Is there a place for love in this modern world, or should we resign ourselves to seeing affective relationships gradually give way to contractual arrangements? The defenders of autonomy must respond to these anguishing questions if they are not ready to admit that we've made a bad bargain.

For the most part, the Moderns agree that the fate of men lies in their own hands; but a good many thought they observed that these men were, by nature, solitary, egotistical beings, hostile to their peers. In particular, this was reputed to be Hobbes's doctrine in the seventeenth and eighteenth centuries (and it hardly matters in the present context if this reputation was justified or not). The political demand for autonomy seems to presuppose the anthropological doctrine of "atomism," that is, the self-sufficiency of individuals — or, in our terminology, individualism.

Social Nature

We should not imagine, however, that these anthropological hypotheses garner any approval from humanist thinkers. Far from it. The "refutation" of Hobbesian ideas is an obligatory trope even for works that aspire to rest in peace with official Christian thought (which does not stop them from simultaneously succumbing to Hobbes's influence). It is precisely the rejection of this individualistic vision that led Montesquieu to criticize Hobbes at the very beginning of *The Spirit of the Laws*. In the state of nature, contrary to what Hobbes claims, men do not try to hurt each other or subdue others. They are weak and frightened, living in need and seeking protection and security. In addition, they have never been truly alone: had they been, they would not have been capable of reproducing, hence of surviving. The attraction between the sexes is much more basic than the strife between rivals. The "desire to live in society" is the "natural law" of humanity (I, 2).

Montesquieu always opposed the idea that the natural state of men was to be alone and outside society. A quarter of a century before *The Spirit of the Laws* (1748), he had written *Traité des devoirs* (A treatise on duties, 1725), the text of which was lost but fragments of which survived in the collection that Montesquieu entitled *Mes Pensées*. Again in opposition to Hobbes, he writes: "The first and only man feared no one. This man alone, who would find a woman alone as well, would not make war on her. All the others would be born into one family, and soon into one society. There was no war then; on the contrary, love, education, respect, gratitude—everything breathed of peace" (615). Montesquieu departs here from the biblical image: the first man has no parents; he was created by God, as was the first woman. Never mind; the main thing is that they would rather make love than war. As for the human beings who follow, they are clearly born of a mother and a father; the protective love of parents precedes any conflict—otherwise the species would not maintain itself. "Childhood being the state of the greatest weakness conceivable, children were perforce dependent on their fathers, who had given them life and gave them the means to preserve it" (616). It is not that hatred is absent in families or in relations between men and women; but had it prevailed, the species simply would not have survived. A few years earlier, in the *Persian Letters* (1721), Usbek declared that inquiries into the origin of society were ridiculous, since every human being is obliged to come into the world within the society that is the family. "They are all born related to one another; a son is born of his father, and he clings to him—hence Society, and the cause of Society" (I, 94).

We may find it strange that in Montesquieu's imagination, children are born and grow up without a mother's ministrations; but what matters is that human beings do not live and cannot live outside of society. To believe that they are asocial by nature is an aberration; to imagine that their goal is to become asocial is to indulge in illusions. Montesquieu is intransigent on this point. We might, however, judge that he is not a typical representative of humanist thought in that certain aspects of his doctrine remain faithful to Aristotle and therefore to the Ancients. It is better, in this case, to confront Rousseau, who is a typical representative of this thought, especially because, as theoretician of the general will and moral autonomy, he is equally famous for having praised natural man as being asocial and for having sung the joys of solitude. Doesn't his work clearly demonstrate the indissoluble bond between the principle of autonomy, on the one hand, and modern individualism, on the other? Since Bonald, this has been the prevalent view. But is it right? To answer this question, we must enter into Rousseau's thought in some detail.

Sociability

"Nature" plays an essential role in Rousseau's conceptual system. In his hypothetical reconstruction of the history of humanity, an original "state of nature" is opposed to a later "state of society." A whole series of oppositions is correlated with this one. And two types of men correspond to these states, which Rousseau calls alternatively "natural man" and "the man of man," or "the man of nature" and "the man of opinion," or "primitive man" and "civic man," or again "the man of nature" and "the factitious and chimerical man whom our institutions and our prejudices have substituted for him" (*First Dialogue*, p. 53)

The contrast between the state of nature and the state of society, between natural man and the man of opinion, leads Rousseau to formulate, in the *Discourse on the Origins of Inequality*, another parallel opposition, between self-love (*amour de soi*) and *amour-propre*. Self-love is a feeling that primitive man shares with the animals; it is, broadly speaking, the instinct of self-preservation. It is "the sole passion natural to man" (*Emile*, II, 92), "a primitive, innate passion, which is anterior to every other, and of which all others are in a sense only modifications" (IV, 213). This is a passion comparable to natural man himself, in that, ignorant of any distinction between good and evil, it is nonethe-

less spontaneously good. Amour-propre, on the other hand, a characteristic only of social man, consists of situating oneself in relation to
others and preferring oneself to everyone else; it leads to the hatred
of others and to dissatisfaction with oneself. It resembles what other
moralists call vanity: it is our dependence on the judgment of others.
"Amour-propre, which is to say a relative [this term in Rousseau is
synonymous with "social"] feeling by which one makes comparisons;
[which] demands preferences, whose enjoyment is purely negative, and
it no longer seeks satisfaction in our benefit but solely in the harm of
another" (*First Dialogue*, p. 9). *Armour-propre* is the source of all vice,
just as self-love is of virtue.

What accounts for all the differences between the state of nature and
the state of society? The fact is that at first, man is alone — not unique,
like Adam, but not taking the proximity of others into account; they are
present in his existence, not in his consciousness. He is alone, he is
solitary, repeats the *Discourse on the Origins of Inequality*; he knows
no "communication with his peers" (199 n. VI). In the state of society,
by contrast (even the name is telling in this regard), man is defined by
his social belonging, by his dependence on others, by communication
with his peers.

Contrary to his popular image (though not among historians), Rousseau does not ignore society and its effect on man — quite the contrary.
In the *Discourse on the Origins of Inequality*, he is engaged in deducing
all the present features of the human race from the single fact of social
life. This is the source of reason, conscience, and moral feeling; private
property, inequality, and servitude, hence all current forms of economic
life; laws, innumerable institutions, and wars; languages, technologies,
sciences, and the arts; our feelings and passions as we experience them
today.

Nonetheless, the popular image of Rousseau as a partisan of the state
of nature and scornful of the state of society is not false. If the man of
nature is good, the man of man is not; or, as Rousseau often puts it,
man is good but men are wicked. The men we see before us are at once
depraved and unhappy; the explanation of this contrast between the
two "men" can be found only in the shift from the state of nature to the
state of society. Our institutions, our social order — in short, society —
are what produce this disastrous effect. Nor is the description of the
two terms of opposition neutral; Rousseau never abstains from passing
judgment. "The pure state of nature is the one above all others where

men would be the less wicked, the happiest, and the most numerous on earth" (*Political Fragments*, II, p. 17). By contrast, in the state of society, "each one takes advantage of the misfortune of others" (*Discourse on the Origins of Inequality*, 202 n. IX). How could we praise such a situation? This is the usual image of Rousseau's doctrine, the position of an unconditional partisan of solitary human nature. Should we resign ourselves to it?

Let us observe, first of all, that it would be mistaken to present Rousseau as a primitivist, a partisan of the *return* to the state of nature. This view seems to be supported in the same *Discourse*, in which he offers his philosophical anthropology in the form of a historical narrative. In reality, however — and this is the first reason why the return to nature is impossible — the "state of nature" is not situated in time. Rousseau has explained this clearly and at length in the preambles to this treatise. The notion of a state of nature is merely a mental construct, a fiction meant to facilitate our understanding of the real facts, not a fact comparable to others. Rousseau's self-proposed purpose, then, is "to know a state that no longer exists, which perhaps never existed, which probably will never exist, and about which it is yet necessary to have correct notions in order to judge our present state" (123). The deductive argument to which Rousseau gives his attention has nothing in common with a historical study. "One must not engage in inquiries into this subject for the purpose of historical truths, but only for hypothetical and conditional reasons; more appropriate for clarifying the nature of things than for showing their real origin, and similar to those that our physicists do every day on the formation of the world" (132–33). In another contemporary text, the "Lettre sur la vertu" (Letter on virtue), Rousseau uses the terms "primitive" and "imaginary" as synonyms (322).

The same will apply later to the "social contract": this is not, as Rousseau's detractors will say, a pact established in common by individuals existing first outside of society, an absurd supposition; but a hypothetical construct allowing a new fact to be brought to light: men no longer wish to consider the norms of the society in which they live self-evident. Kant, who reads Rousseau sympathetically, explained this point effectively in his short treatise *Theory and Practice*. But Rousseau himself already said, speaking specifically of the "state of society": "Let the reader think only that this is less a matter of history and facts than of right and justice, and that I examine things by their nature rather than by our prejudices" (*Ecrits sur l'abbé de Saint-Pierre*, 603).

Moreover, even supposing this state of nature might have existed in other times, no turning back would ever be possible: having passed through the "state of society," man can no longer return to the "state of nature." History is irreversible; one cannot undo what is done: Rousseau was always categorical on this point. "Once a people has been corrupted, it has never been seen to return to virtue," he writes at the beginning of his career, in the *Observations* prompted by a reply to his *Discourse on the Sciences and the Arts* (53); and at the end: "Human nature does not go backward" (*Third Dialogue*, 213).

The "state of nature," then, is not a real state to be attained. What is more, in Rousseau's mind, the "man of nature" *is not really a man*. In his view, real humanity begins at the moment one can distinguish between good and evil. This discovery — of morality — is not one apprenticeship among others: it separates the human from the inhuman. It is "notions of good and evil which truly constitute him as a man and an integral part of his species" (*Emile*, IV, 220). Now, morality and human liberty presuppose one another (for an act to be judged good, the individual must have had the choice between doing it or not doing it); consequently, he who is not free is not entirely human. "To renounce one's freedom is to renounce one's status as a man" (*Social Contract* I, 4, p. 135). Man is distinguished from the beasts, says the *Discourse on the Origins of Inequality*, as we have seen, by perfectibility, that is, his capacity to become other than he was, by the fact that he can escape from pure necessity and enter the realm of freedom. Rousseau's innovative contribution to the tradition of modern natural law that begins with Grotius is not to evoke a state of nature but to decenter it: henceforth it becomes external to human identity. This is what the hasty reader may overlook.

In turn, morality can exist only in society; it presupposes the plurality of men, which must be taken into consideration by the individual. Only mutual company develops the reason and the moral sense. "All that is moral in myself has its relations outside of me, I would have neither vice nor virtue if I had always lived alone" ("Lettre sur la vertu," 320). "It is only by becoming sociable that he [man] becomes a moral being" (*Political Fragments*, II, p. 19). Nor did Rousseau ever waver on this point: in the state of nature, lacking communication between men, one would not know how to distinguish between virtue and vice; the sense of justice is therefore unknown and morality absent. Consequently, in this regard as well, man in this state is not yet entirely man. "Limited to physical instinct alone, he is a cipher, he is a dumb beast" (*Lettre à Beaumont*, 936). As long as he believes he is alone, man is merely one animal among others. "He would be merely a brute had he received nothing from others" (*Lettre sur la vertu*, 325).

We cannot doubt Rousseau's judgment of this state: this passage is "the happy moment . . . that changed him from a stupid, limited animal into an intelligent being and a man" (*Social Contract*, I, 8, 56). Life in society alone "raises us through the greatness of soul above the weaknesses of nature" ("Lettre sur la vertu," 324). Language is born with society, and "speech distinguishes man from the animals" (*Essay on the Origin of Languages*, I, p. 289). Morality is born with society, and "a morality ever unknown to the beasts" is proper to man (*Lettre à D'Alembert*, 79). Rousseau concludes, then, that "as cannot be doubted, man is by his nature sociable or at least made to become so" (*Emile*, IV, p. 290). Does this last clause express some actual reservation? Not at all; it simply recalls the hypothetical history of humanity, its beginnings in the asocial — but not fully human — state of nature. Liberty, morality, and society are three allied terms that together mark the specifically human.

Sociability is neither accidental nor contingent; it is the very definition of the human condition. Contrary to what certain traditional interpretations of Rousseau would suggest, he does not imagine men as already existing and entering only afterward into society, this being but one optional possibility. Quite the contrary, he views social life as constitutive of man; it is only in society that men deploy their properly human capacities. We now understand the solemn tone that Rousseau takes in his *Essay on the Origin of Languages*: "He who willed that man be sociable touched his finger to the axis of the globe and inclined it at an angle to the axis of the universe. With this slight movement, I see the face of the earth change and the vocation of mankind decided" (*Essay on the Origin of Languages*, IX, p. 310). This "vocation" means that one cannot really think of men outside of society except as a pure hypothesis, and that the "state of nature" is inhabited by beings who are not fully human.

Gaze and Attachment

How should we understand human sociability? The Ancients — Aristotle, for example — certainly agree that man is a social being, but they pre-

sent the human plurality as a multiplication of the similar; the idea of
the necessary complementarity of men (of the difference in principle
between *I* and *you*) is alien to them, except with regard to sexuality, as
we can see in the myth of Aristophanes reported in *The Symposium*.
The moralists of Antiquity, as well as those of the classical age in
France, have in turn frequently cited the human need to be admired; but
they consider vanity a fault from which one can free oneself.

Rousseau's thought on this subject passes through several stages. In
the *Discourse on the Origins of Inequality*, in which he considers it for
the first time, Rousseau seems to proceed by way of generalizing the
critique of vanity advanced by the seventeenth-century moralists. But at
the same time he coordinates it with the Aristotelian thesis. Rousseau's
innovation, then, was not to affirm, like Aristotle, the basic sociability
of men but to analyze this sociability in terms of complementarity
rather than resemblance. His contribution was not to observe that men
can be moved by the desire for glory or prestige (something familiar to
ancient and modern moralists alike) but to make this desire, in a generalized form, the necessary threshold that must be crossed before we can
speak of humanity. The need to be seen, the need for "consideration" —
these characteristics of man discovered by Rousseau have a palpably
greater reach than the aspiration to honor or praise.

As soon as they live in society (which in relation to historical time
means always), men experience the need to attract the gaze of others.
The specifically human action is the gaze of mutual recognition: "Each
began by gazing at the others and wanting to be gazed at himself" (*Discourse on the Origins of Inequality*, II, 169). The other no longer occupies a position comparable to mine, but one that is contiguous and
complementary; he is necessary to my sense of wholeness. The effects
of this need resemble those of vanity: one wants to be gazed at, one
seeks public esteem, one attempts to interest others in one's fate; the
difference is that this is not a vice but a basic need of the species as we
know it.

What gives man the sense of his own existence? Sometimes Rousseau
employs this expression as an equivalent of self-love and the instinct for
self-preservation. But when he introduces the perspective of sociability,
he situates this sentiment, with good reason, in the "idea of consideration." This is the conclusion of the *Discourse on the Origins of Inequality*: "The Savage lives in himself; the sociable man [let us not forget that
this means the only truly existing man] lives always outside himself,
knowing how to live only in the opinion of others. And it is from their

judgment alone that he derives the sense of his own existence" (II, 193). That is why we have reason to demand the attention of others: "We would like as much not to be as not to be gazed at" ("Lettre sur la vertu," 325). It follows that "others" are immediately present within the subject — for if he has not internalized their gaze, he is not yet fully human. This statement could also be reformulated by saying that without consciousness, man is not man; and consciousness is the effect of communication, of our internalization of being taken into consideration by others.

We have some difficulty appreciating Rousseau's discovery in the *Discourse on the Origins of Inequality* because the statement of fact — no man outside society — is muddied by value judgment: society is a degradation, indeed a fall of the species. Rousseau never abandoned this dream of a "natural" life in which man is self-sufficient. However, in *The Social Contract* he introduces a term that includes the notion of "society" and is nonetheless positively inflected, namely "the civil state." The social dimension is clearly presupposed by the presence itself of the contract (which would suffice to invalidate the interpretation that for Rousseau, the contract precedes society). The submission of the particular will is justified only to the extent that it becomes the basis of the common law: in this way, "each one, uniting with all, nevertheless obeys only himself and remains as free as before" (*Social Contract*, I, 6, p. 138). "Civil liberty" is a double-edged concept, affirming at once the autonomy of the will and the necessity of a social life; but the first sense of the word *autonomy* already refers as much to the will of the subject, *auto*, as to that of the community provided with laws (*nomy*). It never refers to what Rousseau calls natural liberty, or independence, which consists of doing everything one is capable of doing without any consideration for the framework in which one is situated. The law, like language, presupposes communal life.

When he meditates on the fate of the individual and no longer on that of the body politic, as he does in *Emile* and in the *Dialogues*, Rousseau advances yet another equally positive notion, that of "attachments." It should be recalled here that in Christian theology, this term refers essentially to the bonds established from man to man, as distinct from the "love" one bears the Creator and, through him, his creatures. In this respect, attachment, while not to be condemned, does not deserve to be held in high esteem.

In a fragment of the *Pensées* that Pascal always had with him, even on the day he died, he says: "It is wrong that anyone should become attached to me even though they do so gladly and of their own accord. I should be misleading those in whom I aroused such a desire, for I am no one's goal nor have I the means of satisfying anyone. Am I not ready to die? Then the object of their attachment will die. . . . I am culpable if I make anyone love me. . . . They must not become attached to me, because they must devote their lives and efforts to pleasing God or seeking Him" (bk. 471, line 396). In her *Life of Pascal*, his sister Gilberte insists at length on this character trait. Her brother knew how to be tender and loving toward those near and dear to him, but he fled attachment, both his own and others', just as he fled "amusement." He even amicably reproached his sister, who was less perfect on this point and surrendered herself to an all-too-human attachment to her brother. It is not that he was unfamiliar with creaturely love; but he justified it by the love of the Creator. "Everything which drives us to become attached to creatures is bad, since it prevents us from serving God, if we know him, or seeking him if we do not" (bk. 479, line 618).

Now Rousseau chose to place himself, in his reflections on man, within a purely human perspective. An individual's attachments to others form the very substance of his life. "It is man's weakness that makes him sociable": but man is constitutionally weak, meaning incomplete, and he fills this lack with his attachments. "Every attachment is a sign of insufficiency. If each of us had no need of others, he would hardly think of uniting himself with them" (*Emile*, IV, p. 221). God alone knows happiness in solitude: here Rousseau recovers the thought of Aristotle, who said as much at the beginning of his *Politics*, accepting the idea that society is born of the weakness of the individual. But this is how we are: born incomplete, dying incomplete, always prey to the need for others, always in quest of the missing complement. Rousseau does not believe in original sin, but this does not lead him to conclude (as Pelagius does) that the way to perfection is open to him: man is constitutionally and definitively incomplete. Because he is imperfect, if he were alone, "he would be miserable." It is because he comes into existence congenitally incomplete that he needs others, needs to be considered, needs "to attach his heart" (*Second Dialogue*, p. 116).

Rousseau's man is not only the opposite of God, who instantly knows plenitude; he is also distinct from religious man, who finds his indispensable complement precisely in the existence of God. In this respect, Descartes is not a humanist: from the statement of his own imperfection, he deduced the idea of perfection and the conclusion that "I was not the only being who existed"; which proved to him the existence not of humanity, but of the "perfect Being," God (Discourse on the Method, pt. IV, I, p. 128). In Rousseau, this place beyond the individual is occupied only by other men; that is both the greatness and the wretchedness of man.

In the same *Dialogues*, Rousseau introduces a complementary concept. Sensitivity, or the capacity to perceive the external world, is at the basis of all action. All living beings possess a physical sensitivity. But men, the only free, moral, and sociable beings (in the sense used here), possess also a second sensitivity, a *moral sensitivity*, "which is nothing other than the faculty for attaching our affections to beings which are foreign to us." This sensitivity is at the basis of our capacity for attachment, and "its strength is in proportion of the relationship we feel between ourselves and other beings." Our existence is made up of the whole of our attachments; that is why the exercise of this faculty has the power "to extend and reinforce the feeling of our being" (*Second Dialogue*, p. 112). Relations with others augment the self instead of diminishing it. This characteristic of man makes him what he is; it is the source of his virtues and his vices, of his incessant discontents, and of his fragile happiness.

Human Commerce

If we read him attentively, we perceive that Rousseau, the reputed champion of "natural," asocial man, is in reality one of the most attentive analysts of human sociability. But it might be objected that he is surely a new exception among the "humanists." Could we say as much about a real "individualist" like Benjamin Constant?

As a matter of principle, Constant is so convinced of the impossibility of imagining an asocial man that he refuses to engage in any speculation on man's origins, even as a purely hypothetical construct. Asocial man does not exist and never has existed. This is Constant's reproach against the philosophers of the previous centuries: their insistence on imagining an ancestor of man — "natural man" — wandering all alone in the forest. "If this were the natural state of man, how would he have escaped it?" To answer this question, these philosophers were obliged to imagine men making the decision to live in society — a decision that already presupposes society, debate, the capacity for reasoning. "Society, in this system, would be the result of the development of intelligence, whereas the development of intelligence is itself only the result of society" (*Religion*, I, 8, 83).

This is why Constant explicitly renounces the return to a human state anterior to society. "It was initially assumed that man had existed without society, without language, without religion." Yet "society, language, religion are inherent in man" (I, 1, 46). We must not seek a reason for sociability other than "the nature of man." Apostrophizing Rousseau (without naming him), Constant continues: man "is not sociable because he is weak; he is sociable because sociability is part of his essence." Or again: "Man is sociable because he is man, just as the wolf is unsociable because he is the wolf" (*Filangieri*, I, 8, 213): of course this is the wolf of fairy tales, not the wolf of the steppes. Constant the "individualist" does not demand that "each individual be his own center" (*Religion*, preface, I, 33). Such a formula would be at once false (because there is continuity between interior and exterior) and dangerous (because the isolated individual is particularly vulnerable).

When he leaves the field of political reflection and turns toward the analysis of individual behavior, Constant discovers several new consequences of sociability. Since the subject does not exist alone in the world, he is necessarily constituted in relation to one or several individual, intimate *you*s and impersonal *they*s. There is something excessive and singular in that character *Adolphe*, who observes of himself: "I was sustained by no impulse from the heart" (*Adolphe*, V, p. 95); even Constant, an exceptionally suggestible individual, is not as nonexistent as Adolphe. But in this extreme form he expresses a thesis whose reach is more general, namely, that relationships, affections, loves constitute the very fabric of human existence: no *I* without *you*. Affection is "everything in life" (*Journal*, 1 August 1807). Incomplete egotism is more impossible than immoral.

This truth is too often ignored by those who, like Malthus, built theories based on the idea that man remains exclusively preoccupied with his personal interest. "Man is not only an arithmetical sign," retorts Constant; "he had blood in his veins and a need for attachment in his heart. . . . Everyone knows the reply of the blind man who was reproached for feeding his dog: And who will love me? he says" (*Filangieri*, II, 5, 271). Doesn't a little anecdote like this, whose truth is immediately recognized by everyone, weigh more heavily than volumes of arguments on the rational needs of man? It follows, as Constant wrote to Juliette Recamier, that one finds only what one has given, and that the more one gives, the more one has: affective wealth consists in the intensity of relationships; to love more fully is to live more intensely.

This is not the only lesson Constant draws from his "observation of the human heart" (*Adolphe*, preface, 6). We would immediately have to add: no *I* and *you* without *they*, without others, third persons, public opinion. Rousseau had, of course, discovered that humanity begins from the moment one captures the gaze of the third person; but he bitterly regretted this fall from "natural man" (who was therefore not wholly a man). Constant also aspired, in his youth, to liberate himself from the need to be recognized by the gaze of others, and he boasts about it in his letters to Isabelle de Charrière. Her reply is stinging: "You say that you scorn public opinion because you have seen it go astray. . . . There is no convincing *because*; you do not scorn, you would not know how to scorn public opinion" (13 May 1792).

Constant learns this lesson and assumes without false shame what the earlier moralists could condemn under the name of "vanity." Being human, we need the gaze of others: it is useless to struggle against our very identity. This dependence on others is stronger than the self-interest, which Constant defines narrowly, as we shall see; dependence triumphs when the two come into conflict. "The influence of personal interest is generally exaggerated; personal interest needs opinion in order to act" (*The Spirit of Conquest and Usurpation*, II, 12, p. 122). "In everyone, opinions or vanity are stronger than interests" (*Du Poly-théisme romain*, XI, 3; II, 63). Man "aspires, in his thought and his conduct, to the approbation of others, and outside sanction is necessary to his internal satisfaction" (XIII, 1; II, 130). Relationships with others, we also learned in *Adolphe*, end by becoming "so intimate a part of our existence" (V, p. 99). This is because the separation between outside and inside is entirely relative, since no *I* exists without *you* and *they*.

All of Constant's narratives contain examples of this dependence on the gaze. In *Ma vie*, he remembers one of his earliest love affairs: his goal was not to become a woman's lover, but to make others around him believe that he had. "The pleasure of making and hearing it said that I was keeping a mistress consoled me, for spending my life with a woman I did not love, and not possessing the woman whom I was keeping" (91). If the narrator wants to sleep with Cécile, it is only out of "fatuousness," following a conversation between men (*Cécile*, VI,

161). Adolphe, in analogous circumstances, is in turn moved by "a theory of fatuousness" (III, p. 77), and he describes his own desire for Ellenore as a satisfaction at drawing the gazes of third persons. "Ah, had heaven granted me a woman whom social conventions permitted me to acknowledge and whom my father would not be ashamed to admit as his daughter, then making her happy would have been a source of infinite happiness to me" (VII, p. 125). The gazes of father and society triumph over the desires of Adolphe and Ellenore.

These examples of "vanity," or in more neutral terms, the inevitable dependence on the gazes and words of others, are merely a conspicuous illustration of what constitutes the substance of all human existence: sociability. Often character traits or well-internalized states of mind are revealed to have the same origin. Thus the father's timidity in *Adolphe*, responsible for an "inner suffering . . . which forces the profoundest feelings back into the heart, chilling your words and deforming in your mouth whatever you try to say" (I, p. 48). Yet what is timidity but a fear of the internalized gaze of others? Hence the shame that leads the narrator astray and is present as an invisible witness to his encounter with Cécile: "A remorse, a shame that pursued me in the midst of pleasure itself" (VI, 162). *Cécile* contains another revelatory scene: the two lovers go to the masked ball, where they intensely enjoy the pleasure of being together in public without being recognized by others. The charm is so great that they decide to repeat it the following week; but this impunity is no longer a surprise, and there will be no pleasure in the rendezvous. "The crowd became irksome to us because we no longer feared it" (VI, 167): Isn't this further proof of the constitutive role of the gaze of others in our experiences?

In the network of human interactions, no isolated entities exist but only relations; the very opposition between essence and accident has no place in the world of intersubjectivity. In personal life, the person in himself does not exist. I do not love that being or that class of beings — this is impossible; but I love the being who is in a certain position in relation to me. Constant offered two general formulations of this law in his *Journal*: "The object that escapes us is necessarily entirely different from the one who pursues us" (2 May 1804), and "Everything in life depends on reciprocity" (25 April 1804). Man does not exist outside of other men.

Chapter 4

Living Alone

*B*ecause Rousseau praises nature or the state of nature or natural man does not mean that he ignores human sociability. Because Constant defends the freedom of the individual does not mean he underestimates his dependence on other men. An objection might be raised, at this point, to the effect that the abstract definition of man is one thing, the description of modern man quite another. Man's nature may not destine him to solitude, but what about his history? Isn't Rousseau one of the first to have understood this, describing himself as a solitary walker? Doesn't he reveal by this what the humanists would prefer to conceal, namely, that, in terms of the hidden pact, solitude is part of the price we pay for freedom? Don't the *Confessions* offer a glimpse of what the *Social Contract* leaves deliberately in shadow? In turn, isn't Constant animated by a powerful desire for independence, which makes him turn his back on other men? And hadn't Montaigne, at the very starting point of the humanist tradition, already chosen for himself the solitary life? Now, if solitude is the truth of man, is there still a tenable difference between humanists and individualists?

The Era of Individuals

The truth is that praise for solitude was not an invention of modern times. It is present in Antiquity as the rival of a still earlier ideal, the aspiration to glory. In Homer's time, glory befit the hero; it was the quasi-objective confirmation (because not dependent on the will of the aspirant) of his value. Now, he who declares glory a necessity also declares the need for others, for the multitude, an indispensable echo chamber for amplifying the great deeds of the hero. This system of values would be challenged by the ancient philosophers and, in another fashion, by Christian thinkers, who would see the aspiration to glory as merely egocentric vanity and profane pride. They, by contrast, would praise solitary meditation and withdrawal from the world: the hero on one side, the sage or saint on the other.

These two ideals, heroic and solitary, coexist in the Europe of the Renaissance. The first is embodied in the feudal code of honor, in the love of greatness and glory; the second, the ideal of a life in retirement, is closer to the Christian ideal and draws besides on philosophical reminiscences of Antiquity, as we see, for example, in Montaigne. To liberate oneself from the aspiration to glory, therefore from dependence on the judgment of others, is only a first step; the next consists of not needing others at all. "Let us make our contentment depend on ourselves, let us cut loose from all the ties that bind us to others, let us win from ourselves the power to live really alone and to live that way at our ease. . . . The man of understanding has lost nothing, if he has himself" (*Essays*, I, 39, 177). And in accord with Stoic tradition, Montaigne can proclaim that we must not be too attached to others so as not to suffer from their eventual death. Self-sufficiency, then, is an ideal. Receiving little from others, the individual does not pay them excessive attention. "As much as I can, I employ myself entirely upon myself" (III, 10, 766). "The greatest thing in the world is to know how to belong to oneself," Montaigne repeats after Seneca (I, 39, 178), and turns it into a precept: "You have quite enough to do at home, don't go away" (III, 10, 767).

Perhaps because social allegiances were, in his time, an unquestionable given, and the threat of a society reduced to the juxtaposition of private interests was not yet on the horizon, Montaigne lives his own choices in serenity. One sometimes has the impression that he enjoys a double advantage: he can choose his mode of life as he likes without any risk of destroying the social order. He can prefer the voluntary relations of friendship to the connections imposed by kinship, yet he is firmly inscribed in a family line; he is determined by his birth no less than by his choices. He can opt for liberty, but this does not prevent him from recognizing the hold of culture (custom) and history.

The relation between the needs of the individual and those of society are no more problematic in Descartes. He sees quite well that the interests of the particular person do not necessarily coincide with those of his particular community, yet he thinks that, far from leading us down two divergent paths, the two can be harmoniously reconciled. "Though each of us is a person distinct from others, whose interests are accordingly in some way different from those of the rest of the world," we cannot forget that we are equally part of a greater whole, "the state, the society and the family to which we belong by our domicile, our oath of allegiance and our birth" (to Elizabeth, 15 September 1645, III, p. 266). It is more advantageous for the individual to think that he also belongs to a common body; he will then find the means to arrange all his interests simultaneously. Conflict is not inevitable, either within the person or between eras.

At the end of the seventeenth century, however, the quarrel of the Ancients and the Moderns erupted, and even if at first this turned especially on a judgment of values (which are superior to others?), historical perspective was introduced into the public debate. Men of different eras must also be different. It was in this context that Rousseau would reflect on the evolution of humanity and would, more specifically, contrast the citizen of ancient republics like Sparta or Rome to the individual of modern times. The first, he says at the beginning of *Emile*, is merely a fractional unity that is bound to the denominator, and whose value lies in his relation to the whole, which is the "social body." The second, by contrast, "is entirely for himself. He is a numerical unity, the absolute whole which is relative only to itself or its kind" (I, p. 39). Rousseau's terminology is not ours; still, he casts as opposites two very different configurations: one in which man is merely part of a whole and one in which he himself constitutes that whole.

On another occasion, Rousseau returns to this opposition between Ancients and Moderns, when he compares the inhabitants of ancient republics to those of Geneva. For the first, the private is subjugated to the public; among the second, particular interests are primary: the preoccupation with wealth, the need for protection. "You are merchants, artisans, bourgeois, always occupied with their private interests, their work, their trade, their gain," says Rousseau addressing his Genevan compatriots. The counterpart of this hierarchical change is that the Moderns neglect public affairs, to which the Ancients could devote themselves, freed as they were from material cares thanks to the institution of slavery. "Not being idle, as were ancient peoples, you cannot, like them, unceasingly occupy yourselves with government"; the danger is that public liberties will disappear, becoming the price paid for ensuring one's personal tranquility (*Lettres écrites de la montagne*, IX, 881). Rousseau thus paves the way for the opposition between the participatory liberty of the Ancients and the protective liberty of the Moderns, as Condorcet and Constant would interpret it.

His explorations of himself come to be inscribed in this context and will grant new meaning to the theme of solitude, so important to the view of individualism.

In Praise of Solitude

Rousseau's autobiographical writings indeed give the impression that he is closer to the individualist family than to the humanists, for the happiness of the individual seems to be his sole objective. We might begin here with a statement of Rousseau's, followed by regrets: he is alone, where he would have liked to be with others. "I was born for friendship" (*Confessions*, VIII, p. 304), I was "the most sociable and the most loving of human beings" (*Reveries*, I, p. 3); yet he again finds himself alone and is unhappy about it. This is a "very great misfortune" (*Confessions*, VIII, 338); he dreads "the horror of that solitude" (*Third Dialogue*, p. 245), which is "awful" to him (*First Dialogue*, p. 42). It would seem that he nurtured the hope of finding society again: "We can give him back in his old age the sweetness of true society which he lost so long ago and no longer hoped to find again here below" (*Third Dialogue*, p. 225). The cause of this solitude, therefore, does not reside in him; it is rather due to the hostile attitude of others, or to the fact that they are unworthy of his love. "He who would respond to me is yet to come" (*Mon portrait*, 1124). "It is less my fault than theirs" (*Confessions*, V, p. 158). "He flees men only after searching among them in vain for what he should love" (*Second Dialogue*, p. 127).

Yet, that does not settle the matter. Rousseau can also associate suffering in solitude with the refusal to break out of it: he distinguishes between an authentic communication and a superficial communication; the latter does not remedy solitude, it aggravates it. While being with others, man suffers the same malady, but even more intensely. Thus Saint-Preux describes his arrival in Paris: "I enter with a secret horror into this vast desert of the world. This chaos presents me with nothing but horrible solitude, wherein reigns a dull silence. . . . I am never less alone than when I am alone, said an Ancient; on the other hand, I am alone only in the crowd" (*The New Héloïse*, II, 14, p. 190). Solitude always remains deplorable, but its worst form is experienced in the midst of others: the world is a desert, the social hubbub an oppressive silence. The converse is equally true: as Cicero says (again, the wisdom of the Stoics makes its contribution), surface solitude, purely physical, can be in reality an authentic communication.

Thanks to the distinction between two levels within each of these attitudes, Rousseau can reconcile his nostalgia for society with his condemnation of it. In effect, society valorizes appearance to the detriment of being, public opinion rather than self-love, vanity and not simplicity; social institutions are degrading to man. Granted that the interior is preferable to the exterior, the solitary person is superior to social man.

Rousseau wants to escape the weight of social obligations in order to live freely. This is how he describes himself: "The cause of this invincible disgust that I have always experienced in the company of men . . . is nothing other than that indomitable spirit of liberty which nothing has been able to overcome." Let us make no mistake—here, too, we must distinguish between apparent liberty and authentic liberty: the man who believes he is free is very often a slave to men, for he depends on their opinion and has lost his social autonomy; the prisoner, on the other hand, is free because he is alone. "I have thought a hundred times that I would not have lived too unhappily in the Bastille, since I would not be restricted to anything at all except to staying there" (*Letters to Malesherbes*, III, 573). Rousseau feels "a mortal aversion for all subjugation" (*Confessions*, III, 115); and he knows no half measures: "If I begin to be enslaved to opinion in something, I will soon be enslaved to it in everything all over again" (VIII, 317). So it is better to take refuge in radical solitude. The baneful character of communal life is also expressed on the physical level. "Man's breath is deadly to his kind. This is no less true in the literal sense than the figurative" (*Emile*, I, p. 59).

Society is bad, solitude is good; and solitary man really has no need for others; he is a self-sufficient being. Didn't Epictetus teach us that real wealth is what we find within ourselves? Doesn't Montaigne advise us to stop borrowing from others and draw only on ourselves? One cannot praise too highly the man who "knows how to enjoy his own being" (*The New Héloïse*, IV, 11, p. 396). Through the Stoic tradition with which Rousseau claims affiliation here, we see the image of the "natural man" so dear to him. As his disciple Bernardin de Saint-Pierre will sum it up: "Solitude largely leads man to natural happiness by distancing him from social unhappiness" (*Paul et Virginie*, 136).

Diderot had given one of his characters in *Fils naturel* this retort: "Only the wicked are alone." Rousseau decided that this remark was directed at him, and he was deeply wounded. He repeatedly develops a counterargument: to be wicked, one would have to dispose of victims; therefore live in society, not in solitude. If I am alone, on the contrary, even if I should want to do so, what harm could I do to others? The solitary man is, perforce, good (see *Emile*, II, 341; *Confessions*, IX, p. 382; *Second Dialogue*, p. 99). But perhaps he felt that this argument was a bit mechanical, and returned to the fray: the solitary are good not only because they can do no harm; thirsty for contact, they are, in addition, "naturally humane, hospitable, tender" (*Second Dialogue*, p. 99). Solitude is good, then, both because it is not solitary — "the truly sociable man" lives there, far from crowds and easy contacts — and because it is solitary: "Whoever suffices to himself does not want to harm anyone at all" (p. 100)! Each of these arguments, taken in itself, might be convincing; their juxtaposition in Rousseau makes them both suspect, and reveals how much the defense of the solitary ideal meant to him.

In this way, by a series of displacements and distinctions, solitude, that dreaded state, becomes the ideal to which he aspires — "dearest solitude" (*Art de jouir*, 1173). In any case this is what Rousseau declares. Yet we doubt, not his sincerity, but his lucidity when we perceive how often this declaration recurs. Throughout his autobiographical writings he assures his readers that he has no need of others, that he is happiest without them, that he is grateful for their hostility, for they have forced him in this way to discover unsuspected treasures in himself. "I am a hundred times happier in my solitude than I would be living among them" (*Reveries*, I, 5). If this were true, would he have to repeat it so often? He protests too much: each repetition of the phrase makes us suspect that the last time he was not telling the whole truth. Not to speak of the fact that these declarations appear in letters and books meant to be read; yet readers are also "others"! Rousseau never stops *telling* them that he no longer wants to speak to them; as a result, they have the right to be skeptical when he offers them this description of himself: "As soon as he is alone, he is happy" (*Second Dialogue*, p. 121).

Chapter 4

Rousseau Judges Jean-Jacques

If these declarations were all we had, Rousseau would be an individualist thinker rather than a humanist. But this is not all. Men have passed into the state of society and there is no turning back. So how could solitude be held up as an ideal, with its corollary, the suppression of society? Rousseau knows very well that this is a problem. But he does not say so clearly. We sometimes wonder whether he is not being deliberately evasive by refusing to admit this state of things to himself. Otherwise, how can we explain the ambiguity attached to the word *society* and its derivatives? This word participates, in effect, in two quite separate dichotomies: nature/society and solitude/society. Yet Rousseau acts as if he were always dealing with the same meaning of the word, and he can therefore blame society-the-contrary-of-solitude for all the ills that characterize society-the-contrary-of-nature. It is clear, however, that even in Rousseau's view, solitude and its contrary, society, *both* come after the "fall" into the state of society and are strangers to the state of nature; it is consequently unfair to condemn society for something that its contrary, solitude, equally shares.

Moreover, when he articulates his doctrine, Rousseau avoids any confusion of this kind, and he recalls that real men, sociable beings, cannot live as "natural men" antedating society. The state of nature has never existed, or if it did, it has become inaccessible to us today; we must discuss the only men who exist, those who inhabit the state of society. These men are inconceivable except in relation to others. "Today when my life, my security, my liberty, my happiness depend on the assistance of my peers, it is clear that I must no longer regard myself as an individual and isolated being but as part of a larger whole" ("Lettre sur la vertu," 320). Rousseau takes up this discussion again in *Emile*, speaking of the education of men in the state of society: "Leaving the state of nature, we force our peers to leave it as well; no one can remain there despite others" (321). If one persists in wanting to live in the present as if society did not exist, in other words, if one chooses radical solitude, one is condemned to failure. "A man who wanted to regard himself as an isolated being, not depending at all on anything and sufficient unto himself, could only be miserable" (III, p. 193). So we see that when he is resolved not to do it, Rousseau does not confuse the two very different "solitudes": one belonging to the state of nature and the other that can be lived in society.

Yet, he persists in using the same expression, "natural man," for two entities as different as past man and future man. The concern for winning support takes precedence, here, over the concern for truth. A supplementary meaning is slipped into the word *nature*: a communication seems to be established between the meaning "origin" and the meaning "forest." In the *Confessions*, when he alludes to the conception of the *Discourses on the Origin of Inequality*, Rousseau shows us how these two meanings were forged: "All the rest of the day, deep in the forest, I sought, I found the image of the first times, whose history I proudly traced" (*Confessions*, VIII, 326). The state of nature was therefore depicted according to the experience of the forest, and the man of the woods, aptly named, could participate in both. The first time, nature-forest lent certain of its features to nature-origin; so it was even easier a second time, perhaps, for one to find the dreamed of origin in the real forest, and to identify the imaginary "man of nature" with the solitary woodland stroller and plant collector.

Rousseau is such an intense and rigorous thinker that it is hard to imagine him being fooled by these homonyms and ambiguities. For him to transmit them in his writings, a powerful motive must gradually, over time, have weakened the vigilance of his thought. This motive did exist and was precisely the sort to temporarily blind anyone under its influence: during the "autobiographical" period of his life, Rousseau decided that natural man, that ideal opposite of the citizen, was himself. He explains himself clearly on this point in the *Dialogues*: he designates himself "the man of nature" (*Second Dialogue*, p. 147; and *Third Dialogue*, p. 216) and establishes an equivalence between himself and "the primitive nature of man" (*Second Dialogue*, p. 147). "In short, just as I found the man of nature in his books, I found in him the man of his books" (p. 159). "Where could the painter and apologist of nature, so disfigured and calumnied now, have found his model if not in his own heart? He described it as he himself felt" (*Third Dialogue*, p. 214).

This is what allows us to establish the continuity between Rousseau's doctrinal writings and his personal writings; this is what authorizes us — even obliges us — to turn toward his autobiographical works when we want to be better acquainted with one of the ways of man he has traced, the way of the solitary individual. This continuity was claimed by Rousseau himself: "His system may be false, but in developing it, he portrayed himself truthfully in a manner so characteristic and so sure that it is impossible for me to mistake it" (p. 212). But instead of making Rousseau's system coherent, this continuity makes it problematic. Having decided that the man of nature should resemble him, Rousseau finds himself both judge and plaintiff; as a result, he has not always been able to remain impartial. He who plays on the two meanings of "nature," "natural man," and "society" is an interested party in the debate. Rousseau sins, here, through a fault that is the converse of the one he diagnoses in his friendly enemies, the "philosophers." They defend doctrines they would not in the least care to illustrate by their own lives—this is the characteristic irresponsibility of the modern intellectual. Rousseau himself would like some continuity between saying and doing, between ideal and reality—rightly so. But he goes further: he makes the two coincide, and therefore depicts the ideal according to the real, since it is his own life and being, as he understands them from day to day, that serve him as model.

Yet he could see very well for himself (but outside the autobiographical context) that such inductive reasoning was illegitimate. "If it were permissible to draw proof of their feelings from the actions of men, it would have to be said that the love of justice is banished from all hearts, and that there is not a single Christian soul on earth" (*Préface à Narcisse*, 962). Reflecting on his own existence, and in particular on his abandonment of his children, he still has the lucidity to separate it from his ideal: "As if sinning were not man's lot, and even the just man's!" (to Saint-Germain, 26 February 1770, XXXVII, 279). If this were not the case, how could the Jean-Jacques who abandons his children be at the same time the sage Rousseau who writes a treatise on education? But as he does not follow his own principle and bases his ideals on the description of what he is, we might reproach Rousseau for just what he holds against others, namely, deducing right from fact. This process, even if it is not used here in the service of tyranny, never serves the interest of truth. This is why all of Rousseau's philosophical conclusions, when he takes himself as the example of his ideals, are subject to caution: sincerity is not wisdom. "From pure and architectonic meditation," Philonenko observes, "Rousseau tumbles down the steps that lead to biography" (*Rousseau*, III, p. 260). The "philosophers'" hypocrisy (or cynicism or lack of conscience) must be condemned; yet there is no need to embrace the opposing party and eliminate all distance between ideal and real. Continuity does not mean correspondence; the ideal can guide a life without being confused with it.

Radical solitude could not constitute an ideal for man, for the simple reason that it is impossible. What Rousseau offers us under the name of solitude are two complementary experiences, which we might call restrained communication (in particular in the *Confessions*) and the quest for the self (in the *Reveries*), in which he aspires to a pure feeling of being. This quest remains a legitimate path for the individual; it is clear, nonetheless, that this is a private and extreme experience that can be cherished for itself but not elevated as a public ideal. We must examine more closely, then, "restrained communication."

This is not solitude. And how could a writer — a man who spends his life manipulating words that come to him from others in order to arrive at new constructions again meant for others — how could he embody the solitary man? He is in constant communication with others: a mediated communication, of course, but no less intense for that. What is Rousseau if not a writer; what else does he do in the course of his life? Not only does he cover thousands of pages with his writing, but he knows that in this way a particularly solid communication is established that even death will not disrupt. Hence his concern for his reputation, for the opinion of his future readers, throughout the autobiographical period and even in the worst moments of his misanthropy: "I would easily consent to have no existence at all in the memory of men, but I cannot consent, I admit it, to remain defamed. . . . I cannot consider as something indifferent to men the reinstatement of my memory" (*Third Dialogue*, pp. 227–28). Is he a true solitary who confides his manuscripts to reliable persons, gives them precise instructions on the course they must follow, makes multiple copies and takes multiple precautions?

Like all of us, Rousseau wants to be loved. "Devoured by the need to love, to be loved, and hardly sensible to any others" — this is how he describes himself in a letter to Sophie d'Houdetot (from 17 December 1757, IV, 394). He would like to live with others, even if he knows they are imperfect. "I feel too strongly in my particular case how little I can forgo living with men as corrupt as myself" (*Letter to Philopolis*, 131). But fate does not smile upon him. Two factors are aligned against him (in a proportion that does not have much bearing in the present context): the hostility that such an extraordinary personality provokes, and his own suspicious character (in other words, persecution and the delusion of persecution). So he falls back on a double strategy. On the one hand, he disqualifies all other men so as to seem indifferent to their judgment (this is a variant of the saying "sour grapes"): All men are wicked, I alone am good. On the other hand, he has recourse to "supplements": the vegetable kingdom, escape into the imaginary, writing, persons reduced to the role of instrument or object. But—we know him now—he is always aware that the substitute is not worth the original. As Julie says apropos another "supplement": "What are you enjoying when you take your enjoyments alone? These solitary pleasures of the senses are dead ones" (*The New Héloïse*, II, 15, p. 195).

Yet Rousseau is led to erect this substitute as an ideal after he decides to depict natural man in his own image. And it is here that his reasoning breaks down. What provided a legitimate model for autobiographical research could not become, without some adaptation, a way for all men, a common ideal. This ideal must answer to criteria other than chance, which makes us one way rather than another, and gives us the courage to say so. Seen from this point of view, the "supplements" practiced by Rousseau are of unequal value: if the preference for isolation, for escape into the imaginary, for being surrounded by plant life, for writing are morally neutral behaviors and reveal the liberty (the right) of the individual, this is not equally true of the depersonalization of other beings. And this is what defines Rousseau's relationships with the individuals around him, beginning with his beloved "governess," Thérèse. To reduce others to mere appendages of the self, refusing them the status of wholly separate subjects, is to renounce equality between men—something Rousseau would not, moreover, want to admit.

We should therefore read Rousseau's project by ignoring the personal tastes of their author, insofar as this is possible; otherwise, we are condemned to aporia. The life of Rousseau the individual is dominated by a susceptible and suspicious temperament; this man believes he is being persecuted (a well-founded belief most of the time), and often prefers solitude to company—a solitude all the more desirable for its rarity. His autobiographical writings contain the defense and the illustration of this agoraphobic inclination. But the personal predilection for isolation is not confused, even in his mind, with a doctrinal declaration of the essential solitude of man. Rousseau makes very clear the distance between the general rule (the recommendations he addresses to Emile) and the exception (his own fate): He keeps himself apart from men; Emile must "live amidst them" (V, p. 474).

A page of the *Dialogues* is still more eloquent in this regard. Rousseau first reiterates his taste for solitude; yet he tries also to distinguish between the particularities of his life and his ideal for man, and adds: "Absolute solitude is a state that is sad and contrary to nature: affectionate feelings nourish the soul, communication of ideas enlivens the mind. Our sweetest existence is relative and collective, and our true self is not entirely within us. Finally, such is man's constitution in this life that one never is able to enjoy oneself well without the cooperation of another" (*Second Dialogue*, p. 118).

The *Rêveries* are a melancholy reminder that the self always includes others, that one never manages to be free of them. When he reflects on the world rather than trying to justify himself, Rousseau confirms that a part of the self is found in others, and he does not complain about it. As he writes in his *Lettres morales* addressed to Mme d'Houdetot: "In your deepest solitude your heart says that you are not alone" (VI, 1801). Our happiness is that of a social man; and even from an egotistical point of view, the other is indispensable to us. Julie already said: "the purest soul does not alone suffice for its own happiness" (*The New Héloïse*, II, 11, p. 185), and the "Profession of Faith" ends with these words: "It is in forgetting oneself that one works for oneself" (*Emile*, IV, p. 313). Society is not a blind alley, a "supplement"; it generates qualities that do not exist without it, and communication is a virtue in itself. Saint-Preux said this in his own way: "It is not good that man should be alone. Human souls need to be coupled to realize their full value" (*The New Héloïse*, II, 13, p. 188).

The Desire for Independence

Rousseau the thinker rightly belongs to the humanist family, even if Rousseau the individual sometimes flees from it. The first, unlike the second, does not believe that man without others is still man; he does not believe that life in society is the price we must pay to the devil in exchange for the freedoms he grants us. We would arrive at a similar conclusion if we examined the declarations strewn throughout the literary and private writings of Benjamin Constant, in which we read a need for solitude and a demand for definitive "independence." The "freedom" of the individual in relation to his affections cannot be conceived according to the model of the freedom of the citizen in relation to the state: affective independence is not equivalent to political autonomy. The independence Constant dreams of is only one moment in the game of desire-as-absence, in which the subject no longer has anything to desire and seeks to escape ennui. Aspirations to solitude are formulated repeatedly in the *Journal* and in the correspondence — but this is a desire that could not be realized and that conceals another. Once separated from his first wife, Constant writes to Isabelle de Charrière: "For more than a year I would desire this moment, I would sigh after complete independence; it has come and I am shivering! I am dismayed by the solitude that surrounds me, I am frightened of having nothing to hold onto, I, who groaned so at having to hold on to something" (31 March 1793). Twenty years later, he notes in his journal: "I have so desired to live alone and today I tremble at the thought" (*Journal*, 27 October 1814). Constant's appeals to "independence" cannot be read independently of their context.

This is also the lesson of *Adolphe*. The hero believes he has such an "ardent desire for independence" (I, 14) at the beginning of his story, and later regrets his free life of yesteryear. But these declarations are not to be taken literally, unless we are satisfied with the psychology professed by Adolphe's father: "With your spirit of independence," he writes somewhat naively to his son, "you are always doing what you do not want" (VII, 54). It is Adolphe himself who will discover the bitter truth at the end of his story: "freedom" and "independence" were merely relative values — relative to Ellenore and to his relationship with her. Once Ellenore is dead, they mean nothing to him; or rather they show him their underside: independence is the "desert of the world"; freedom is "isolation" and the absence of love (X, 76). "How it weighed on me, this freedom I had so regretted! How my heart missed it, that dependence which had often revolted me! . . . Indeed, I was free, I was no longer loved: I was a stranger to everyone" (X, 79). "Freedom" in relation to others cannot be an ultimate goal; it is rather the mask that our desire dons to replace one unsatisfying relationship with another, more intense one, the alibi for one's wish to turn away from the object that is pursuing you. An entirely "independent" life would be a life without meaning, and it would threaten the very existence of the subject.

It is true that we must distinguish once again between the general theory and the analysis of a historical period, the contemporary era. It is not only in the abstract that men are necessarily social; in the modern era, when the forces of disintegration act on them, they must seek to balance their new freedom by a concern with public matters. The new role of the person, with the private world where he reigns as master, seems yet so essential to Constant that when he seeks a name appropriate to modern times he spontaneously dubs this "the era of individuals" (*Histoire abrégée de l'égalité*, 389). He regards the evolution that led European peoples (the only peoples who really interest him) to this point as largely positive. They have arrived at an era in which the collective — whether the state, the corporate body, or the family — can no longer dictate the individual's conduct. "Instead of the subjugation of the individual by the family, itself merged with the state, each individual lives his own life and claims his freedom." There is no more unity in ideas, no more automatic social consensus, but this is an advantage, not an inconvenience. "The intellectual anarchy they deplore seems to me an immense progress of the intelligence" (*Les cent jours*, "Introduction to the Second Edition," 71), for the search for truth has taken the place of absolute truth guaranteed by authority, and this is a good thing.

Superior on the level of values, the modern era is also one that facilitates the greatest happiness in its subjects. Now, "to be happy, men need only to be left in perfect independence in all that concerns their occupations, their undertakings, their sphere of activity, their fantasies" (Constant, *The Spirit of Conquest and Usurpation*, II, p. 104). Must we believe that liberty alone is sufficient to the happiness of the Moderns, as Constant resolutely claims here? Is a whole life consecrated to the private world the best life imaginable? This may be doubtful. But it must be said that Constant himself does not entirely endorse this unconditional praise of the Moderns.

In the same text in which he introduces the opposition between the liberty of the Ancients and that of the Moderns, the *Principes de politique* of 1806, Constant establishes five differences between the two eras; and the advantages are not always on the same side. The Moderns enjoy individual freedom, but the Ancients actively participate in the government of their city (and find their happiness in this). The Moderns love repose: "Repose — and with repose, ease, and in order to arrive at ease, industry — is the unique goal toward which the human race is heading" (XVI, 3, 361); the Ancients prefer war, which brings glory and social cohesion. The Moderns are more sympathetic, the Ancients sterner. Finally, the Moderns are more lucid, but they are lacking the enthusiasm of the Ancients. "The Ancients had a whole-hearted conviction about everything. We have the hypocrisy of conviction about almost everything" (XVI, 6, 368). We doubt everything, are weary of each enterprise in advance, do not believe in the strength of our institutions. "Domestic affections replace larger public interests" (XVI, 7, 370).

That the Moderns are content with civil liberty becomes for Constant, then, not a reason for satisfaction but a source of worry and a matter for reproach. The lack of all enthusiasm, courage, patriotism, therefore of all social concern, cannot be a mark of glory. Throughout his first political pamphlet, *De la force du gouvernement actuel* . . . (1796), Constant already sounds this theme, which he shares at the time with Mme de Staël. "Repose is a good, but inactivity is an evil." The "loss of a goal, of interests and hopes beyond the narrow and personal," makes life futile; "there is always something dull and withered in what concerns only the self." Each of us also needs to let ourselves be carried away by enthusiasm, and to be "electrified by the acknowledgment of one's equals" (VII, 71–72).

There is something even more serious to the community than the moral collapse of individuals: in order to be maintained, civil liberty itself needs a certain dose of political liberty. In other words, if each man is only concerned with his own affairs, the tyrant can seize power; and under tyranny, one has no more leisure to tend to one's own affairs: one is obliged to submit and to follow.

By practicing the "domestic virtues" only, one easily forgets that their exercise itself presupposes a society that respects those virtues and protects them—something all societies do not do. "Its natural effect [that of modern society] is to make each individual his own center. Yet when each is his own center, all are isolated. When all are isolated, there is nothing but dust. When the storm comes, the dust turns to mire" (*De la religion*, preface, I, 133). By caring only for his personal pleasures, the individual sheds his interest in public affairs and tries to ignore the misfortunes of others, forgetting that his own private well-being depends on the public well-being. "The cause of the fatherland has been deserted because enlightened self-interest dictated no compromise on a daughter's dowry" (32). If the country is in flames, isn't the dowry threatened? For Constant, this is not a purely imaginary danger but what was in fact emerging under the rule of Napoleon, whose intention was to reduce society to this state. "The art of governments that oppress citizens is to keep them apart from one another and make communication difficult and meetings dangerous" (*Additions*, 628). The isolation of individuals is perhaps not an inevitable consequence of modernity, but it is certainly one of its possible consequences, which modern tyrants will attempt to bring about.

So we must not simply hope that the storm passes and preserve our personal pleasures. The Moderns cannot allow themselves to desert the public arena. From his first political pamphlet in 1796 to his last great work, *De la religion*, which he started publishing in 1824, Constant repeats the same message: let us mistrust the modern tendency to fall back on the private sphere, let us not be content with the egoistic happiness accessible to each person. We need something more, something that goes beyond the individual; in addition, if each person confined himself to himself, this very happiness would vanish. It is imperative that the public spirit, political liberty, be maintained. The independence of the individual cannot be an ultimate goal.

The Active Life and the Contemplative Life

We must come back at last to Montaigne, who, as we have seen, could also participate in the praise of solitude. Does that leave him out of the humanist family? Reading the *Essays*, we perceive that he does not propose choosing between solitude and society, but rather between two forms of social life, the active life and the contemplative life. He never had any doubts on the point of departure: man is endowed with a sociable nature. The very identity of our species resides in this. "There is nothing to which nature seems to have inclined us more than to society" (I, 28, 136). What is more social than conversation? Now, this is "the most fruitful and natural exercise of our mind" (III, 8, 704). The weakness of individual reason will be at least partially compensated by this constant exchange between individuals. It is the communication between men that yields the very definition of humanity. "We are men, and we hold together only by our word" (I, 9, 23). Society is natural to man: "There is nothing so unsociable and so sociable as man; the one by his vice, the other by his nature" (I, 39, 175). Human nature is sociable; only its perversion can cease to be so. Sociability is part of the human condition itself.

If Montaigne prefers to live in relative solitude, it is not in order to rediscover a lost nature, or because solitude is in itself superior. He is not unaware that to dispense with the approbation of others can simply be another way of flattering one's pride (II, 17, 492). The reason for his choice, as he willingly concedes, is something different: it is because he dreads the inherent constraints of public life. He loves being his own master, and this "has made him useless for serving others" (487). He does not love the world of rewards and dependencies that constitutes the "court of the great," and therefore declines the proposal that he live in the king's entourage, preferring to withdraw to his home and his library. It is not that one vocation is superior to the other; it merely suits him better. For him, the inconveniences of dependencies outweigh the advantages flowing from power. And from his point of view, the fate of the king himself is hardly enviable: "A king has nothing that is properly his own; he owes his very self entirely to others" (III, 6, 689).

Montaigne's position is clear: what he is fleeing, in the final analysis, is not human society in general but "servitude and obligation"; what he cherishes is not solitude as such, but the possibility this offers him to focus and find himself, so as finally to communicate better with others. "I throw myself into affairs of state and into the world more readily when I am alone" (III, 3, 625). Solitude is the means, but not the end; in Montaigne's case, it improves his sociability. The demand for solitude is obviously not situated at the same level as the fact of our sociable nature: solitude, like vanity, comprises attitudes proper to a social animal. The framework in which we live must not be confused with the strategies one chooses, once this framework is recognized, nor with the rules of the game, with its greater or lesser mastery. There are numerous forms of sociability and one chooses among them according to one's inclinations.

These values, therefore, are not absolutes. Montaigne does not claim, like the Ancient Stoics, that his choice is basically objective and deserves to be set up as a rule: he bases his ways of being on his "dreamy way" (622). Man is social by necessity; public or private, part of the crowd or solitary, by choice. We are no longer dealing here with a matter of principle but with the way of life that best suits each individual. There is no *single* ideal conduct in this regard but several, and everyone has the right to act according to his penchant. It is true that these preferences no longer involve humanist doctrine, which is content to proclaim our constitutional sociability but does not teach us how to choose between the forms it can take. It has, however, two limits. At one extreme, a life entirely devoted to the need for glory and honors no longer conforms to humanist thought, because this heroic ideal cannot suit everyone. And the humanists posit an ideal that is universally accessible; one must be able to reach it not only by accomplishing exploits but also by leading an ordinary life. The everyday is not an obstacle to merit; quite the contrary. At the other extreme, excluded from the spectrum of laudable conduct, is an exclusive concern with the inner life and indifference to any aspect of the social order. One cannot peacefully cultivate one's garden while Rome burns: that is to deny the presence of others within us, and ours in them. Within the vast space between these two exclusions, divergent choices are acceptable: Constant engaged in parliamentary debates and Montaigne withdrew to his library: both remained faithful to humanist thought.

When he seeks to rank these kinds of social life, Montaigne conforms, on several occasions, to a doctrine that can be inspired equally by Platonism, Stoicism, or Christianity, and that prefers the interior to the exterior, the spiritual to the material, the contemplative life to the active life. Yet the global message of the *Essays* is a little different. Montaigne declares: false language is less sociable than silence (I, 9, 24). On the lowest level, then, is false language, superficial worldliness; silence and solitude are preferable to these. But the very usage of the qualification "false" implies that all language is not false: there is also true language, which is superior to silence. Montaigne comes back to this when he evokes the possibility of traveling in company. The human being is made to live with his peers, and Montaigne recognizes himself in the common condition. "No pleasure has any savor for me without communication" (III, 9, 754). But there are companions and companions. People of quality with whom one can enter into friendship are irreplaceable. "It is rare good fortune, but inestimably comforting, to have a worthy man, of sound understanding and ways that conform with yours, who likes to go with you." Such a meeting is rare. Insipid companions, on the other hand, are legion, and rather to be avoided. "But still it is better to be alone than in boring and foolish company" (III, 9, 754–55). Just as silence cedes to true language but remains preferable to false language, solitude is inferior to the rare friendship but superior to communal promiscuity.

On another occasion, Montaigne takes things to a higher level. One must transcend the superficial opposition of life for others and life for oneself; each of these solutions, which might satisfy only one part of man, in reality mutilates him. He who demands everything from others is a fool, but he who gives them everything is unnatural. In order to bypass these extreme choices, one must recognize the part of others in oneself, and the expansion of the self toward others; they need me no less than I need them. "The main responsibility of each of us is his own conduct," of course, but "he who lives not at all unto others hardly lives unto himself" (a variation on Seneca: "Live for others if you want to live for yourself") (*Lettres*, 48, 2). The wise man knows "that he is to apply to himself his experience of other men and of the world, and, in order to do so, contribute to public society the duties and services within his province." He must also distinguish between superficial sociability, which makes us seek glory and honors or easy encounters, and authentic friendship, the source of both inner joy and merit. He who knows how to practice this last form of sociability is superior to both the worldly man and the solitary one, for he situates himself beyond their opposition; "he has attained the summit of human wisdom and of our happiness" (III, 10, 769). This hierarchy itself is not a rigid rule: Montaigne lives in ease and does not repudiate the acquisition of a little glory; he simply knows that higher and more powerful joys exist.

The human being is not necessarily fated to live life in society: Montaigne privileges the life of the mind, the company of books and private relations, to the detriment of public engagements; he feels no remorse at leaving the mayorality of Bordeaux and shutting himself up in his library. But this freedom in relation to public life merely shows more clearly man's need for other men: pleasure and happiness, truth and wisdom are based on this discovery. This is indeed why conversation among friends, the free search for truth in respect and love for the other, is what Montaigne cherishes in this world more than "any other action of our life" (III, 8, 922). In this respect, Descartes is a faithful disciple of Montaigne. Like him, he prefers the solitude of retirement—relative and not absolute—to the affairs of the city. This ideal solitude is found (and here Descartes is inventive) in the midst of the big city, yes, but a foreign city—as it happens, Amsterdam. "In this big city where I am, there being no man but myself who is not a practicing merchant, everyone there is so attentive to his profit that I could stay there all my life without ever being seen by anyone," he writes to Guez de Balzac (5 May 1631). Several years later, he confirms this in the *Discourse on the Method*: "Amidst this great mass of people, of busy people who are more concerned with their own affairs than curious about those of others, I have been able to lead a life as solitary and withdrawn as if I were in the most remote desert" (pt. III, I, p. 126). He knows very well why he needs solitude: it is the condition of success in the kind of work he has chosen. "When my mind would be wearied by the attention required by the troubles of life," he could no longer concentrate on study, which is dear to him (to Elisabeth, 28 June 1643). A choice must be made between public honors and action that consists of cultivating one's mind; having chosen, Descartes prefers his "desert" to all the royal courts.

Having chosen, he does not deny his sociability but chooses the form that suits him best. He who has decided to make thinking and writing his profession does best to lead a retiring life; worldly distractions and public appearances ill suit him. This does not mean that he refuses to communicate, but that by preference he chooses one form of communication over others. Nearly half of Descartes's work is made up of letters sent to individuals; he is surrounded (though at a distance) by loyal friends, and if he is prepared to go anywhere, it is to enjoy meeting with them.

To be honest, if this choice dictates his life most of the time, Descartes does not always follow it: no one could become entirely indifferent to the desire for honors and reputation. We find him going off to Paris, attracted by a promise of gratification — only to discover that the invitation to meet conceals merely vain curiosity. "What disgusted me most, was that none of them [his hosts] evinced the wish to know anything about me but my face; so that I have reason to believe that they only wanted to have me in France like an elephant or a panther, for the sake of rarity, and not at all for any useful reason" (to Chanut, 31 March 1649). He has not, however, learned his lesson: dazzled by the supposed greatness of high-ranking royalty, Descartes — despite his reticence — accepts an invitation from Queen Christina of Sweden. Once confronted with the reality, he perceives his mistake and dreams only of returning to his desert, outside of which "it is difficult for me to make progress in the search for truth; and this constitutes my chief good in this life" (to Elisabeth, 9 October 1649). But this is impossible: every day he must continue giving lessons in philosophy to Queen Christina, who is available only at five o'clock in the morning! Leaving the warmth of his stove to go to the palace, Descartes takes a chill and dies of pleurisy in February 1650.

The philosopher was wisest when he preferred the solitude of his desert and written communication of the results obtained by his search for truth. Rousseau understood this and readily admits, after all, that his own choice of solitude is hardly different from that of Descartes; or, one might add, of Montaigne, and so many other thinkers and writers, humanists or not. Writing is that paradoxical activity which demands that one flee from others in order to meet them more effectively. So Rousseau could reply to Diderot's supposed reproach: "For me, I do myself honor by imitating the villainous Descartes, when he spitefully went off to be philosopher in his Northern Dutch solitude," he writes ironically to Saint-Germain (XXXVII, 281). Solitude is still a way of living with others.

Chapter 5

The Ways of Love

*L*et us grant, with the humanist thinkers of the past, that solitude is not inevitable, that communal life could not possibly be weakened, since being itself is made up of relations with others. All this still gives us nothing but a negative assurance: sociability is not endangered by the freedom of the Moderns. But can we hope that this freedom also creates a positive gain? Is there something in the situation of modern man that contains the promise of richer, more gratifying human relations than in the past? We must turn here to love, and ask ourselves: What is the relation between love, on the one hand, and, on the other, the idea that modern man must pay a price for his freedom? What is the specifically humanist conception of love?

To begin, we must circumscribe the meaning of the word — one of the most durable and depleted words in our vocabulary. In the pages that follow, I will designate by *love* only the affective interpersonal relationship. This will allow me to set aside at the outset all uses of the word in which the object of love is not a human being but a thing, or an animal, or God, or an abstraction such as homeland, liberty, or even humanity; for the same reason I will not deal here with love of self. On the other hand, we will preserve hypothetically the same term whatever the agents of the relationship — whether between lovers, parents and children, or friends; not that these differences don't count, but they modify a sentiment that maintains its identity through all its transformations.

The Impossible Substitution

Let us begin with this statement: in human relations, the substitution of persons is sometimes easy, sometimes difficult, sometimes impossible. So we have three groups of instances: either everyone can appear at a certain place, or only certain persons, or only one person. This distinction allows us to identify three relational spheres in which every individual participates: the *humanitarian* sphere (for example, I must help a person in danger, whoever it is), the *political* sphere (in some respects, all my fellow citizens are interchangeable, yet they are not interchangeable with foreigners), and the *personal* sphere, in which no substitution is possible: I am attached to my father, to my lover, to my friend, to my child as irreplaceable individuals. Clearly, love refers to this last sphere, as one of its first great theoreticians, Aristotle, already knew quite well: "Love, which means, as it were, an affection pushed to its supreme degree, is addressed only to a single being" (*Nicomachean Ethics*, IX, 10, 5). Not that one cannot love several people at once; but love is characterized by the radical impossibility of substitution: if the loved person is different, the love is different as well.

The logic that governs these different domains is not the same. In the personal sphere, individual identity is irreducible; in the political sphere, on the contrary, it is parenthetical. In a democratic society, this sphere rests on the principle of equality; the personal sphere has no use for this principle but implies individual recognition, valuing what is unique in each person. If I love this person among all others, it is not because she is equal to others but because she is different. Benjamin Constant describes the separation of the two spheres in this way: "Magistrate, judge, public man, his duty is surely justice; but the most precious part of his private existence, over which society must have no hold, is to surround himself with exceptional beings, cherished beings, his peers in excellence, distinct from all the beings of his species. When it comes to others, it is enough for him never to harm them and sometimes to serve them; but to this favored circle, to this circle of love, of emotion, of memories, belongs his devotion, his constant occupation, and all forms of partiality" (*Godwin*, 565).

Justice must prevail in the political sphere. But it is clearly out of place in the private domain, woven of preferences and rejections — perfectly legitimate in their place; it would be ridiculous to want to submit my choice of the object of my affection to the rules of justice. If I am attached to someone, it is not because he or she is similar to all those who might take his or her place, but because he or she is different and, in my eyes, better: more beautiful, more attractive, more touching than his or her potential rivals; in short, a superior and not an equal. The purest embodiment of the bonds that define this domain is love.

This salient feature of love has several consequences. The first is that once we speak of relations of love, we also postulate the existence of individuals, of singular beings who are not interchangeable. The individual as a unique being is not a historically belated aquisition; the oldest narratives in our tradition already introduce us to beings as individual as we are today. Andromache does not love the Trojan warriors in general but her unique and individual husband, Hector. Priam has several sons, but when Hector is killed, it would not occur to him to console himself by reflecting that his sons are interchangeable: only Hector is Hector. Love and death, death in love: nothing is better proof that the substitution of one being for another is impossible. It seems likely that the first representations of individual human beings in painting or sculpture are bound precisely to this kind of situation: the death of someone dear. Other social relationships do not require the same kind of individual uniqueness: I employ a worker, I deal with a merchant — another might do as well, provided that he knows his job. There is only one king, but it is the office that is unique, or the category, not the individual who embodies it; this king dies, another will replace him and demand from his subjects the same respect, the same humility.

Now, if the love object is unique and irreplaceable, he must also partially escape the causes of which he is the outcome; he is shrouded by a certain indeterminacy that is responsible for his difference. If the individual could be entirely deduced from the causal series we discern to be operating in the world, if it were enough to know the biological, social, and psychic conditions acting in him in order to exhaustively describe his identity, there would be no reason why the same causal series might not produce a second individual strictly identical with the first, or an infinite series of such individuals — who would be no different from copies of a book. The intervention of will is not indispensable in the affirmation of individuality, and one face never precisely resembles another, even if the individual is not responsible for it.

When we say love we say individual and freedom. If I love this woman, I am not unaware that she shares a number of features with other women, with other French people, with other forty-year-olds; but she cannot be reduced to them. Without this aspect of individuality and freedom, and even if it is not its chief cause, my feeling does not deserve to be called "love." As a consequence, there is a primary secret affinity between humanist thought and the experience of love, to the extent that both affirm or presuppose a certain freedom of the individual — here, that of the love object, not of the loving subject.

The fact that the love object can never be replaced by another influences our image of the relationship between love and sexuality. By placing ourselves in a sociobiological perspective (that is, one that seeks immediate biological explanations for social facts), we are prepared to consider that love is derived from sexuality through "sublimation." Yet such a conception not only poses formidable problems as soon as we include the relations between parents and children or between friends; it is also revealed to be inadequate as soon as we acknowledge the uniqueness of the love object. Rousseau strongly insisted on this specificity of love, which distinguishes it from animal sexuality. As a general rule, animals know only sexuality, in which the partners are interchangeable; a few rare species are the exceptions to this rule — and we perceive them as close to humans precisely for this reason. Human love is therefore, in this sense, "antinatural," since it pushes us to the exclusive choice of a partner. It is "an artificial factitious feeling, born of the usage of society," which fixes desire "exclusively on a single object" (*Essay on the Origins of Inequality*, I, 157–58). Again, not that we cannot love several beings at once, but that every love is defined by its particular object. "Far from arising from nature, love is the rule and bridle of nature's inclinations. It is due to love that, except for the beloved object, one sex ceases to be anything for the other" (*Emile*, IV, p. 214). Rousseau's formula may be hyperbolic, but it identifies a distinctive feature of human affections. Love and sexuality are two entities that intersect; each can exist with or without the other.

What distinguishes love from other interpersonal relationships is indeed this impossibility of replacing the love object with another. If we situate ourselves in the political sphere, where certain substitutions but not all, are possible, we are faced with *solidarity*. All residents of France are in solidarity with one another through their Social Security or their pension funds. In a less institutional way, I also feel solidarity with all people of my age, my gender, my profession, or my origin; I am ready to act on their behalf, indeed to sacrifice myself. But this feeling is not love, even in the broad sense that includes friendship, precisely because members of the group are interchangeable. If the restriction of the group were to disappear, if all human beings could benefit from the same feeling, we would enter the humanitarian sphere. This feeling of universal love has been exalted by the Greek pagan tradition under the name of *philanthropy*, and by the Christians as *agape*, or love-charity. This is a love of particular individuals, but a love whose objects are, indeed, interchangeable; enemies deserve it no less than friends. From our point of view, then, these relations do not strictly belong to the domain of love but rather to that of morality.

Love-Desire

The impossibility of substitution concerns all love; yet all forms of love are not the same. Greek thought has bequeathed us a distinction that we can use here by adapting it to our needs, the distinction between *eros*, or love-desire, and *philia*, or love-joy. In order to pursue our enquiry into the relations between love and humanist thought, I would now like to evoke these two broad categories.

First, a few of the characteristics of love-desire: it is constituted by a lack (nonsatisfaction is its initial necessary condition); it starts with the loving subject, not with the love object; its advertised (but never attained) goal is the fusion of the two lovers. On this canvas — bequeathed to Europeans by Greek thinkers and Roman writers, transmitted by the troubadors of the Middle Ages — French authors from the Renaissance to our day, humanist or not, have untiringly embroidered their personal variations.

A lack: love is interpreted here as the desire for an absent object. Desire is therefore constituted by this lack; if the lack is filled, desire dies, and the subject is frustrated instead of satisfied. He would not know how to be otherwise: the singularity of desire comes from the fact that, falling on a person rather than a thing, it can only be experienced, never fulfilled, unlike the need that can be satisfied or the wish that can be realized. The subject loves love more than its object; and to make it last, he is quite prepared, in the extreme instance, to keep this object forever at a distance. His desire is fueled by the rivals and jealousies it conjures up; obstacles are indispensable to it: in their bed, a sword separates Tristan from Iseult. Albertine vanished is the only lovable Albertine. A celebration of absence, eros culminates in death, absence par excellence, which is its secret ally.

Thus Montaigne thinks "that our desire is increased by difficulty" (*Essays*, title chap. 15, bk. II, p. 463), that "difficulty gives value to things" (463–64). The woman who resists, or the woman protected by a jealous husband, is all the more desirable to her admirer; the presence of rivals activates desire; jealousy, envy, the forbidden create love rather than follow from it. One scorns what one has, one desires what one lacks. One can become conscious of this logic and turn it to advantage: "I wanted to sharpen this pleasure through difficulty, through desire, and through a little glory" (III, 3, 826). Love is experienced only as an absence: "In love there is nothing but a frantic desire for what flees from us" (I, 28, 137).

Rousseau's characters believed that by preventing passion from succeeding, one could make love-desire yield a remedy against its withering. "Love is a desire that is whetted by obstacles," therefore "it is not good that it should be satisfied; it is better for it to endure and be unhappy than flicker out in the bosom of pleasures" (*The New Julie*, III, 7, p. 263). The satisfaction of love provokes its demise, and a frustrated love is preferable to the total absence of love. Love without pleasure is worth more than pleasure without love. "The sight of spent love frightens a tender heart more than that of an unhappy love, and disaffection for what one possesses is a condition a hundred times worse than regret for what one has lost" (III, 7, p. 263). The important thing is to love; the greatest enemy of love is the disappearance of every obstacle, therefore of any possibility of new conquest: happiness palls; this would be the law of human desire (cf. VI, 8, 570). Novelty fuels desire, habit diminishes it. From the moment apotheosis is attained, happiness can merely decline; to reach the summit means that one is compelled to descend.

Julie agrees with her cousin Claire (who was the author of the preceding analysis): the accomplishment of love is its death knell, "sensual love cannot do without possession, and with it dies out" (*The New Héloïse*, III, 18, p. 280); conversely, obstacles only make it more intense. Emile's tutor asks in his turn: "Would Leander have wanted to die for Hero if the sea had not separated him from her?" (*Emile*, V, p. 433). Julie has therefore found a solution to make love immortal: "In order to love each other forever we must renounce each other" (*The New Héloïse*, III, 18, p. 299). Her love will stay alive, and her consciousness will grant her a secondary bonus: "In a way, one enjoys the self-imposed deprivations thanks to the very sentiment of their cost and of the motive that leads one to make them" (III, 7, p. 262).

For centuries people wanted to see in this variety of love, also called passionate love, the truth of all love. We may well wonder whether the success of this conception, which was enormous throughout the history of the West, despite its patent inadequacies, was not due to its affinities with the structures of narrative, itself based on something lacking and attempts to fill the void. In both we find a quest that is always suspended, always begun anew, a discovery of unexpected obstacles. But because a narrative is comely, does it follow that it must be true? Surely there are also other ways to explain this success: it corresponds to the initial (and often the only) form of any amorous relationship, and it is also connected in our minds to the strong physical experience of this phase (don't we use the terms *physical* and *erotic* interchangeably?).

This is the first feature of love-desire, then, the result of the need to conceive of its object as absent. Its second feature — its egocentrism — comes from the fact that the other exists here only from the perspective of the self. Is eros egotistical? One might think the contrary, since the lover praises the love object to the skies, believes him to be the handsomest, the strongest, or the most elegant, desires her above all, believes he will waste away if they are separated. Yet nearly everyone has experienced this paradox: I am ready to do anything for this person, but only on the condition that she loves me. If, on the contrary, she stops loving me, hatred replaces love: taken to an extreme, I would prefer to see her dead than living in the arms of another. Jealousy and possessiveness go hand in hand. Through the love object it is still me whom I love: eros arises from relational egotism, or, as the theologians used to say, it is a love of concupiscence, in which I want to take rather than to give. We see here that love-desire does not very effectively embody that feature of love which wants its object to be irreplaceable. If my love is determined by the absence of its object, I retain a feature of this object that does not characterize it in itself but uniquely in relation to me. It is no longer the unique other whom I love, it is her absence — which any other individual could reproduce.

The love object is ignored if love serves the interests of the loving subject above all else. He or she is also ignored, but in another way, in the project that aims at a fusion between subject and object. This, too, is a commonplace that dates from Antiquity; this ideal is attributed as much to love as to friendship. Aristophanes, in Plato's *Symposium*, maintains that two lovers are animated by the "desire to mingle together in a single being" (191a), that "love tries to make two beings into one" (191d), that what each of them desires is "to be submerged in the beloved" (192e). Aristotle recalls, in the *Nichomachean Ethics*, the proverb holding that "friends have but a single soul" (IX, 8, 2) and speaks of the "friend being another self" (IX, 4, 5). The image passes into Latin literature: "friends form a single being, have a single soul," according to Cicero; each possesses part of a single soul, Horace continues; and Saint Augustine describes his friend as "another myself": "I thought of my soul and his soul as one soul in two bodies" (*Confessions*, IV, 6, p. 56). Yet, in commenting on the image in Aristophanes, Aristotle already warns against the dangers of fusion: the formation of a single being, which is in any case merely an image, a pressure put on the real relationship, will inevitably have as its price the obliteration of their prior singularity. "To become both a single being from the two they were" necessarily involves the "disappearance of the two individualities, or at least of one of them" (*Politics*, 1262b).

Montaigne, who places no great value on love, limits the ideal of fusion to friendship. Here the two souls, he writes, "mingle and blend with each other so completely that they efface the seam that joined them" (*Essays*, I, 28, 139). The friend's will is lost in mine; "neither of us reserved anything for himself, nor was anything either his or mine" (139). Here, notions of generosity, gratitude, and duty have no more currency: since all is common to them, the friends form "one soul in two bodies" (141). The friend "is not another man: he is myself" (142), since his death "only half of me seems to me to be alive now" (143).

Rousseau, on the other hand, reserves fusion for love. "The first of my needs, the greatest, the strongest, the most inextinguishable was entirely in my heart: it was the need for an intimate society and as intimate as it could be; it was above all for this that I needed a woman rather than a man, a lover rather than a friend. This peculiar need was such that the closest union of bodies could not even be enough for it; I would have needed two souls in the same body; since I did not have that, I always felt some void" (*Confessions*, IX, 348). Rousseau appropriates the traditional image, but gives it a paradoxical spin: it is no longer one soul in two bodies that he seeks, but two souls in a single body. He seeks physical fusion, that is, the impossible. Woman is differentiated here from man (and love from friendship) only because she gives a heterosexual man the impression of total contact.

The pinnacle of the relation with the other, then, would be his absorption, which also means his demise. On another occasion, Rousseau uses the same image: "To read while I eat has always been my whim for lack of a tête-à-tête. It is the compensation for the society I lack. I alternately devour a page and a bite: it is as if my book was dining with me" (*Confessions*, VI, 225). Books are a substitute for friends, but, on the other hand, they belong to the same realm as the brioches. Is this also the fate of friends? Fusion—or rather, since this is impossible, a life together that appeals to it—leads to the same result as ignorance of the other, only by a different path. The other does not exist as a wholly separate subject; he is not lost, here, amidst things but disappears into me, he is nothing but one of my parts. If indeed the love between two beings ends in the creation of a single being, this is because one of the two has chosen or has been forced to sacrifice himself for the sake of the other. The result of fusion is, in reality, hardly different from that of submission.

In the end, if we are to believe these descriptions of it, love-desire would be condemned to failure by its very structure. This is a perpetual frustration, as Montaigne already observes: either the object of desire is absent, or desire itself. "Desire and its enjoyment make us equally dissatisfied" (*Essays*, II, 15, 465). The logic of love-desire is diabolical: I love only if I am not loved, I am loved only if I do not love. It would follow that one is always at the mercy of two complementary forms of unhappiness: unrequited love, and being loved without being able to love in return because of that love itself. The assurance of being loved atrophies love, prevents loving; yet it is the goal of all love. We all aspire, without always knowing it, to our own unhappiness: we want to be loved, which will prevent us from loving in return, a state that will then condemn us to disappointment and discontent. Yet we cannot stop seeking love; we are, then, by the very structure of our desire, fated to oscillate between the two frustrations of not being loved and of not loving.

Constant often uses this image of an impasse. Subject to its implacable logic, the human subject seems to have no chance to find happiness in love. To be loved does not make us happy, and therefore we should not wish for it. We should not, and yet we do: such is the ordinary tragedy of desire. I love; but my choice is between two forms of unhappiness: either the object of my love responds to my demands and desire dies; or she does not and desire is frustrated. Constant sees a fatality in this, and says that he conceived his character Adolphe in order to make this point. "His position and Ellenore's had reached an impasse, and that is precisely what I wanted. I've shown him tormented because he loved Ellenore only weakly; but he might not have been tormented less had he loved her more. He suffered by her for lack of feeling; with a more passionate feeling, he might have suffered for her" (*Adolphe*, preface, 8). Should the whole of human life be reduced to such a "choice between two evils"? This sometimes seems to be what Constant believes. All his life is an "alternation between suffering and exhaustion," he writes in a letter to his aunt, the Comtesse de Nassau (2 August 1808). But, to believe him, the life of his friend Germaine de Staël is not much different: "She has always had that kind of anxiety about our liaison that prevented her from finding it exhausting" (*Journal*, 19 August 1804).

Nothing in this conception of love relates it to humanist thought. The will of the subject is reduced here to nothingness; love obeys impersonal laws that guide the conduct of all men: egotism, the desire for what is lacking, the aspiration for an impossible fusion, inevitable frustration. These psychic laws have the rigidity of biological codes; an individual's conduct is explained by a causal series over which he has no control. This conception would suit scientistic doctrines. Yet it is present in the writings of thinkers related to all the families of modernity, and it was by design that I have chosen to cite the formulas penned by humanist writers.

Love-Joy

Love-desire, then, is a form of love that guarantees neither the uniqueness of the love object nor her freedom, and even less that of the loving subject. This is not true of the other form, love-joy, which can be observed in a sexual relationship but also between parents and children, or between friends. This love can also be experienced in absence (it is the usual fate of parents to live far from their children, once they are grown), but it is not this absence that creates it or nourishes it, rather it is an accident that does not abolish love, and in principle its presence is preferred; its horizon is reciprocity. Its underlying feeling is the joy one feels at the simple existence of the love object; so, speaking again like the theologians, it is a benevolent love, not a concupiscent love. The goal of this love is not fusion: I cannot rejoice in the existence of the other unless he remains separate from me. The description of this love — sometimes under a different name — is found in the same authors who were capable of depicting love-desire; but this new variety of love, unlike the first, will be in accord with humanist doctrine. Why is this so?

In Montaigne, this relationship is best embodied in the nonsexual friendship between two men, illustrated in an exemplary way by his own relationship with Etienne de la Boétie. In his description of friendship Montaigne recuperates most of the features attributed to it by the Ancients. Friendship implies the friends' resemblance and equality. This is why the tyrant is to be pitied: he doubts the sincerity of those around him and cannot trust anyone; reciprocity is off limits to him. By contrast, trust between friends is total, and the law of ordinary human relations is reversed: "I give myself to my friend more than I draw him to myself" (*Essays*, III, 9, 746). Reflecting on love, Montaigne concludes that it is impossible to apply to human relations a purely economic logic: here, to give is to take. "In truth, in this delight the pleasure that I give tickles my imagination more sweetly than that which I feel" (III, 5, 682).

Rousseau's appreciation of this second form of love evolves over time. In *The New Héloïse*, he is close to Montaigne: the reciprocity and joy provoked by the existence of the other characterize friendship rather than what we usually call love, which demands fusion. Several years later, however, in his *Pygmalion* (1762), Rousseau portrays the choice for or against fusion differently. The sculptor Pygmalion is tempted to merge with Galatea, but he restrains himself: if he became her, he would no longer love her. "If I were her, I would not see her, I would not be the one who loves her. Ah! May I always be another, so as to want always to be her, to see her, to love her, to be loved by her" (1228). Fusion (be it only imaginary) makes love, at worst, impossible: love exists only at the moment of separation between self and other, therefore the self must remain a distinct entity. At the same period, love in *Emile* seems to be something different from what is described by Julie and Saint-Preux, since instead of fusion we find here reciprocity as the goal of love, understood as the recognition of the other as a wholly separate subject that cannot be reduced to the self. If one can still speak of possession, this is rather paradoxical because it is mutual. "Possession which is not reciprocal is nothing. It is at most possession of the sexual organ, not of the individual" (*Emile*, IV, p. 349). By claiming to absorb someone, one makes him disappear; by valuing him, one maintains him as a separate being.

In addition, this new love is no longer centered on the sole insatiable demand of the *I*. "Love, which gives as much as it demands, is in itself a sentiment filled with equity" (V, p. 430) and "true love" can never be a love that does not value the other. This love is less a victim of illusions than passion, for it engages the mind of the lover, not only his heart; it is action assumed by its subject. Finally, there is another great difference from love as it is described in *The New Héloïse*. In the novel, we could observe a "scale of love" of the Platonic type (from physical to spiritual, from particular to general): Saint-Preux had to raise himself to the quasi-Christological love of Julie. In *Emile*, by contrast, the young man's love for Sophie (or Sophie's for him) is not meant to be transformed into anything else; it is its own end. Rousseau interprets love here (and not only friendship) as a joy in presence. It is that love, going beyond the good feelings between Julie and Wolmar, that is meant to flower in marriage.

Isn't this second kind of love in turn threatened by the same danger as the first, namely, wear and tear? Rousseau writes: "I have often thought that if one could prolong the happiness of love in marriage, one would have paradise on earth. Up to now, that has never be seen" (*Emile*, V, p. 476). Montaigne was content to make a similar disillusioned statement. Rousseau, however, reflects on ways to overcome the obstacle. The recipe is simple, he says: "It is to go on being lovers when one is married" (V, p. 476). Rousseau's suggestion is as much concerned with physical love as with the emotional rapport of the two spouses: each of them must remain a free subject, a being entirely separate, never surrendering his or her will, acting only out of love and not out of duty. "Neither of you ought to be the other's more than he pleases." This means, too, that married or not, lovers have the right of refusal: Rousseau had a good understanding of conjugal rape. "Let each of you always remain master of his own person and his caresses and have the right to dispense them to the other only at his own will" (p. 477). The love object is not presented in love-joy in the same way as in love-desire: not only is he or she strictly irreplaceable, but in addition the beloved's autonomy is preserved. This freedom is not incompatible with fidelity: to refuse to give oneself to the other does not mean giving oneself to a third person; simply, the individual is not sacrificed to that community, the couple. The existence of love-joy, then, confirms the compatibility between autonomy and sociability: the free man is not condemned to live in solitude.

In its chief characteristics, love-joy is opposed point by point to love-desire: joy in presence is substituted for the cult of absence, the *you* is not defined as a function of the *I*, so the fusion of the two is no longer the regulating ideal of their exchange but is replaced by reciprocity. The *you* is no longer a means, it becomes the end; in addition, he must preserve the autonomy of his will: these two characteristics relate love-joy to humanist doctrine. Yet the relationship is still loose, and our initial question has not yet been answered: How does any conception of love respond to the challenge addressed to the humanist project?

The Individual as End

When there is love, no substitution of its object is any longer possible, as we have seen. But the place and role of this object are not always the same. In love-desire, she is defined in relation to the subject (*you* are what *I* lack) and finally instrumentalized to my advantage; moreover, relations between the two obey immutable laws. In love-joy, the love object is defined by herself, therefore unique and definitively free, at the same time the beneficiary of my love. This does not mean, however, that I cannot go beyond the person of the beloved.

The question "why" has a double meaning, for what reason and to what end, *warum* and *wozu*, *pochemu* and *zachem*. In the Greek tradition, the question bearing on the cause is not considered vain; on the contrary, it is often said that only he who has certain qualities is worthy of love. Through his person, it is these qualities that we love and cherish. The individual is not instrumentalized to the advantage of another individual, but love is justified by the person's merits; in this sense, it is put in the service of an abstraction, namely, beauty or virtue. This is the meaning of the "scale of love" described in Plato's *Symposium*: love of the individual is merely the love of beauty in him, and this in turn is merely an imperfect incarnation of the idea of beauty, to which one aspires oneself, the beautiful itself finally merging with the good. To love the individual for himself would reveal, in Plato's eyes, a scarcely admirable idolatry.

For Aristotle, too, the qualities of the beloved person are not irrelevant: real love-friendship (*philia*) can flower only between virtuous and worthy individuals; that is why it remains so rare. Aristotle carefully distinguishes this love from self-interested, utilitarian friendships; nonetheless, even without finality, love can have its reasons. The idea that every human being, even a slave, might be worthy of becoming the object of love is alien to this way of thinking. The example of maternal love, to which Aristotle resorts several times, does not constitute a refutation: every child, unworthy as he may be, can have a mother who will love him — but only on the condition that he is her child.

The specifically Christian form of love, love-charity (or *agape*), is extended to everyone, and therefore does not require justification. One must not love this person because she is rich or beautiful or good, nor because she is close to us. "The pagans themselves — don't they do as much?" Jesus exclaims in the Sermon on the Mount (Matt. 5:47). One must love her because she is a human being like others. God loves all his children, good and bad, just and unjust. Jesus, who is his earthly incarnation, shows how this type of paternal love can become a rule of life in relations between men. Particular persons, unless they are saints, will not be as perfect as Jesus; nonetheless, they will preserve this ideal, which refuses to seek any justification for love.

The causal "why" is summarily dismissed here, in contrast to Greek thought, but the final "why" is not. Saint Paul says: to love God is nothing but loving one's neighbor, "he who loves others has fulfilled the Law" (Rom. 13:8; cf. I Cor. 13:2–7; Gal. 5:6 and 14; I Tim. 1:5; etc.). But this also means that one must continue to love God through others. Christian philanthropy is derivative and subordinate. Saint Augustine contrasts the two loves by evoking the death of his best friend: he loved him in himself, and that was his mistake; moreover, he has been punished for it by the sorrow he felt. "I had spread my soul on the sand by loving a mortal being, as if he did not have to die," he writes. No such thing threatens the believer, who never risks anything: "Happy is he who loves You. . . . He alone will lose no one dear to him" (*Confessions*, IV, 9, 74). Through particular beings, Augustine now addresses his love to God.

Certain mystical currents within Christianity will go so far as to cast aside the love of men, thus reorienting the original message. In the sev-

enteenth century, Saint Francis of Salesia enjoined a believer to renounce all human love: "Our Lord loves you, my Mother, he wants you
all for himself. . . . Think no longer of friendship, nor of the unity that
God made between us, nor of your children" (to Mother Chantal, 21
May 1616). Such is the spiritual nakedness of the Christian: God is all
for him, the rest is nothingness. "That which is not God is nothing to
us. . . . I love nothing at all but God and all souls for God" (1620–21).
Nicole, another author close to Jansenism, spells it out: "God properly
does not ask men only for their love; but also he asks for all of it.
He does not want to share it, and as he is their sovereign good, he does
not want them to become attached elsewhere, or to find their repose in
another creature, because no creature is their end" (*Les Visionnaires*,
463). Neither love nor death makes this act legitimate, makes the individual an ultimate end. We may recall the injunction that Pascal—
certainly the greatest of the antihumanist thinkers in France—kept on
himself the day of his death: I must prevent attachments, mine for
others as those of others for me, for the individual being must not become "anyone's end."

For Christians no less than for Plato, then, the adoration of the particular human person smacks of idolatry. Christian love is without reason, to be sure, but it is not without purpose. The justification of love is
not necessary, in the final analysis, because I love this individual not as
such but insofar as he is one child of God among others, all equally so.
This explains why, in love-charity, the substitution of the object is possible: I must not attach myself to this or that person, but bring the same
love to everyone. Ideally, I must not even try to know the name or face
of the person to whom my charity is addressed.

Men have always sung the praises of love, but their reasons have not
been the same, since they have invested the same words with different
meanings. If love allows one access to beauty, if its practice coincides
with that of virtue—since in both cases one desires the benefit of others
for themselves—it is because one esteems beauty and virtue; the value
of love would therefore be a reflected or instrumental value. Love coincides with divine Law only because the Law gives this love its meaning.
But this is not how the humanist authors understand it.

First, let us recall one of the most moving if ancient formulations of
love, which tradition attributes to Héloïse in her letters to Abelard. This
would be around 1135, at the very beginning of the period of "courtly
love," and the former lovers are both confined to their respective mon-

asteries, engaged in the fulfillment of their religious duties. It is in these circumstances, and certainly not forgetting the Christian doctrine of love, that Héloïse writes to Abelard in her first missive: "God knows, never have I sought in you anything but yourself. It is you alone that I would desire, not what belongs to you or what you represent" (*Letters of Héloïse to Abelard*, 127). And following Abelard's warnings, she returns to the subject in her second letter: "In all the states into which life has led me, God knows, it is you, more than he, whom I fear to offend; it is you rather than him whom I have sought to please" (160). This simply human love is no longer Christian.

Montaigne, who describes the blossoming of the same idea in the perfect friendship he knew with La Boétie, says straightaway that not only is this friendship not in the service of any external goal, but also that the only reason for his choice of La Boétie is the man's individual identity. Therefore, the person of the friend is not reducible to any general notion, the individual as friend illustrates no concept; he is a unique instance that, contrary to the former examples, is worthy in itself. This is the source of the celebrated line: Why did I love him? "Because it was he; because it was I" (*Essays*, I, 28, 139). It is revealing to see that the formula did not come to Montaigne whole cloth; he had first written, in the margin of his copy, "because it was he"; only later did he add the second half of the formula (we shall return to its implications). The existence of the friendship proves that one cannot "generalize" the person.

Montaigne's originality in relation to classical thought lies, then, neither in the superlative place granted to friendship, nor in the proximity of the two friends that would lead to fusion; rather, it lies in the unique character of the person of the friend, and in the refusal to seek any justification for his love of him. Nothing comparable to the Platonic "scale," which presents the love of the person as a simple step in the love of the beautiful; the individual, here, represents only himself. Aristotle and Cicero praise friendship because it is the best embodiment of virtue, Montaigne because it celebrates the achievement of individual identity: for him, moral reasons have nothing to do with it. Aristotle also says, "because it was he," "because he is what he is"; but by this he means, because he is that admirable being. Like the Christians, Montaigne does not seek justification for his love; but unlike them, he does not make the individual being into a means of access to God, love of the creature does not lead here to love of the Creator. He loves La Boétie for himself, as an ultimate end.

There should be no misunderstanding: to say "because it was he, because it was I" does not mean that the person of the beloved does not matter to me, as long as it is this one and not another. This interpretation would be fitting strictly for the love between parents and children (I will love my mother or my son whatever they do, whatever they become), not for the love between two adults. Here, the identity of the beloved is decisive; I do not love only a proper name or a physical continuity, I love a person because I find him or her full of qualities that delight me. And I refuse to give third parties any explanations that might become matters for dispute: "because she is intelligent," "because he is handsome." Montaigne admires La Boétie for what he is, a brilliant, generous, and courageous man. Indeed, that is why love does not always last: "he" is not fixed, nor am "I"; what constitutes an identity today can disappear tomorrow — for the lover, the friend, or both. Not to see the individual as the illustration of a concept, which is the mark of love in the humanist conception, does not mean that one is indifferent to what he becomes, nor that one is condemned to the purely passive role of unconditional admirer.

We cannot avoid facing the formidable problem formulated by Pascal (*Pensées*, B. 323, L. 688): one does not love the abstract substance of a person, but only his qualities. Nonetheless, all our qualities are not "borrowed," and it is their accumulation and conjunction that make my "I." It is the I itself that is perishable — such is the wretchedness of man, which here becomes the source of his greatness. That is not all: not only is the configuration of moral characteristics so complex that it is unlikely to repeat itself (it is as improbable to encounter a person's moral double as it is his physical one), but in addition, the capacity for freedom that defines every human being makes his behavior unpredictable and therefore unique in a more powerful sense. We seek to capture the gaze of the beloved also because we cannot be sure of his response: the gaze of the other, in which indecision is always possible, is our way of reaching his freedom. That singularity is radical, and is not limited to the complexity of the person. The blind can compensate for the absence of vision by developing their other senses; but we sighted people are handicapped in the face of the blind, since we can no longer use that privileged means for reaching their freedom and singularity — their living gaze.

We are witness here to the veritable emergence of the second humanist postulate, which I have called the finality of the *you*, the refusal of any instrumentalization of the other, which finds its culmination in love-joy. The referent for this postulate is no longer an anthropology but a morality, in the broader sense: it does not describe how men are, but how one should behave toward them. Yet this elevation of man to a place where God used to be does not lead to idolatry (this humanism is not "naive"): Montaigne does not tell us that his friend was perfect or that he should have been treated like a god; he simply states his own attachment to this singular being. Descartes will follow him on this point when he declares: "There is no person so imperfect that we could not have for him a very perfect friendship" (*The Passions of the Soul*, 83, I, p. 357). The quality of the feeling is not determined by the virtue of its object, the absolute is not given in nature but produced by the subject.

Almost two centuries later, Rousseau will put into Julie's mouth—the new Héloïse!—the expression of this principle, according to which the individual must always be an end in human relations, and not only a means. "Man," she says, "is too noble a being to have to serve merely as an instrument of others, and he ought not to be used for purposes that suit them without consulting also what suits him" (*The New Héloïse*, V, 2, p. 439). The lover does joyfully what morality enjoins everyone to do: in both cases, the reduction of the individual to an instrumental role is rejected. This is the profane version of Saint Augustine's celebrated formula: "Love, and do what you will" (VII, 8, 328–29).

Loving the Imperfect

The love object does not have to be good; he does not have to be beautiful; yet the lover thinks he is. The power of love to create illusion, to lend its object the greatest virtues (which Stendhal called "cristalization"), is a theme familiar since the time of Latin literature; but its meaning changes. La Rochefoucauld, for example, sees it as additional proof of our inadequacy, of our mind's powerlessness to tease out the strategies of desire. Otherwise, how do we explain the fact that one becomes clear-minded only after ceasing to love? "Lovers do not see their mistresses' defects until the rapture is over" (*Posthumous Maxims* 545). "There are few people who, when their love for each other is dead, are not ashamed of that love" (*Maxims*, 71).

Rousseau knows these texts, and he cites one of them to Julie, who confirms this opinion: it is our imagination itself that induces illusion, by adorning the loved one with all the virtues; it is myself that I loved in you, she adds in another moment of lucidity (III, 8, p. 280). If by any chance we should desire something, the imagination is entrusted with embellishing it (*The New Héloïse* VI, 8, 693); Rousseau sets so much store by this statement that, after confirming it in the second preface to the novel, he repeats it in *Emile* (V, p. 447). Emile's tutor is categorical: "what is true love itself if not chimera, lie and illusion? We love the image we make for ourselves far more than we love the object to which we apply it. If we saw what we love exactly as it is, there would be no more love on earth" (IV, p. 329). Rousseau again takes up these assertions in his own life. He writes in a letter: "Love is merely illusion. . . . [O]ne sees nothing as it is as long as one loves" (to Deleyre, 10 November 1759, VI, 192). Yet the meaning of these lines is not La Rochefoucauld's.

If we required true beauty, real goodness, we would no longer love that being for what he is but for his qualities; if those qualities were absent, one would cease to love him. Rousseau would like every individual to be loved; it is useless to search for justifications, and in any case these would be illusory. We have the luck to see the beloved adorned with all perfections. To recognize the illusion is at the same time to renounce the requirement that a person must have particular virtues in order to be loved: human life is an imperfect garden; for Plato, individuals are only shadows, only ideas, therefore beauty as well, truly exist. For Rousseau, on the contrary, beauty is a lure, while relations between beings are quite real. Far from demonstrating human weakness, this capacity to embellish the object of love illustrates greatness of feeling. For even if the virtues of the love object are imaginary, those that create love in the heart of the lover are quite real. Rousseau writes to Saint-Germain: "The love that I conceive, that I have been able to feel, inflames the illusory image of the perfection of the loved object; and this illusion itself carries it to the enthusiasm of virtue" (*Correspondence*, XXXVII, 280).

"Where is the true lover who is not ready to immolate himself for his beloved?" we read in *Emile* (V, p. 391); the act would be authentic even if it were motivated by an illusion. This is the most precious feature of human love: as Descartes said, for the sake of highly imperfect beings, for the sake of entirely relative value, it manages to produce the absolute. The human race therefore has the unique capacity to fabricate the infinite from the finite, the eternal from the transient, to transform a chance encounter into a life's necessity. When the lover experiences the mysterious feeling that the beloved is not the most desirable for him alone, but that he has objectively superior qualities, he is not suffering under any illusion. That is why we are not lying when we declare: "I will always love you," even if most of the time the prediction proves to be false; these words translate our will to introduce the absolute into an existence that is devoid of it. "The lover," Julie says, "does not lie as he utters lies" (*The New Héloïse*, I, 46, p. 105).

When Rousseau thinks, long after the events, of the woman he loved most, Sophie d'Houdetot, he draws us a physical portrait of her in which we do not recognize the gaze of the lover. "Mme the Comtesse d'Houdetot was approaching thirty and was not beautiful. Her face was marked with smallpox; her complexion lacked delicacy, she was near-sighted, and her eyes were slightly too round" (*Confessions*, IX, 369). We stumble here on the very first step of the ladder of love: how can we love a being if she is not the incarnation of beauty or virtue?

Happily, men have at their disposal a capacity to see the loved object as they would like her to be. Rousseau was then in the midst of describing the perfections of Julie, his literary character: "I was intoxicated with love without an object, that intoxication fascinated my eyes, that object became fixed on her, I saw my Julie in Mme d'Houdetot, but invested with all the perfections with which I had just adorned the idol of my heart" (370). This is not a matter, as it sometimes is in Rousseau's autobiographical writings, of praising a life passed in the company of chimeras, but of putting our capacity to fabricate the real in the service of our relations with concrete human beings. Illusion is no longer a blind alley, a substitute; it is the means that allows men to fabricate the absolute from the relative, to make things such that the imperfection of individuals is not an insurmountable obstacle to the perfection of their feelings. In this respect, this love overlaps with the ancient category of benevolent love (or "pure love"): not only is it disinterested, but I even love the other in his imperfection, knowing that my imagination will supply the rest.

We now have a better understanding of why the humanists give such importance to love. For Montaigne, his friendship with La Boétie was the high point of his life, and he reserves a place of honor for its evocation at the center of Book I of the *Essays*. There is a qualitative leap between this relationship and what Montaigne calls somewhat scornfully "common" or "ordinary" friendships, simple bonds of circumstance or convenience. What justifies this exceptional place is not, as we have seen, the friend's personality but the quality of the experience itself. Montaigne's wisdom suggests that life finds its meaning in the very fact of living; but as a humanist, he does not think that the individual being is complete in himself: man achieves his plenitude only through friendship. The other is external to the *I*, but friendship-love is an indispensable part of my life and, as such, serves no purpose.

Montaigne insists on this several times: just as the person of the friend is the sole justification for his choice, friendship is an end in itself. "The object of this association is simply intimacy, fellowship, and conversation: exercise of minds, without any other fruit" (*Essays*, III, 3, 625), that is, but friendship itself. This is what distinguishes it from other human relationships that are meant to be instrumental, such as physical love, whose aim is sexual pleasure. "Friendship, on the contrary, is enjoyed according as it is desired," and not an instrument at all: "whereas in friendship there are no dealings or business except with itself" (I, 28, 138); it "has no other model than itself, and can be related only to itself" (139).

Love and Humanism

Individuals cannot explain the value they attach to love, even if they are ready to confirm it. The troubadours who sing of courtly love repeat: "What is life worth without love?" "One is worth nothing without love," declaims Bernard de Ventadour; Benjamin Constant echoes him almost seven centuries later: "What is life when one can no longer be loved?" (to Juliette Recamier, 8 October 1815). What modern men — whose unformulated thought is expressed by the humanists — value in love is not necessarily beauty, virtue, or wisdom, even if these are part of it. They dimly understand that human beings are not self-sufficient, and that in order to exist, they need others. Love in all its forms satisfies this need and embodies their most intense experience. This praise is found at the center of the humanist tradition, in which love also becomes an ideal. The reason is simple: love promotes the other man as the ultimate end of my action, as humanism would have it. It is true that Christianity was already called the "religion of love," but, as we have just seen, human love had to be given a divine justification. It is humanism, however, that inaugurates a new era here, by stripping this love of any supernatural motivation. Reserving this place for love at the summit of its hierarchy, humanist thought again counters the accusation that it reduces men to solitary and self-sufficient individuals.

This humanism is not, however, "naive": man is appreciated here as value, not as fact. Love is valorized not because its object is perfect (it is not), but because to love someone this way, in and for himself, is what we can do best. In the mother's love for her child, it is not the child that is admirable but the love. The loved individual is an embodiment not of perfection, but simply of the human. Cherishing the human — practicing "the humanism of the other man," as Emmanuel Levinas says — is the supreme value. The set of features I have just defined — the impossibility of substituting another for this object, his status as an ultimate end in itself, the maintenance of his distinct identity, the joy in his very existence — tell us nothing about the intrinsic qualities of either protagonist; they all speak to us of the bond that has grown between them.

The irreducible individual, the end of human action, is therefore no less characteristic of this thought than the autonomy of the subject. At first glance, however, one might think the opposite. If humanist thought were limited to praising the will, to praising autonomy in moral, political, and social life, then nothing would be more contrary to it than the very existence of love. For the loving subject is not the one governed by his will: one cannot love because one has decided to love. On the contrary, love is the clearest example of an action that does not originate in an act of will. Rousseau, who knew this perfectly well, is set, it is true, on hedging this statement with several qualifications. First of all, he wishes that love would preserve the right of the subject to act according to his own will — but this is a question of the loved subject, of the other, whose freedom was already presupposed by his individuality. Now, man as goal is not the same as man as agent, the *you* cannot structurally be reduced to the *I*, even if both are simple human beings. On the other hand, the loving subject himself is not condemned to passivity. If the choice of the love object is not a matter of will (of his autonomy), the relationship that he will live with that object is up to him; thus he can surmount the antitheses of submission and freedom by accepting chance, but progressively assuming responsibility for that decision. These two qualifications, however, do not diminish the force of the main point, namely, that no one can force himself to love: chance and mysterious affinities decide in the place of the subject, and control over the forces operating at this moment eludes him.

This impossibility of subjecting love to the will demonstrates why every "proud" doctrine postulating human omnipotence is condemned to failure. Will cannot govern everything since it cannot govern love. The liberty of the subject will never be complete; his will depends in its turn on elements that remain involuntary: even the taste for freedom, Tocqueville says, is an instinct that one cannot choose freely. Being what one is, one can choose to act according to one's will, and this justifies the demand for political autonomy; but can one choose to be what one is? The individual can never be conceived as a tabula rasa; a certain "given" always precedes the "chosen." The subject's total mastery of himself is impossible; all "pride" would be misplaced here. Yet this does not make *liberty* a futile word: "Does it follow that I am not my own master, because I am not the master of being somebody else than me?" (*Emile*, IV, p. 280). But love reinforces the humanist doctrine in quite another way: by making the human being no longer the source but the goal of his action. The praise of love enters into humanist doctrine not through the autonomy of the *I* but through the finality of the *you*. Yet, the two are not isolated, for they are both linked to the irreducible freedom of the human being: the freedom that allows him to resist his "nature," that makes him unpredictable.

The choice of such a purely human end distinguishes humanist thought from the other families of modern thinking. Conservatives and scientists usually assign men ends that transcend them: God, nature, or simply community for some; the proletariat, the master race, or the happiness of humanity for others. To die for the king, for the fatherland, or for the revolution are, after all, similar options: in each case it is an entity superior to the individual that is the goal, while he himself is reduced to the role of means. As for the individualists, they refuse to subject the individual to a superior objective, whatever it may be; my own flowering is considered an end worthy of respect. The humanist family equally rejects all instrumentalization, only the goal of action is no longer the subject himself, but others.

Humanism affirms values that surpass the life of each individual; yet these values are in no way linked to the divine, as the conservatives often require them to be. We might say that this involves a lateral or horizontal transcendence, not a vertical one. The human being takes the place of the divine. But not just any human being: only one who is embodied in individuals other than myself. In any case, the religious is not replaced here by the political, God by the state, the nation, or the party, as in other forms of conservatism or scientism. And no one will confuse this love for individuals with the veneration of the leader, required of all members of society. Even if this leader is an individual person, it is his office one worships here, not the person who assumes it. And perfection cannot be dissociated from the venerated object, whereas one bestows love on imperfect beings.

This does not mean that in the humanist view, one ought to consecrate one's life to a single person: this other can be multiple. The main thing is that the "other" is always composed of particular human beings instead of an abstraction, even one like "humanity." If we sacrifice singular human beings for the good of humanity, we have left the humanist family behind. And the same is true if, conversely (as happens in scientism), we subject our entire existence to what should be only its means: work, money, success. Here we would have two, opposite antihumanist choices: one that would transform man's means into ends, and one that would reduce man himself to a means in view of a transcendent end — divine, natural, or simply abstract.

Love escapes this double reduction. Therefore it becomes the best embodiment of what I called earlier *active* humanism: not only does it demand the equality or autonomy of citizens, which prevents certain injustices from being inflicted on them, but also the promotion of positive values that allow every existence to be given meaning. At the same time we see that this activity values the private sphere, in which preference in relations of attachment, devotion, friendship, and love can flourish, even if the public sphere of political action is not condemned. It is not an accident that humanism became increasingly compelling just as people began to appreciate domestic and everyday virtues, family life, and marriage for love. And Benjamin Constant, who certainly demanded a balance of the private and public spheres, bore witness in his fashion to the predominance of love, by declaring: "A word, a look, a squeeze of the hand have always seemed to me preferable to all reason, as indeed to all earthly thrones" (to Annette de Gerando, June 5 1815).

Chapter 6

The Individual:

PLURALITY AND UNIVERSALITY

*T*he humanists have shown that the devil's first threat was empty: life with others is not the price we pay for liberty. The autonomy of the *I* does not force each individual to isolate himself and cut himself off from other men. But as we know the devil has other cards up his sleeve: he also claims that this individual who boasted about becoming the subject of his own actions was in reality impressionable, fickle, distracted—a thoroughfare rather than a coherent being.

The autonomy of the individual can in fact be understood as having a double meaning: in relation to the larger entities that contain him, or in relation to those smaller ones that create him. The great French humanists, from Montaigne to Tocqueville, believed in the possibility of the freedom of modern man in relation to his particular community. This does not prove that he can meet a second challenge from the other side unscathed. For if the individual is merely a bundle of multiple characters over which he has no control, if he is merely the label haphazardly slapped onto a series of discontinuous states, if he can never take advantage of any unity, can we still speak of his autonomy? Having escaped the grip of the powers he should have served, doesn't man risk succumbing to the elements that should serve him? Wouldn't the appropriate price for the enjoyment of freedom be the dissolution of that man who was meant to become the beneficiary of the pact?

The internal analysis of the person will be conducted by humanist thought, not within the framework of a general theory, but in the margins of self-knowledge. Montaigne and Rousseau embody, in France, its two decisive moments, prompting unexpected developments in humanist doctrine.

Man, Diverse and Undulating

The idea that the particular being is multiple has been understood in two different ways: on the one hand, as a variation in time, a segmentation of life, modifications in a "horizontal" unfolding we call inconsistency; on the other hand, as a simultaneous multiplicity, in space and no longer in time, and more specifically, as a stratification of the inner being, which is this time dissected "vertically."

What is the cause of "spatial" plurality? Montaigne straightaway points to the answer by encapsulating the plurality of men and the plurality of inner man in the same analysis. The exchange in which we are engaged with others can be pursued within ourselves. "You and one companion are an adequate theatre for each other, or you for yourself" (*Essays*, I, 39, 182). The interior dialogue is set on the same level as the dialogue that unfolds outside, the internal plurality is similar to that which surrounds us. "And there is as much difference between us and ourselves as between us and others" (II, 1, 244). If this interior dialogue is possible, that is because I am multiple in myself, or as Montaigne says: "We have a soul that can be turned upon itself" (I, 39, 177). We can conclude from this that the individual is made up — also — of contacts with others, and that since these others are multiple and occupy various positions in relation to him, he himself is condemned to infinite diversity.

Montaigne does not linger over the different characters that inhabit us simultaneously. On the other hand, he is inexhaustible on our mobility in time; the endless discussion he describes takes place between successive incarnations of the same being. This is how Montaigne first depicts himself: he is prey, so to speak, to permanent change. "Me at this moment and me this afternoon are indeed two" (III, 9, 964). Is this, after all, a singular characteristic separating Montaigne from other men? Not at all. It is man in general who is "a marvelous, vain, diverse and undulating object" (I, 1, 5). "Nothing is harder for me than to believe in men's consistency, nothing easier than to believe in their inconsistency" (II, 1, 239); they are unstable and fickle. That is why the legal profession provides an eloquent image of the human condition: the causes defended are different, but lawyers always plead them with the same conviction.

The primary reason for this internal diversity is, as for "vertical" plurality, the diversity outside us. If I change so easily, it is because my interior depends on the exterior — which is necessarily shifting. There is a permeability between self and other. "Our actions are nothing but a patchwork" (II, 1, 243). "Man in all things and throughout is but patchwork and motley" (II, 20, 511). Circumstances decide for me; and I am much more shaped by successive influences than by internal resources; the acquired wins out over the innate. "I will perhaps be other tomorrow, if I learn something new which changes me" (I, 26, 109).

Book II of the *Essays*, which is the last part of the work's first edition, ends with these words, a conclusion and echo of all that goes before: "And there were never in the world two opinions alike, any more than two hairs or two grains. Their most universal quality is diversity" (II, 37, 598). Book III offers the same opinion: "The world is but a perennial movement. All things in it are in constant motion — the earth, the rocks of the Caucasus, the pyramids of Egypt — both with the common motion and with their own. Stability itself is nothing but a more languid motion" (III, 2, 610). It is this diversity and this mobility in the world that make men so changeable. Our reason itself, which is internal to us, readily lends itself to this: "It is an instrument of lead and wax, extendable, pliable and accommodating to any bias or measure" (II, 12, 565). That is why Montaigne himself gives up representing things as they are and becomes attached to the process of becoming: "I do not portray being. I portray the passing. Not the passing from one age to another, or, as the people say, from seven years to seven years, but from day to day, from minute to minute" (III, 2, 611).

One consequence of this extreme nominalism (only instantaneous states exist) is the impossibility of knowing the world with precision or having a coherent image of it: this is the conclusion of the "Apology for Raymond Sebon." It is folly to want to fix this movement and aspire to unity. "Only fools are certain and assured" (I, 26, 111). Only fools resist change. On the contrary, flexibility and changeableness are the characteristics of wisdom. "It is being, not living, to remain attached and compelled by necessity to a single movement. The most beautiful souls are those that have more variety and flexibility. . . . It is not being a friend to the self, much less a master, it is being its slave to follow oneself incessantly and to be so much in the grip of one's inclinations that one cannot part from them, that one cannot bend them" (III, 2). The autonomy of the *I* would be affected if one allowed oneself to be driven by habits. Montaigne adopted this attitude, so that his book of inquiry into the self ends on a surprising note: Montaigne's "ruling quality" is "ignorance" (I, 50, 219). But if the self is merely in passage, how can anyone be held responsible for his actions? And how can we still count Montaigne among the humanist thinkers, who do not believe that the autonomy of the *I* is an empty notion?

The Ruling Pattern

Having come this far, the reader of Montaigne is overtaken by doubts. The book he has in his hands, which he had just come to understand, is not as chaotic as this manifesto would suggest. Montaigne's thought may not form a system, but it is coherent nonetheless; and while the image its author leaves us of himself is certainly complex and subtle, it is not disorderly. Does this mean that his programmatic declarations are subverted by the very movement of the text? Not really: they must be read in context. Montaigne strongly states a thesis, that of human changeableness, and he describes it in detail; the first edition of the *Essays*, in particular, begins and ends with this statement. The individual, Montaigne declares, has no essence that would resist the vagaries of existence. But this does not mean, on another level, that this individual has no stability or that one can never generalize from one individual to another.

The *Essays* do not only imply this claim, they spell it out. Apprenticeship changes me, of course, but not to the point of blending the acquired with the innate. I have "natural faculties that are in me," I use "my own natural resources" (I, 26, 107), and education must not try to "force natural propensities" (109). Without this qualification we would topple over into proud humanism and believe, like Pico de la Mirandola, that we might become animal, vegetable, or mineral, as we like. "There is no one who, if he listens to himself, does not discover in himself a pattern all his own, which struggles against education and against the tempest of the passions that oppose it" (III, 2, 615). Dependence on others need not become servitude. We may well consist of impressions received from the outside; what is indigenous is still distinguishable from what is foreign. The individual is like the city: the difference between citizens and foreigners remains relevant. We harbor desires that are alien, borrowed, and those that are natural to us, even if the first are sometimes likely to supplant the second, "neither more nor less than if, in a city, there were such a great number of foreigners that they were to displace the natural inhabitants or suppress their former power and authority, entirely usurping it and seizing it for themselves" (II, 12, 472).

And this man who spoke of himself as in permanent division and perpetual motion also declares: "For virtually since its birth, [my judgment] has been one; the same inclination, the same road, the same strength" (III, 2, 616). He who observed that no quality could define him, also informs us: "My actions are in order and conformity with what I am"; he has, he tells us, a "tincture with which I am stained all over" (617), meaning something general and dominant, and which is no longer a matter of ignorance, in other words, the undifferentiated opening to all. Montaigne is even certain that if he were to live a thousand years, he would always react similarly in the same circumstances; and he claims he is prepared to return from the other world to refute those who would distort the truth of his being (III, 9, 784): therefore such a being exists.

How do we explain this double claim of both changeableness and stability? By the fact that in principle we are free, but that freedom can be limited by facts. Man does not have a single and eternal nature, but lives in a certain space and time; now, the fact of existing in this place, at this moment, gives him an identity, although it is other than the absent essence. Place is our belonging to a culture or, as Montaigne says, a custom. Men are not born in a vacuum but within an already existing society. "We take men already bound and formed to certain customs, we do not create them like Pyrrha or Cadmus" (III, 9, 730), like imaginary characters formed by men out of stones or dragons' teeth. "It is for habit to give form, just as it pleases" (Montaigne, III, 13, 827). Usage carries us along with it: for the individual, custom seems as powerful as nature. "Habit is a second nature, and no less powerful. What my habit lacks, I hold that I lack" (III, 10, 772). The examples Montaigne gives are eloquent. He learned Latin before French: the second is customary for him, the first is natural (III, 2, 605). Was nature, then, merely a first custom?

Montaigne's social conservatism is based on making custom absolute. Since nothing exists beyond custom, since the sole consecration comes from length of use, we must think twice before rebelling; better to accept "and not easily change an accepted law" (title of bk. I, 23). We must not be shocked at all peoples' ethnocentrism; things would be no better if they decided to change by trying to imitate others. As it is often impossible to know if one value is superior to another (for example, if Protestantism is better than Catholicism), it is preferable to stick to the values transmitted by tradition—those into which one is born. "The most beautiful human lives, to my mind, are those that conform to the common human pattern" (III, 13, 857), and this is as true of the group as of the individual: "Change alone lends shape to injustice and tyranny" (III, 9, 731).

Man belongs not only to a cultural context; all of life unfolds in time, so he has an individual history as well. The outcome of a life is the identity of the person. That "essence" is the product of existence, not of its source; yet it is solid. The provisional has become permanent, the soul takes on wrinkles it will never erase. "I am no longer headed for any great change or inclined to plunge myself into a new and untried way of life. . . . It is too late to become other than I am. . . . By long usage this form of mine has turned into substance, and fortune into nature" (III, 10, 772–73). And once again, this does not characterize him alone: it goes for everyone, like those sages of Antiquity for whom "so perfect a habituation to virtue . . . has passed into their nature . . . the very essence of their soul, its natural and ordinary gait" (II, 11, 310). The striking consequence of this discovery is that man becomes more and more authentic as he ages: life is a process of becoming oneself; compared to the child, the old man has the privilege of coherence over chance. Now, as we have seen, individuation is partly tied to freedom: to the extent that my freedom increases, I become increasingly myself, a unique being; and there is infinitely more difference between the faces of mature men or women than between the faces of newborns.

The human being is therefore, we note once more, that strange animal who has no real identity at first, but who spends his life producing one: he converts form into substance, fortune into nature, habit into essence. It is not enough to say that societies know only customs and are ignorant of "nature"; it must be added that adaptation itself becomes a nature. Montaigne, says Marcel Conche, "assimilates history to nature" (*Montaigne*, 95). And what custom is to country, biography is to man. Montesquieu (after Pascal) will understand this lesson and put it in his own terms: "What was arbitrary has become necessity . . . what was merely convention has become as strong as natural law" (*Mes Pensées*, 616). Are we to conclude from this that the "historical" and "cultural" humanism inaugurated by Montaigne is opposed to a more substantial humanism based on a conception of "human nature"? No, for this "nature" consists precisely of our indeterminacy, of our capacity to supply ourselves with an individual and collective identity: nature has put us into the world free and unfettered.

The imposition of this ruling quality is inevitable; but it is also a value, for it gives unity and meaning to a life. It is in the name of friendship that Montaigne makes such an effort to preserve the image of La Boétie from fading. "If I had not supported with all my strength a friend that I lost, they would have torn him into a thousand contrasting appearances" (*Essays*, III, 9, 752). We must therefore conclude that outside even the physical nature with which we are all apparently provided, the interior diversity of the person and his interior dialogue also has a limit that is "natural," but of another kind. At the outset man is, of course, diverse and undulating, and the confrontation of his different aspects can take the place of company; but the course of human life leads everyone to discover his ruling quality, and to stick by it. Interior dialogue, in this sense of the word, becomes after some time more repetitive, and no longer really bears comparison with the dialogue in which we engage with our friends, our loves, those people we love for themselves and for who they are. This dialogue is unending.

Humanist thought, embodied here by Montaigne, asserts the liberty of the individual but by placing limits on it: one physical, given at the outset; the other moral, situated at the point of arrival. Nature does not determine in advance what each man or each people will become; chance, liberty, and will each have its place. But what one was not initially, one ends by becoming, even if this is never 100 percent: history is transformed into nature. History, here, finds a new function: although the humanists refuse to consider it an acceptable justification for the present state of affairs (because something exists does not mean it is just: history consigns victories to might, not right), they see it as the place for the constitution of being. Montaigne is, and is only, what his life, his work, his dealings with others have made him. The inner plurality culminates in a new unity.

The Individual as End (again)

The work of self-knowledge in which Montaigne was engaged allowed him to discover the identity of the person beyond his inner multiplicity.

This is not a threat to the autonomy of the *I*. But this work contributes to humanist doctrine in yet another way, by making the particular individual into an object worthy of being known. From this point of view, the *Essays* break new ground.

Actually, their project was not fixed from the outset. Early on, it seems that Montaigne had in mind a genre quite common in his time, a sort of compilation of ancient wisdom drawn from philosophers as well as writers, embellished by the reflections that these sentences or exempla might suggest to Montaigne himself. But along the way, the project changed; the result was the book of *Essays* as we know it today.

The new conception, which increasingly imposed itself on its author, consists of subjecting knowledge of the world to knowledge of the self, of making the object into an instrument for knowing the subject. This compilation of instructive curiosities and sentences, on the one hand, and the self-portrait, on the other, seem to belong to two, entirely independent if not contradictory, projects. Montaigne fuses them, however, into one by granting them the roles of means and end, respectively. His readings will find a new place: other authors now provide only raw material, or a means of appropriated expression; the true subject of the book is Montaigne. "It is myself that I portray" (I, "To the Reader"). "I aim here only at revealing myself" (I, 26, 109). "These are my fancies, by which I try to give knowledge not of things, but of myself" (II, 10, 296). "In fine, all this fricassee that I am scribbling here is nothing but a recording of the essays [experiments] of my life" (III, 13, 826). This project of making a portrait of the self becomes its distinctive feature. "The world always looks vis-à-vis; as for me, I turn my gaze inward, I fix it there and keep it busy. Everyone looks in front of him; as for me, I look inside of me: I have no business but with myself; I continually observe myself, I take stock of myself, I taste myself. Others always go elsewhere, if they stop to think about it; they always go forward. . . . [A]s for me, I roll about in myself" (II, 17, 499).

Why does Montaigne take this path, when he himself acknowledges its singularity? He gives several answers to this question. Often, he tells us that he is writing for his friends, so that they might keep a faithful image of him, an accurate likeness and a lasting memory (see "To the Reader" II, 8, 18; III, 9, and so on). However, this justification seems tainted by the desire to please. Otherwise, why would Montaigne publish his essays instead of distributing them privately (as Malebranche already observed)? He knows, moreover, that he is not writing for his friends alone: "Many things that I would not want to tell anyone, I tell the public" (III, 9, 750). At other times, he asserts that knowledge of the passions can contribute to their moderation (III, 13), but this moral lesson is in fact almost absent in the *Essays*, and by the end of his enterprise Montaigne is not even certain that he has advanced very far along the path he had marked out for himself: "I have seen no more evident monstrosity in the world than myself. We become habituated to anything strange by use and time; but the more I frequent myself and know myself, the more my deformity astonishes me, and the less I understand myself" (III, 11, 787).

Let us observe Montaigne's project from a closer vantage point. Its novelty does not lie in the autobiographical material, but in the fact that he removes this self-knowledge from any objective that might be exterior to it. Montaigne does not tell us about his being because it is in any sense remarkable; he is even careful to caution against any such inference on the part of the reader, who might infer the subject's intrinsic importance from the place he grants it. "Someone will tell me that this plan of using oneself as a subject to write about would be excusable in rare and famous men who by their reputation had aroused some desire to know them. . . . It ill befits anyone to make himself known, save him who has qualities to be imitated, and whose life and opinions may serve as model" (II, 18, 503). Montaigne will therefore regularly remind his readers that his person is not in the least admirable, that it is even very often to be criticized. "Others have taken courage to speak of themselves because they found the subject worthy and rich; I, on the contrary, because I have found mine so barren and so meager no suspicion of ostentation can fall upon my plan" (501).

One hundred fifty years earlier, Robert Campin and Jan van Eyck decided to paint the portraits not only of the great of this world but of more common people, since the singularity of the individual was becoming reason enough to represent him. In the sixteenth century, the movement reached writing, even if preference was given to publishing the life stories of famous men; Benvenuto Cellini justifies the existence of his own *Life* only by the "great success" he achieved in his art (11). The first modern autobiographies, which interest themselves in the individual as such, and not, as with Saint Augustine or Abelard, in the individual's fate as an illustration of divine will, date from the second half of the century, but Montaigne could not know them, since they were published only after his death.

Montaigne himself will produce the theory of this approach. Hence his claim for originality: "It is the only book in the world of its kind" (II, 8, 278), and he explains: "I am the first to [communicate with the people] by my entire being, as Michel de Montaigne, not as a grammarian or a poet or a jurist" (*Essays*, III, 2, 611). This celebrated formula declares both an anteriority and a "finality" of the individual: poet, grammarian, or jurist are categories that transcend him and might be illustrated equally by other individuals; he is alone in being universally, that is entirely, Michel de Montaigne. What he claims is not that the qualities illustrated by his person are good, but that he has the right to interest himself in that person without it being illustrative of anything. The individual in himself deserves to be known. Montaigne drew all his conclusions concerning the human race from the nominalism of William of Occam, which he embraced: there are only particular objects in the world; where humanity is concerned, only individuals exist. Psychic or social laws do not exhaust individual identity: "I have a singular desire that we should each be judged in ourselves apart, and that I may not be measured in conformity with the common patterns" (I, 37, 169). It is in this way that the *Essays* participate in humanist thought.

Montaigne tries to conceal nothing of himself: his goal is not to tell how he should be but how he is. Since Machiavelli, the Moderns have known how to separate the two, the ideal and the real, and have preferred to dedicate themselves to the knowledge of what exists. "I want to be seen here in my simple, natural, ordinary fashion, without straining or artifice" (I, "To the Reader," 3). The face that he paints may not be perfect, but were it "bald and graying" (I, 26, 108), it has the merit of being his. "I want people to see my natural and ordinary pace, however off the track it is" (II, 10, 297).

There is an additional advantage here, even from the moral standpoint, in harmony with the practice of confession but transposed into the secular space of human commerce: confessed sin weighs less heavily. "Free and generous confession weakens reproach and disarms slander" (III, 9, 749). Why is this so? Not because the confession itself offers absolution but because the exposure of the self to the public eye leads to a certain behavior. "He who would oblige himself to tell all would oblige himself not to do anything about which we are constrained to keep silent" (III, 5, 642). To enter into the arena of public speech and thereby recognize its legitimacy is worth more than giving free rein to one's inclinations (as La Rochefoucauld also says); confession is therefore a step in the right direction. This is why "lying seems to me even worse than adultery" (642) that is, sin itself. At the same time, sincerity toward others guarantees sincerity toward the self. "Those who hide it from others usually hide it from themselves" (642). For Montaigne, the public ear has replaced the ear of the confessor. But it must be added that the change is more radical than he says: there is really no more confession if this speech is not addressed to God but remains confined to the purely human space. The addressee of the message changes its contents: one does not speak to one's brothers and sisters as one does to an omniscient and omnipotent being.

Montaigne does not write his book in order to know the world, nor to offer himself as an example, but to know himself — intransitively. He might repeat here the explanation offered for his choice of friend: Why describe himself? Because it is he. The individual does not need a justification that transcends him; he himself is the ultimate justification. Just as the impulse toward friendship needs no moral finality and is explained only by that particular other who is the friend, self-knowledge is justified by the uniqueness of the subject and by the exceptional position he occupies in relation to himself. There is, however, also a difference: the *I* is as unique as the *you*, but the uniqueness of the *you* is a source of value, while that of the *I* is a simple fact. Montaigne does not justify love of the self, here, but knowledge of the self. In the present case, that leads him to a progressive identification of his being with his project of knowledge: Montaigne is only the man who seeks to know who he is. "I have taken a road along which I shall go without stopping and without effort as long as there is ink and paper in the world" (III, 9, 721). "We go hand in hand and at the same pace, my book and I" (III, 2, 611–12). It is no longer the man who produces the book, it is rather the book that makes the man.

A Unique Being

Montaigne wants to know the individual Montaigne, because of his uniqueness: because it is he. When Rousseau engaged in his own autobiographical enterprise two centuries later, he remembered Montaigne's project but was not satisfied with it. His would be different: if he wanted to know the individual Rousseau, it was because there was no one like him. This individual not only could not be reduced to others;

he was not like them. He was not only unique, he was different. It is at the beginning of Book I of the *Confessions* that Rousseau expresses this thought most vigorously. "I am not made like any of the ones I have seen; I dare to believe that I am not like any that exist. If I am worth no more, at least I am different." Nor is there anyone who resembles him among those who preceded him on this earth; more significant still, there will be no one in the future either, for nature has broken "the mold in which it cast me" (I, 17). He is a being of a separate species and consequently requires an entirely new analysis. By asserting this rupture between himself and others, Rousseau steps outside the framework of humanist thought to enter, as he does several times in the autobiographical writings, into the realm of militant individualism: every individual is an isolated and incommensurate being.

What exactly is this absolute difference between him and other men? The first answer Rousseau gives is based on the very existence of the *Confessions*, since it is a book unlike any other. "I am forming an undertaking which has no precedent, and the execution of which will have no imitator whatsoever" (I, 17). "My purpose is to display to my kind a portrait in every way true to nature, and the man I shall portray will be myself" (I, 17). What is new, if we are to believe Rousseau, is that not only will he tell the truth, but he will not be selective about what he tells (whether the best or the worst is unimportant). He will bare *all* to the reader, leaving him the freedom to draw his own conclusions. Rousseau behaves as if the only rule of his enterprise were the one that psychoanalysts impose on their clients today: tell everything. "I will be true; I will be so unreservedly; I will tell everything, the good, the bad, in short everything" (*Ebauches des confessions*, 1153). In this respect, his book is a unique work.

The language of autobiography would be transparent, the pure mediator of total experience, which would come on its own to fill the pages of the book. Rousseau knows, however, that to tell everything is impossible, for lived experience is inexhaustible; he also knows that he must choose not only from experience undergone but also from forms of representation: words do not flow by themselves, they are inscribed in neither things nor acts. "For what I have to say I must invent a language as new as my project: what tone, what style should I take?" (1153). When he thinks about it, Rousseau discerningly identifies the characteristics of the genre: "In surrendering myself both to the memory of the impression received and to present feeling, I will paint doubly the state of my soul, namely the moment when the event happened to me and the moment when I have described it; my style . . . will itself become part of my story" (1154). Yet such "professional" remarks betray a concern for the reader, an attention to form that no longer corresponds to the simple project to tell all, to make experience transparent.

In the abandoned preface to the *Confessions*, Rousseau reproached Montaigne for not conforming to this singular rule: "Montaigne paints a likeness of himself, but in profile" (1150). Reflecting with detachment on his own *Confessions* as he is writing *Rêveries*, he admits that they were written with as much imagination as truth, that he embellished one moment and omitted another, that he obeyed verisimilitude and not truth: "I spoke of things I had forgotten as it seemed to me they must have been" (*Rêveries*, IV, 37). He admits with humility that he has not necessarily done better than Montaigne: "Without thinking about it and by an involuntary movement I sometimes hid my malformed side and depicted my good side" (37). Isn't it the case that any portrait, whatever it may be, is always "in profile"?

Several years pass after the formulation of the project, and Rousseau himself states: the self-portrait he realized is not as different as he claimed from the self-portraits of his predecessors. Does this mean that the author is finally like others? Rousseau would not like to admit it and first attempts several alternative answers. All the same, he is different from everyone, he says, because of the pleasure he finds in living alone: all people need the proximity of others in order to satisfy their self-regard; he alone hardly feels the need for this. Or, he is exceptional in the impartiality of his judgment: "But above all something I have seen in him alone in the world is an equal attachment to the works of his cruelest enemies" (*Second Dialogue*, p. 111). His tolerance is unique: "I hear everyone talk about tolerance, but he is the only truly tolerant person I have known" (p. 117). At the end of his life, at the period of the *Rêveries*, he believes that he is the only man to free himself from all fear as well as from all hope, therefore to live in peace and serenity.

These new explanations of absolute difference are hardly more satisfying than the earlier ones. Even assuming that Rousseau is telling the truth, the feature he identifies is only the superlative of a quality that already exists elsewhere, if only to a lesser degree. Others have loved solitude, practiced magnanimity or tolerance, others have achieved serenity; the difference may be only quantitative and relative, it is no longer absolute. This is perhaps why Rousseau attempts a final explanation of his difference in the *Dialogues*. What separates him from all others, he now claims, is that he alone is a "man of nature." All others are in the grip of prejudices, of the passions of self-regard. "They all seek their happiness in appearances, none is concerned about reality. They all place their being in appearance. Slaves and dupes of amour-propre, they live not to live but to make others believe they lived." He alone escapes this rule, and the proof is that if he hadn't, he would have been incapable of writing his books and constructing his doctrine. "A man had to portray himself to show us primitive man like this, and if the Author hadn't been as unique as his books, he would never have written them" (*Third Dialogue*, 214). It follows that Rousseau is not only different, he is in addition the best of men, seen as the unique representative of the "man of nature," a species superior to the "man of man."

We have already noted that Rousseau's projection of the personal example onto his rhetorical construction has dire consequences for its coherence. But it is unclear that it provides a better definition of its author's singularity. After all, what is he telling us here? That he is different from all men because he never compares himself to them. His own Rousseau, he says, loves himself "without making comparisons," and "in his life it never entered his mind to measure himself against another" (*Second Dialogue*, p. 106). Now, this assertion, like every similar claim to absolute singularity, cancels itself out: in order to establish his difference, Rousseau must surely have compared himself to other men (otherwise, his claim would be unfounded); but if he had done this, he can no longer say that he is so different from others: like them, he compares and measures himself. The statement of difference results from comparison; this difference therefore cannot consist of the absence of self-regard, that is, of comparisons.

Rousseau is well aware that this is the case, and that knowledge cannot be arrived at without comparison, which alone discloses to him the secret of similarity and difference: "For how indeed to determine a being only in relation to himself, and without comparing him to anything?" (*Ebauches des Confessions*, 1148). This ultimate justification for his absolute difference therefore collapses in its turn, and it must be said that nothing emerges to shore up Rousseau's exorbitant claim, which remains a pure petitio principeii.

I and Others

Rousseau does not always, however, take such an extreme position; other formulations that date from the same period as his work on the *Confessions* testify to a more measured ambition. He wants to think that the exploration of his life and his person in which he is engaged will be useful to his contemporaries and readers. In what way? Still through the knowledge of his own being, which is singular but no longer radically different from others.

Here Rousseau takes exactly the opposite view of La Rochefoucauld. For the earlier writer, knowledge of the self is impossible (because of vanity), knowledge of others fertile ground. For Rousseau, on the contrary, knowledge of others quickly reaches its limits, for we have no direct access to them; knowledge of the self can go infinitely farther. Rousseau rejects the argument of vanity (whether as a vice to be avoided or as a source of blindness). To admit his vanity is not a vain act, and one can go beyond the prejudices of one's amour-propre. On the other hand, "no one can write the life of a man but himself. His inner way of being, his real life is known only to him" (*Ebauches des confessions*, 1149). I can *feel* only my own being, Rousseau also says; as for others, I must be content with *knowing* them from the outside. He has confidence in the capacity of the human being to overcome any obstacle, but this does not become an affirmation of omnipotence; it is rather the refusal to see any limitation whatsoever as definitive, provided one is not compelled to leave the natural world. It may not be of much interest to try to settle this debate between Rousseau and La Rochefoucauld: each of the two kinds of knowledge is irreplaceable in its way; what matters here is the description of the path chosen by Rousseau.

One can know only the self, yet this very knowledge is hampered by the absence of all comparison. How does one surmount this obstacle? Not by mechanically transposing from the self to others, but by becoming acquainted with the narratives that others have constructed of their own inner explorations. This narrative, then, must be at once scrupulously true and made public. If such a narrative exists, everyone will be able both to explore his own being and to compare himself to another individual who has gone before him along this path. "Outside of oneself, one would have to know at least one of one's peers in order to untangle in one's own heart the part of the species and the part of the individual" (1158). This is precisely the rather ambitious mission that Rousseau assigns himself: to produce a narrative, the knowledge of an individual, that will allow all other individuals to discover themselves. "I want to endeavor that in order to learn to appreciate oneself, one might at least have a point of comparison; that everyone might know himself and one other, and that other will be me" (1149). Rousseau will be the Jesus Christ of autobiographical inquiry: he sacrifices himself on the altar of knowledge in order to permit those who come after him to reveal themselves to themselves.

The role Rousseau reserves for himself remains exceptional, but there is no more radical rupture between him and others; he simply allows them to profit from his exceptional capacities for introspection and re-membrance. Contrary to what he has said elsewhere, everyone can fol-low this path: "Let each reader imitate me, let him come back into himself as I have done" (1155). His work will be facilitated by Rous-seau's sacrifice, but the result will not necessarily be different from it. By this detour, Rousseau arrives at a point that contradicts his initial state-ments: we love to believe that we are different from others, whereas we differ very little. "If I were in that fellow's place, we say, I would do otherwise than he does; we are wrong. If ever we were in his place, we would do the same as he" (1158–59). We can choose our actions, we can base them only on our actual being; but we would not even know how to freely choose our being: freedom is real but relative. Auto-biographical research, then, does not separate an individual from all others; on the contrary, every autobiography paves the way for those that follow.

The Human Condition

And Montaigne? In a sense, the *Essays* are only a last resort (a supple-ment, Rousseau would say): they take the place of letters and words that, had it not been for La Boétie's death, Montaigne would have ad-dressed to his friend. Or rather, they restore the memory that La Boétie would have kept of him. "He alone enjoyed my true image and carried it away. That is why I decipher myself so painstakingly," readers were informed in the edition of 1588 (III, 9, 752 n. 14). If he set about writing, it was to pull himself out of the dazed solitude into which the death of his friend had plunged him, and he does not stop hoping that another "honest man," recognizing himself in the *Essays*, will come one day to seek his friendship (III, 9, 750).

The cult of friendship and knowledge of the self form a complex hierarchy in Montaigne's project. The *Essays* are first conceived as a monument to the memory of La Boétie, somewhat like a mausoleum: The center of Book I must be occupied by the major work of the deceased friend, the discourse on *Voluntary Servitude*. However, Montaigne then decides that such a publication would be inappropriate in the context of the religious wars that were tearing France apart (La Boétie's text was used by the Huguenots in their struggle against the monarchy); so he substitutes a less offensive text by La Boétie, his love sonnets. The substitution is made easier since, as François Rogolot so effectively demonstrated, "voluntary servitude" can designate not only the effect of tyranny but also the virtuous submission to the interests of the friend. Now things take a new turn: after a moment's thought Montaigne judges that these sonnets themselves no longer have a place at the heart of the *Essays*; they will be removed from it. In the end, La Boétie certainly had his mausoleum, but there is emptiness at its heart; or, according to another comparison Montaigne employs, what should have constituted the center of the tableau was invaded and finally replaced by what formed its frame, the "fantastic paintings" (I, 28, 135) by Montaigne himself. La Boétie is no longer really present in it as an individual, he is no more than the pretext for a general reflection on friendship; he is no more than the absence that makes writing the *Essays* necessary, then possible. The individual La Boétie is no longer an end but a means.

"Because it was he," Montaigne had first written, perhaps inspired by a formula of Aristotle's; then he added: "Because it was I." It's as if the discovery of the individual La Boétie, before the period of the *Essays*, had allowed Montaigne to conceive of the individual other than the self as an end; however, in order to discover himself as an irreducible individual in his turn, and therefore to write the *Essays*, La Boetie had to die—first physically, then symbolically, meaning that he is content to play an auxiliary role within Montaigne's book. The "I" does not simply add itself to the "he," it supplants it. The *Essays* are no longer a monument to the glory of La Boétie; they have become the site where Montaigne's uniqueness spreads its wings, and he is the only individual-as-end in the *Essays*.

This statement takes on its full meaning in the light of a narrative that Montaigne wrote in 1570, seven years after La Boétie's death and ten years before the first edition of the *Essays*. Montaigne tells his own father, in great detail, about the course of his friend's fatal illness, before coming to his last words. "He began to entreat me again and again with extreme affection to give him a place; so that I was afraid that his judgement was shaken. . . . 'My brother, my brother, do you refuse me a place?' This until he forced me to convince him by reason and tell him that since he was breathing and speaking and had a body, consequently he had his place. 'True, true,' he answered me then, 'I have one but it is not the one I need; and then when all is said, I have no being left" (*Letters*, p. 1055). As if by a supernatural prescience, La Boétie not only demands that he should have a place in his friend's discourse, but he anticipates his progressive disappearance. The *Essays* are made possible by the friendship of the two men, then by the death of the first; but La Boétie has no more place in the finished work: when all is said and done, his being is not there. Montaigne should not have forgotten these words.

Montaigne is not content simply to declare that every individual is worthy of being known in himself. In fact, one difficulty would certainly have arisen: How would he make the self the exclusive addressee of this work? How could he claim that his goal was to address himself rather than others, while at the same time claiming that there is no rupture between self and others (he has taught us this himself), that we are made by others, contain others within us? If he were at one with his friend La Boétie, how could Montaigne address only himself? Through self-scrutiny, Montaigne has identified his own ruling quality: it makes him see the ideal of his own existence in successful human exchange. "My essential pattern is communication and revelation. I am all in the open and in full view, born for company and friendship" (III, 3, 625). Books are not worth more than beings: superior to children as works, they nonetheless remain a poor substitute for friends.

And once a friend is dead, the book continues to address others: young readers who will not be able to understand it at the moment, but also, beyond these, to all readers of goodwill. "I speak to my paper as I speak to the first man I meet" (III, 1, 790). Since words belong to everyone, one cannot describe oneself, that is, convert one's being into words, without addressing others at the same time; which also means that one could not reach through writing a self isolated from its relations with others. This is why, Montaigne tells us, he has modified his way of writing. Initially, indeed, he had chosen the brief form of the short essay to suit his inclination: he does not like long expositions and prefers "detached pieces" (II, 10, 300). But, taking his reader into serious consideration, he decides to write in the way that will be most comfortable for him and not for the author: "Because such frequent breaks into chapters as I used at the beginning seemed to me to disrupt and dissolve attention before it was aroused . . . I have begun making them longer" (III, 9, 762). For the same reason Montaigne has contempt for those who want to give an impression of depth by being obscure, and prefers Socrates, who speaks in a way that each person might understand. "The speech I love is a simple, natural speech, the same on paper as in the mouth" (I, 26, 127). This simplicity of language is nothing more than a respect for readers.

Rethinking his project of self-knowledge from this perspective, Montaigne now adds that it is addressed not only to himself but to everyone. It is possible to move to this generalization because, as different as men are from one another, "each man bears the entire form of man's estate" (III, 2, 611). The statement is strong, even if Montaigne will continue elsewhere to question the possibility of a shift from the singular to the universal. He himself, seeking to know himself, does not stop at the variegated array of events but aspires to grasp an underlying identity; in this respect, the project of the *Essays* is more ambitious than an autobiography. "It is not my deeds that I write down, it is myself, it is my essence" (II, 6, 274). In the same way, this individual project does not prevent him from speaking of "man in general, the knowledge of whom I seek" (II, 10, 303) or of "the study I am making, the subject of which is man" (II, 17, 481). Indeed, quite the contrary, one leads to the other: "This long attention that I devote to studying myself trains me also to judge passably of others" (III, 13, 824). There is no more contradiction between "portraying oneself" and "addressing others," and Montaigne can write in a single sentence: "I owe a complete portait of myself to the public" (III, 5, 677). Knowing oneself better fosters better communication with others.

Montaigne does not want to offer his life as an example, for it is not better than others; his inquiry into the truth, on the other hand, can help others, since it may inspire each person to know himself. "There is no description equal in difficulty, as certainly in usefulness, to the description of oneself" (II, 6, 273). Therefore, he conducts his own inquiries "not without ideas of instructing the public" (II, 18, 504). Knowledge of the self fosters the communication between men; reciprocally, the best friendship and the best dialogue between two men are animated by the impulse to know: "The cause of truth should be the common cause for both" (III, 8, 705).

In the final analysis, then, the individual can be universalized. How shall we reconcile this conclusion with the other conclusion Montaigne seemed to reach in his reflections on friendship, namely, that there is nothing beyond the individual as he is embodied in the person of the friend? It is as if Montaigne's idea (never explicitly formulated) were the following: taken one by one, men resemble one another; considered in their interaction, their friendships, and their loves, they cannot be reduced to one another. Contrary to what all future narcissists will think, it is not me in my own identity who is absolutely different from all other men (indeed, there is a permeability between me and others, between the one and the universal); it is me as other, that is, a me in relation to another. Different, of course, not in his substance (from his own point of view, he is in his turn an instance of the human condition) but in his position in relation to me: He was my friend and no one else. The first individual is *you*, not *me*, for every *you* presupposes a *me*, and the individual exists only in relationship. Every *you* is unique, every *I* is common. Considered one by one, men are alike; but when they are seen in the constellation of their relations, it must be admitted that they become different and irreplaceable: my mother is that woman, my son that child; I love this individual, not that one.

The inquiry into his own being to which Montaigne gives himself reunites these two dimensions of the human world. On the one hand, doubled as knowing subject and object to be known, Montaigne can envisage his own person as if it were another; the hero of the book, the author's double, occupies a position in relation to him as unique as that of his friend La Boétie, and makes him in turn a unique being: he who attempts to know the hero. The *I* can become a final end, like the *you* elsewhere, because he himself is caught in the net of intersubjectivity. On the other hand, knowing a single individual, Montaigne discovers man: far from constituting a final end, his person becomes an instrument for interrogating the human condition.

Porphyrus had written in his commentary on the logic of Aristotle: "Beings of this kind are called individuals, because each of them is composed of particularities whose combination would never be the same in another being" (*Isagogès*, 7, 20). This is substantive individuality. Montaigne, through his skepticism and his nominalism, carries this assertion to its extreme. But when it comes to what human beings are, he goes further: every man is a matchless individual, and yet each one bears within him the imprint of the human condition as a whole. It is another kind of individuality, positional and not substantive, that is irreducible: because it was he (for me), because it was I (for him). La Boétie is not unique in himself. He is an individual in this new sense because for me, he occupies a place that no one else can claim. As for myself, I can become unique provided I become double, subject and object. The individual is truly different from others only through the relations he establishes with them. *I* is all others, and yet the other himself is irreducible. In this way, the uniqueness of the individual and the universality of men are reconciled.

Montaigne's thought on man, as I said at the outset, contains all the basic ingredients of humanist doctrine. Here we find them brought together: the autonomy of the authorial *I*, who is deliberately engaged in this work of knowledge, construction, and communication; the finality of the *you* being addressed: every individual occupies a unique position in relation to me, and in friendship this other leads to nothing beyond himself; the universality of the *they*, of all men who share the same human condition. There is a reason for this plurality of requirements: it is that the dimensions of the human itself are multiple and cannot be reduced to one another. In the objective world, everyone is a member of the same species; in the intersubjective universe, everyone occupies a unique position; in communion with oneself, everyone is alone, and responsible for his actions. Unique and universal, alone and with others: this is the man Montaigne bequeathed to the humanist tradition.

Chapter 7

The Choice of Values

$\mathcal{T}$he devil claimed that the price of freedom consisted, first of all, of the need to become isolated from other men; Montesquieu, Rousseau, and Constant have shown that it was nothing of the kind. He added that the modern individual would also have to renounce his identity and all control over the self; Montaigne has effectively explained how and why modern man could be both multiple and one. We are left with the devil's third threat, which is as follows: having preferred liberty to submission, modern man has lost all possibility of claiming affiliation with any values other than purely individual ones. God is dead, and the idols one attempted to substitute for him are perishing ever more quickly. The loss of common values leads in turn to new disasters, no less grave: in a world with neither common values nor ideals, society collapses or is transformed into an enterprise governed by bureaucratic rules and power relations; and the individual himself becomes nothing but an animal or a machine. In order to escape these dangers, then, it is better to renounce freedom.

The great humanist principles — the autonomy of the *I*, the finality of the *you*, the universality of the *they* — are accountable, however, as I have said, to an anthropology, a politics, and a morality; they refer at once to characteristics of the species and to common values. The autonomy and equality of rights constitute the chief political values and the essence of "passive" humanism. The time has come for us to examine "active" humanism more closely, and to analyze its articulations. I use the word *morality* in its broadest sense, covering everything related to values situated in the individual sphere. It therefore also includes questions having to do with love or religion, and is contrary only to "anthropology" and to "politics," not to "ethics." Before going any further, however, we must note the place that moral values occupy in the doctrine of the other modern families (the subject of this chapter).

The position of the conservatives on matters of morality is relatively simple: they prefer heteronomy to autonomy. In other words, they believe in the existence of common values fixed by the society in which we live. To be moral is to conform to the current norm. The origin of this norm is another question; in Europe, it is usually tied to Christian doctrine. In the world of the Gospels, it is not enough to conform to the law to become a moral being; but for the conservatives, it is enough to conform to precepts of the Gospels to be worthy of praise. Bonald does not always refer to Christian principles; he is content to exalt blind submission — the contrary of autonomy — as the primary virtue. "The repression of curiosity and the submission of reason to faith is a more effective and more general means of fixing the mind of men, and of all men; therefore it suits society better" than free inquiry (*Théorie*, II, 300–301).

As we have seen, values should have no place in the scientistic family: in a world where necessity is everything, the words *good* and *bad* have no meaning. If my acts are entirely determined by my heredity, my social situation, or my psychic history, why should I take pride in them or, on the contrary, feel ashamed? They would deserve neither praise nor blame. Nonetheless, the scientists do not refrain from formulating imperatives saturated with values, which should be followed even more strictly as they lay some claim to a scientific basis. As Taine says, "science ends in morality while seeking only truth" (*Derniers essais*, 110). These values discovered by science are necessarily the same for everyone, since science is one. So, those who paved the way for scientistic thought in France — the materialists of the Enlightenment, Condorcet, Saint-Simon, Auguste Comte, and the positivists — are also universalists who dream of instituting a single world government.

It must be said that when this scientistic doctrine is taken as the foundation of a governing politics, as it will be in the totalitarian states of the twentieth century, it undergoes a visible reorientation. These values, theoretically based on science, cease to be universal and become those of a single group. The transformation was made easier in German national socialism by the choice to base itself on Social Darwinism — a simplistic interpretation of the law of "survival of the fittest," as we have seen. Soviet communism advocated in principle a universalist ideal; but the means adopted to attain it — a merciless class struggle whose goal was the total elimination of the bourgeoisie — annulled the contents of this ideal and legitimized war, not peace. In the final analysis, all men are *not* worthy of the same respect, since some of them are enemies; and enemies are less than human and deserve to be exterminated.

In addition, ideological demands quickly become a pure pretext for repression, whose sole objective is to keep power in the hands of the group that manages to grab it. Those states who claim the authority of science are in practice busy discarding any spirit of free inquiry, any argument basing itself only on reason; in their actual existence, they curiously ally themselves with authoritarian regimes inspired by conservatism, and cultivate the same virtue of submission. In a totalitarian state, one seeks to control the conformity to morality rather than leaving it up to each person to decide for himself. In this sense, we can say that morality is replaced by politics. Instead of asking oneself questions, the individual must submit to the rule of the group as a whole.

These two types of value choices are relatively simple and clear. This is not true for the individualists, who are split into a number of factions.

The Individualist Arts of Living

Unlike the members of the two preceding families, the individualists believe in the autonomy of the subject, but they do not assign a particular role to human interaction: each individual makes his own way toward his ideal. That is why it may be preferable not to speak here of "morality," which always implies a common transindividual rule, but only of values, and designates their codification as an "art of living." In the individualist perspective, the meditation on values does not lead to observing the effects of common life on each of the members of society, but to teaching them to move toward their greater realization, toward the accomplishment of their own destiny, toward what can be their happiness.

In reorienting themselves toward an art of living rather than a morality, the individualists break with the long Christian tradition and reconnect with the pre-Christian conceptions of the Greeks and Romans. There are, of course, many ways of framing the opposition between Greek and Christian morality. It is sometimes said that the first aspire to happiness, the second to the good; that the Greeks cultivate the perfection of the person, the Christians their relation to God; that the first seek to complete nature, whereas the second aspire to tear themselves away from it; that the Greeks respect the ends of man, the Christians their duties. But in the present context, the great difference between these pagan and Christian sources is in the role attributed to life in society, even if this role is implicit rather than presented as a part of the agenda.

For the pagans, the ideal is that of a good life, meaning, finding a good place in the cosmic and natural order of things. Socrates aspires to the perfection of his soul. What exactly is this ideal nature of man? On this point, opinions diverge. For a number of ancient thinkers, man's nature namely, his rational and spiritual capacities, is what separates him from the beasts. The best life is therefore one that allows these capacities to be cultivated at leisure — the contemplative life, which the philosopher leads in his retirement. Certain authors, however, such as Aristotle and Cicero, also claim that, as man is a social being, he can achieve excellence only in the active life and in the most exalted human relationship, that is, friendship. "Nature has given us friendship . . . to allow the virtue — which in man alone can be perfect — of associating with others and thus tending toward perfection," writes Cicero, for example (*On Friendship*, XXII, 83).

The goal is the excellence of the individual; the means — conditioned by man's social nature — will be friendship. In both cases, the relation to others is not an ultimate objective; at most it can serve as an effective means of attaining virtue. But whether one chooses the active life (with others) or the contemplative (solitary) life, the goal is always the harmony of the individual with the natural order in which he is established. Human "virtue" is continuous with that of objects, a warrior can be excellent, like a shield — provided they both achieve the perfection of their function and embrace the ends inscribed in their essential nature.

For Christians, on the other hand, the good coincides with the love of one's neighbor (because all men are God's children); morality, then, is interpreted as benevolence and charity, a capacity to act decently toward others, and no longer solely as unqualified aspiration to a good life. The framework of morality is not a relationship to nature but one between men. The whole Law, says Christ, is summed up in these two commandments: to love God and to love one's neighbor as oneself (Matthew 22:37–40). Saint Paul adds: to love God is nothing but loving one's neighbor; without the love of charity, faith is not enough. Setting aside the relatively marginal tendencies of mysticism and praise of the monastic life, Christianity chooses to situate itself in the world of human exchange, and piety becomes synonymous with pity. The other side of this equivalence, as we have seen, is that one does not love human beings for themselves, but insofar as they lead to God.

The "neighbor," it should be recalled, is not a relative or friend: the Christian loves not only his relatives or his fellow citizens but everyone, including foreigners, enemies, and people down on their luck; his love is not individualizing, it is, as we sometimes say, *agape* and not *philia*. The difference between Christian and Greek morality lies less in the content of this or that proposition than in the place these occupy in the structure as a whole. The Greeks were also familiar with philanthropy, or universal love, and even xenophilia, or love of foreigners, and not only the love of friends; but the moral requirement as such is oriented differently, namely, toward perfection understood as the realization of one's being. When they think of human sociability, they reserve the same place for the individual and his peers. In the Christian tradition, on the other hand, there is no more question of personal excellence eventually reached through friendship; we can no longer speak here of a good life in itself, but by definition the good depends on benevolence toward others. This new need of others for the self is rooted in the exceptional place attributed to Christ, who is not simply our peer: he must die on the cross so that all others might be saved; those others do not identify with him but profit from his sacrifice. By imitating Christ, we do not confuse ourselves with our neighbor, we are not simply content to affirm our common humanity; we do for this neighbor what he cannot do, we are complementary to him and therefore indispensable. It is in this sense that the intersubjective dimension plays a decisive role among Christians.

The Greeks want to live in conformity with nature in order to attain happiness, which is also the good. The Christians think that nature is bad (this is expressed in the doctrine of original sin), and that instead of aspiring to conform to it, we must subdue it; the ideal is distinct, indeed opposed, to nature (it is the Law). And the search for the good in itself should make the good Christian happy.

Some Greek virtues therefore disappear in the Christian perspective. If the perfection of my being is my ultimate end, I can achieve it by being stronger than others: Achilles is admirable. But in the Christian view, he may be simply proud. These conflicts resurface in the Middle Ages, when, for example, Christian ideology seeks to use chivalric tales for its own ends: if the desired goal is the Holy Grail, a Christian relic, valiant fighters are no longer the most appropriate candidates. For the Greeks, courage is a virtue in itself; for the Christians, it is a virtue only if it is in the service of God and other men.

Having no particular place for sociability, the individualists can therefore more easily reconnect with the ethical tendencies of the Ancients (Mill, the eloquent spokesman for Utilitarianism, readily allied himself with Epicurus). Like them, in order to attain full flowering and happiness, they seek to discover their own nature and to conform to it. But they separate themselves from it at the same time; the great difference is that modern individualists have simultaneously opted for autonomy. While the Greeks possess an image of the cosmos that includes the social norm, the individualists renounce the claim to any common representation and are content for each man to seek his proper nature in his own way. Therefore they offer a double challenge to sociability: both in the content of their choice, of the good life rather than benevolence (like the Greeks rather than the Christians); and in its form, since each person freely chooses the life that suits him best (like the Moderns rather than the Ancients). In a society without common norms, the aspiration to the good life (of the Ancients) is transformed into a cult of authenticity (of the Moderns). Let each person do what suits him: this is the motto of the individualist order, one of whose earliest formulations is found in Theophile de Viau, at the beginning of the seventeenth century (as Gouhier reminds us):

> *I condone each person following his nature;*
> *Its empire is pleasant and its law is not harsh.*
>
> . . . .
>
> *Never will my judgment find fault with*
> *Him who attaches himself to what he finds aimiable.*
> ——*Satire première de Viau* (1620), in *Oeuvres complètes*
> (Minard, 1951)

Within this general framework common to individualists, there is a great variety of options, some significant examples of which I will offer here.

Montaigne's Wisdom

Certain aspects of his thought rank Montaigne in the humanist tradition; others suggest that he paved the way for individualism. His anthropology can be viewed as fundamentally humanist. He believes in the indeterminacy of human nature, which will be guided by custom but also by the "voluntary freedom" of the subject. He knows that this nature is sociable. He does not forget, finally, that all men belong to the same species and that this belonging weighs more heavily than national determination, however meaningful. He knows that class differences vanish in the face of one's common humanity. Any human being represents humanity as well as any other. "A little man is a whole man, just like a big one" (*Essays*, I, 20, 67). "The souls of emperors and cobblers are cast in the same mold" (II, 12, 350). "I see that males and females are cast in the same mold; except for education and custom, the difference is not great" (III, 5, 685). These lines contain a revolutionary potential that Montaigne does not exploit; he affirms human universality nonetheless.

Montaigne's moral vision, while related to that of the humanists, is distinct from it, however, because of its structure as a whole. He approaches other humanists in his preference for our free actions rather than for those decided by natural or human laws (the autonomy of the *I*), and his interpretation of friendship as an ultimate goal requiring no other justification (the finality of the *you*). He distances himself from them, however, by his ethical thought, which is not in the service of the good but of happiness and, as with the ancient sages, is not seen from the perspective of benevolence but of the good life. The way of wisdom, in Montaigne, is plotted without any specific reference to others. It leads the individual to follow his destiny on earth, which is simply to be. Here, the goal of the wise life, we might say, is to erase the difference between ends and means, to find the meaning of human actions in those actions themselves.

More precisely, Montaigne knows very well that a great number of objects are meant to be used as instruments, and that the same is true of numerous human activities. Justice is not done for the sheer pleasure of doing it but to confound the guilty and protect the innocent. The physician by practicing his profession does not seek his pleasure but the relief of the sick. Knowledge of various kinds is useful; but Montaigne does not aspire to knowledge. What he seeks is wisdom, a state in which one achieves happiness despite one's own imperfection; and in this domain the goal of action is in the action itself. Self-knowledge, the activity to which Montaigne dedicated his life, has no end that transcends it. It is true that, as we have just seen, Montaigne aspires to know man through himself, but this is because each individual is already the whole man; universality is in the object before being in the action aimed at it. Friendship itself is interpreted along the same lines: the movement that carries me toward the other aims at nothing beyond that other. Friendship does not constitute the goal of life; rather, in the best friendships one lives without a further goal — as one ought to do in the rest of life. Friendship is the most beautiful part of existence, it would be a shame to miss it; still, to serve the *you* is not an obligation for the *I*.

Certain actions, certain objects find their end outside themselves; but life as such has no purpose but itself. "The advantage of living is not measured by length, but by use" (I, 20, 67). "The practice of everyday life should be an aim unto itself" (III, 12, 805). Living "is not only the most fundamental but the most illustrious of your occupations. . . . Our great and glorious masterpiece is to live appropriately" (III, 13, 850–51). The sage will try to achieve this intransitive state, this rejection of instrumentalization, in each of his actions." "I undertake to move about while I like moving" (III, 9, 749). "When I dance, I dance; when I sleep, I sleep" (III, 13, 850). "Alexander said that the purpose of his work was to work" (III, 13, 854).

Human life unfolds in time; to renounce seeking an external purpose leads to an acceptance of living in the present. Montaigne learned from Seneca and Horace that those who endlessly project themselves into the future are condemned to perpetual frustration, while those who know how to live in the present are blessed. We should not quarrel with those dear to us during their lifetimes and appreciate them only after death, nor should we seek to spend our time as if our true life were to begin later: it's now or never. Of course, it is impossible to entirely purge our consciousness of the thought of a before and an after for each thing; but one can find joy in the present rather than pushing it back to an inaccessible elsewhere. Equally, each action potentially contains man in his entirety. "Each particle, each occupation of a man betrays him and reveals him just as well as any other" (I, 50, 220). And if he truly had to choose, Montaigne would prefer the common life to the exceptional life of the greats of this world. "The most beautiful lives, to my mind, are those that conform to the common human pattern, with order, but without miracle and eccentricity" (III, 13, 857).

Since the whole of humanity can be embodied in any being, any action, Montaigne teaches us that one should be content with the fate one has been dealt, without seeking to modify it: just as his refusal to base values on nature led him to conservatism (to respect the law of the country of one's birth), his appreciation of all the facets of an existence pushes him to accept life as it is, rather than seek to improve it. "For all actions, say the philosopher, are equally becoming and honorable in a wise man" (III, 13, 852): one must learn to take pleasure in the self, whereever we are, whoever we are. "As for me, I love life and cultivate it just as God has been pleased to grant it to us" (854). The art of living to which Montaigne aspires here is the opposite of any program of collective or militant action: wisdom consists of taking pleasure in life as it comes. It is in this sense that we must understand the old precept to conform to one's nature. This acceptance of the self and the world is the result of wisdom. "It is an absolute perfection, and virtually divine to know how to enjoy our being rightly" (857) — a being that is itself anything but perfect. It is not the purification of the self but its realization that leads to happiness. "And I am so made that I like as well to be lucky as wise" (III, 10, 784). Duty and inclination should not run in contrary directions. "Meanwhile favor yourself; believe what you like best" (III, 12, 804). Here, liberty and nature are reconciled.

In all these choices, Montaigne approaches the ancient conception of wisdom. Yet at the same time, he separates himself from it, precisely because he chooses a way that, although known from history, is not the way of his society. Rather than remaining a devout Christian, as the custom of his time and country dictate, Montaigne divides his life into two parts: his knees bend, his public actions conform to custom; but his reason and his judgment remain free, and he chooses for himself an art of living that suits him personally, with no concern to impose it on others. This amounts to saying that, opting for autonomy, deciding to live according to principles that he has freely adopted, Montaigne remains a Modern; and more precisely, he paves the way for that individualist attitude which consists of choosing an ideal from history that is not necessarily that of one's contemporaries: I have decided to become a Buddhist, or a Confucian, or an animist, or — why not? — a Christian.

Montaigne is modern also in that he does not regard the distance between the ideal and the real as a curse. He endeavors to be a man who seeks, and does not regret that he is not one who has already found. In philosophy, we know, thinkers are split into three groups: those who know where the truth lies, those who have renounced seeking it, and those who stubbornly pursue it. Montaigne ranks himself among the last, thus preferring imperfection to perfection: he writes "not to establish the truth but to seek it" (I, 56, 229). Men must be blamed not for failing in their search for the truth, but for renouncing it. "Agitation and the chase are properly our quarry; we are not excusable if we conduct it badly and irreverently; to fail in the catch is another thing. For we are born to quest after truth; to possess it belongs to a greater power." As Lessing would say two centuries later, possession of the truth properly belongs to God; its search to man alone. Situating himself in a simply human perspective, Montaigne can therefore conclude: "The world is but a school of inquiry" (III, 8, 708), of research and study; success lies in the attempt.

The same is true of happiness. Montaigne has decided to accept the human condition in its very imperfection, and to find a reason for contentment in the impossibility of achieving complete contentment. "For there is no satisfaction here below except for souls either brutish or divine" (III, 9, 755). Aristotle said that only the gods and the animals could live in isolation; as if he were implying that the common life could not be perfect, Montaigne transfers this impossibility to any aspiration to complete happiness. But this is man's nature: "Life is a material and corporeal movement, an action which is by its very essence imperfect and irregular; I apply myself to serving in its own way" (756). To be wise and happy does not mean that one has attained plenitude but that one has agreed to live in incompleteness and finitude. Montaigne concludes, "I want death to find me planting my cabbages, but careless of death, and still more of my unfinished garden" (I, 20, 62).

Gentility in La Rochefoucauld

A hundred years after Montaigne, La Rochefoucauld formulated another version of individualist morality. He judged that, as far as the people are concerned, obedience to current norms is sufficient. But for "gentle folk," members of the elite, such as La Rochefoucauld himself, the requirement is different: It is conformity to the self that is desirable, not to the expectations of others or to prevailing norms. In his *Reflections* (notably I, III, and XIII), La Rochefoucauld would insist on the two steps of this requirement: a critique of social conformity ("false") and a defense of fidelity to the self ("true"), implying a plurality of equally acceptable ways of living, anchored in turn in the plurality of men themselves. This positive side of his thought is often forgotten and deserves to be recalled.

"The only good copies are those which show us the absurdity of bad originals," declares La Rochefoucauld (M 33): this adjective can never be applied to this noun; what is good implies fidelity to the self, not to another; "imitation is always unfortunate" (M 43). Yet the common people seek to imitate: "They neglect their own goods for the goods of strangers, which usually do not suit us" (*Reflections*, III). These imitators are condemned to falseness and either knowingly deceive others or are dupes themselves. However, truth in relation to the self is more important than the conformity to virtue: one is false "in the desire to make oneself worthy through qualities that are goods in themselves but which do not suit us"; this is how people behave who do not know how "to discern what is good in general and what is proper to us" (XIII).

The basic rule of the good life becomes truth in relation to the self (M 626, pp. 122–23, *Maxims*), a modern interpretation of what the Stoics (Panetius) called living in conformity with the dispositions nature has bestowed upon us. "Let each person judge precisely what is good for him, let him govern his own inclination, and let him refrain from seeking whether it suits him to act as others may be inclined to do: the most suitable conduct for each person is what is properly his own" (Cicero, *Treatise on Duties*, XXI, 113). La Rochefoucauld employs the term *truth* in a sense that is compatible with plurality: this is not an objective and absolute truth (or a value) but rather an adequation between what one is and what one does. People are true "insofar as they are truly what they are," each according to his work and his inclinations. That is why "a subject can have several truths" (*Reflections*, I), a single person can show several aspects of himself, and therefore eventually realize himself in several characters; toward each of them the same requirement of adequation to the self is maintained.

Reciprocally, several beings can aspire to the truth of the same quality, that is, to its optimal expression; since their ways of approaching it are multiple, their identities, although different, are of "an equal truth." This is because "there is no general rule for tones and manners" (*Reflec-

tions, III); and each must therefore be content to follow his natural bent. "What is suitable above all," Cicero already declared, "is to remain in accord with oneself in one's conduct and one's designs" (*Treatise on Duties*, XXXIV, 125): La Rochefoucauld's individualism is rooted in the doctrine of the Stoics, while reorienting it in the direction of plurality. We shift here from a morality of duty (we must act this way because it is the law) to an ethic of authenticity (we must act so as to be faithful to the self, in order to fulfill our individual nature). At the same time, we glimpse the possibility of converting the hereditary aristocracy into an aristocracy of character (the "gentleman"). A self exists, then, that is more authentic than the social roles with which we are usually identified; it is incumbent upon us to seek that self, and having found it, to conform to it (here we recognize the first steps of an approach that will become familiar to the Moderns).

La Rochefoucauld is certainly a moralist, in the sense that he is an observer and analyst of mores, of passions that move the human heart; however, when it comes to formulating positive recommendations concerning our conduct, he does not formulate a morality but rather a rhetoric (or, as we would say today, an aesthetic). Benevolence has no particular place here. It is in the rhetorical tradition that La Rochefoucauld was able to find his precepts by transposing the rules of writing into a code of living — in that rhetorical tradition which moralists (in the common meaning of the word) have always held suspect. Doesn't it offer to teach us to uphold any thesis, just or unjust, as effectively as possible? Doesn't it instruct us that there is not a unique beauty but as many beauties as there are subjects, and that the writer's art consists of finding the one suitable to each person?

Now, La Rochefoucauld in his turn considers *convenience*, a key notion of rhetorical doctrine, the master word for our code of conduct: we must always seek what suits each person, instead of imposing the same requirements on all subjects; suitability is the contrary of conformity. "There is an air that suits the figure and talents of each person, what suits some does not suit everyone." The same requirement will be transposed to the individual's inner life: we do not possess a unique identity, we must adapt to circumstances. We do not walk the same way "at the head of a regiment and out for a stroll." Different tones, manners, and feelings are suitable to every state; every kind of work, every house has its own beauties. The other terms La Rochefoucauld uses to describe the ideal conduct all lead in the same direction: one must seek the accord of one's different ingredients (III), a *proportion* between them (XIII, cf. M 207), a *harmony* between words and thoughts, tones and feelings, manners and figure (*Reflections*, III).

In the war of every man against all, in the rivalry of self-regard, each person is fundamentally alone. In social conformity, in the hypocrisy that allows us to disguise our vices, the individual submits to the multitude. The decent man is neither alone nor with all others: he has opted for a restricted and select company, of a few other decent men. The most valued activities are therefore social activities — but not just any social activities; in his *Self-Portrait*, La Rochefoucauld mentions only two: "And above all I find very great enjoyment in sharing my reading with an intelligent person" (27) and "the conversation of [decent] people is one of the pleasures that I enjoy most" (27).

These two activities, moreover, easily shift back and forth: reading in common provides the material for agreeable new conversations, which in turn result in the production of new readings. This is indeed how the *Maxims* were created in the salon of Mme de Sablé, first as a game of wit between decent folk — the mistress of the house, La Rochefoucauld himself, their friend Jacques Esprit, and occasionally a few others — then as a text that circulated through letters and thus served as a pretext for new conversations by the fireside, and for new commentaries. Each of the friends not only produced maxims in turn, but contributed improvements to those of others, so that we can see it as a truly collective enterprise: the partner elicits the maxims by his expectation, he or she then corrects their form, and only their final approbation makes them an object of public circulation. "The sentences are sentences only after you have approved them," La Rochefoucauld writes to the Marquise de Sablé (17 August 1663). Speaking, listening, reading, and writing between "gentlemen" is the superior activity to which one might devote oneself.

It is possible, between members of the elite, to tactfully satisfy one's vanity without wounding that of others, to reconcile the intransigence of each *amour-propre* with the existence of others outside it. Conditions requisite for the unimpeded flow of "commerce between decent persons" include, first, a reciprocal trust between participants, which is not to say that each one must reveal himself entirely to the other, or demand of him total trust; rather, one need not fear that something said in passing might be used indiscriminately. On the other hand, this common life should not be experienced as a constraint, "each one must preserve his liberty: he must reveal himself or not, without constraint." The essential thing is to open up with a view to the same goal: "To contribute as much as one can to the diversion of people with whom one wants to live," to add "to the pleasure of society" (*Reflections*, II). And in a letter, La Rochefoucauld recommends that his friend "occupy himself, if possible, with what is most diverting" (it is true that he immediately adds: "This advice is much easier dispensed than followed" [to Count de Guitaut, on 19 November 1666]). We see that by starting from the same condemnation of our false virtues as do Pascal and the Jansenists, La Rochefoucauld arrives at the opposite result: far from blaming the spirit of diversion, the label with which Pascal stigmatized all social life, La Rochefoucauld wants to contribute to its perfection.

La Rochefoucauld reminds us less of an educator than of an artist, whose raw material would be the human being himself. "We must try to become acquainted with the expression that is natural to us, not to cast it aside, and to perfect it as much as possible." As the Stoics already recommended, the "gentleman" chisels his being the way a sculptor seeks to free the forms contained in a block of marble, to unlock the truth of the material. A good life is that which a person has known how to model as a successful work. Or again, without in the least expressing indignation that we should all be engaged in a great theatrical performance, the "gentleman" decides to intervene, like a director, in the unfolding of the "human comedy," in order to make it more harmonious and more pleasant. Every actor must find the role that suits him and adapt himself to it; the whole troupe must advance, little by little, toward greater cohesion. The theater, which Pascal regarded as the worst threat to the virtuous man, becomes a tool for understanding the life of man and the course of the world. La Rochefoucauld is 180 degrees from the Jansenists here: like them, he has a dark view of human nature, but his pessimism is not despairing, and the cruelest painter of the human heart can bequeath us an art of living.

La Rochefoucauld shares with the humanists a certain faith in the capacity of the individual to shape himself, therefore a certain autonomy of the *I*; but this feature is common to humanists and individualists. It is true that he reserves this privilege for a very few; however, on this point the difference between him and the democratic humanists is merely quantitative. He parts ways with them definitively in his anthropological hypothesis: he thinks that egotistical interest and self-regard govern our acts exclusively, and relegates social norms to the role of belated (and hypocritical) remedies, provided for the primary rule of individual appetites. As for his morality, the *you* plays no particular role: it is certainly not the ultimate goal of my actions.

The Aestheticism of Baudelaire

Under the Old Regime, spiritual power was meant to pertain to the Church, even if in practice the civil authorities could act in its stead. Beginning in the middle of the eighteenth century, another social group, the men of letters, aspired to replace the priests in this function, aspired to what Paul Bénichou has called the "consecration of the writer." Shortly after the Revolution, this dream seemed within reach, since the Christian church had lost its prerogatives. After the fall of the Napoleonic empire, which had not allowed men of letters to come to power, a first generation of writers—Hugo, Jules Michelet, Alphonse de Lamartine—attempted to address the spiritual concerns of their contemporaries. The values they defended were not new; what had changed was the place from which they were endorsed.

However, disenchantment followed on the heels of the dream. The poets and thinkers who wanted to seize spiritual power had to yield to the evidence: the change that had just come about was still more radical than they had hoped. It was not only the former actor—the Church—who was dismissed; it was no longer the same play, and in the new drama there was no role for a repository of spiritual power distinct from and independent of the nation. It was not so much so-called humanitarian values that were contested—the politicians did not refrain from appealing to them—as the right of men of letters to control of them. A reversal then happened in the thought of the new generation of poets, the generation of Baudelaire. Their elders claimed that art should rule public life. "When the people are lacking faith," Victor Hugo exclaimed, "they need art. In place of prophets, the poet" ("Explanatory Notes from *Inner Voices*"). Having perceived that this claim was futile, the younger brothers renounced the external hierarchy but chose subversion of the inner world: without much caring to know whether the multitude would follow their example, they declared that we must replace ethical values with aesthetic values. This choice can be called *aestheticism*.

The substitution takes two chief forms, both of which we already find in Baudelaire. He is still bitter about the failure of the earlier project and complains of "a world where action is no sister to the dream" ("Le Reniement de saint Pierre," CXVIII, vol. I, p. 122). He adapts himself to this, on the one hand, by praising the life transformed into a work of art; and on the other, by regarding the production of works of art as the crowning achievement of a life.

To ask a life to be beautiful rather than good — this is the morality of the man who, in Baudelaire's time, was called the *dandy*. "These beings have no other condition but to cultivate the idea of the beautiful in their person, to satisfy their passions for feeling and thinking" (*Le Pientre*, II, 709–10). The primary form of this cult is the unconditional admiration of physical beauty; and Baudelaire affirms:

> That physical beauty is a sublime gift
> Which exacts forgiveness for all infamies.
> (Allégorie, CXIV, I, 116)

Like other individualists, Baudelaire seems to bypass Christian traditions and reconnect with pagan values. For him, as for Plato, the Beautiful is necessarily allied with the Good. But the surface agreement conceals a major difference: for Plato, physical beauty is a likely index of virtue, but its presence is not required: proof being the ugliness of Socrates. For Baudelaire, on the contrary, beauty coexists with infamy, but counts far more; in addition, it stands as a praise of art, not of nature. The Platonic hierarchy is turned upside down here. It is the entire person of the dandy, and not just his body, that must subject itself to this aesthetic ideal, rejecting any other requirement as meaningless, either because beauty automatically produces a higher good or because it excuses evil.

> Let it be heaven or hell you came from, what do I care,
> O Beauty, huge, terrifying, innocent monster
>
> . . . .
>
> From Satan or from God, what does it matter? Angel or Siren,
> What matter if you — velvet-eyed fairy,
> Rhythm, perfume, gleaming, o my only queen! — make
> The universe less hideous and time less heavy?
> (*Hymn to Beauty*, XXI, I, 25)

The quality of experience, for the dandy, supersedes any other consideration: "What does it matter, the eternity of damnation, to him who has found the infinity of pleasure in a moment?" (*Le Mauvais vitrier*, I, 287).

It is not only the poets who demand that beauty replace or subjugate the good. Ernest Renan was a scholar and a philosopher; yet in 1854 he writes: "I conceive similarly for the future that the word morality shall become improper and be replaced by another. For my particular use, I prefer to substitute the label aesthetic. Faced with an action, I ask myself if it is beautiful or ugly, rather than good or bad" (*Le Desert et le Soudan*, 542). But it is in his first great work, written in 1848, that he declares: " 'Be beautiful, and then spend every moment doing what your heart desires'—this is the whole of morality. All other rules are inaccurate and false in their absolute form" (*L'Avenir de la science*, 871). To do good is therefore to behave like an artist, since action obeys the aesthetic requirement of coherence rather than the moral requirement of conformity. "For me, I declare that when I do good . . . I perform an act as independent and as spontaneous as that of the artist who draws beauty from the depths of his soul in order to realize it outside him. . . . The virtuous man is an artist who realizes beauty in human life, just as statuary realizes it in marble, as the musician does through his sounds" (1011). If the immanent criterion of beauty (the harmony of parts of a being or a life) takes the place of the transcendent criterion of the good, aesthetics replaces ethics. Participating in the surge for emancipating aesthetics from all moral, religious, or political tutelage, offspring of the movement of art for art's sake, aestheticism results in a new union of these domains, but this time under the dominion of beauty.

The other variant of aestheticism consists of asserting that it is the professional artist who accomplishes the noblest act, namely, the creation of a book, a painting, a piece of music. The prayer of the poet then becomes: "Oh Lord my God! Grant me the grace to produce a few beautiful verses that prove to me that I am not the last of men, that I am not inferior to those I scorn!" (Baudelaire, *A une heure du matin*, I, 288). The production of art becomes here a redemption of life; no action is superior to it. That is why God reserves for the poet a place in the immediate vicinity of his throne. Now, since everyone is not a poet, it follows that one man's meat is another man's poison: one morality for artists, another for common people. "There are several moralities. There is the positive and practical morality that everyone must obey. But there is the morality of the arts. This is entirely different. . . . There are also several kinds of Liberty. There is the Liberty of the genius, and there is a very restricted liberty of scamps" (*Notes pour mon avocat*, I, 194).

As in La Rochefoucauld, the world is divided between people of quality and commoners. There are two moralities, and two only: the traditional sort, which is imposed from the outside, and the sort practiced by the superior individual, which consists of producing the beautiful. It is at this point that Baudelaire's friend Barbey d'Aurevilly, who had defended the publication of *Fleurs du mal*, parts company with him: "We do not believe that Art is the chief goal in life, and that aesthetics must one day rule the world" (Baudelaire, *Marginalia*, II, 342).

This will not prevent Baudelaire's numerous posterity from equally committing themselves to this second version of the aesthete's ideal. Mallarmé shares neither his predecessor's illusions, nor hence his disappointments, with regard to the role of poetry in public life: "A modern poet has been foolish enough to be distressed that Action was not the sister of the Dream," he writes to Cazalis (3 June 1863). Nonetheless, he is the author of the famous formula: "Everything in the world exists to result in a book" (*Le Livre, instrument spirituel*, 378). And Marcel Proust, despite his reservations about Oscar Wilde's dandyism (the attempt to impose the criteria of art on life), comes close to the variant favored by Mallarmé: "The true life, life finally discovered and illuminated, hence the only life fully lived, is literature. . . . The supreme truth in life lies in art" (*Le Temps retrouvé*, 474, 481).

In what way is aestheticism estranged from humanism? Chiefly in that it does not grant a significant role to the relation with the other and, more crucially, the finality of the *you*. Aestheticism may or may not reject the universality of the *they* (it does in Baudelaire), but in any case it does not reserve a specific place for human sociability. Consequently, it valorizes only the qualities of the *I*. Humanist doctrine neither confirms nor contests the existence of an ultimate agreement between ethics and aesthetics; but it prohibits interpreting ethics as a pure translation of aesthetic requirements, since the whole of ethics pertains, for humanists, to the intersubjective world.

Chapter 8

A Morality Made
for Humanity

We can now turn to humanist morality itself. For the purposes of closer examination, I would like to invoke two of its greatest representatives in France, Rousseau (in this chapter) and Constant (in the chapter that follows).

Rousseau thinks that humanist morality must challenge two attitudes simultaneously: the destruction of common values, which we observed among those I have called individualists; and the submission of values to dogma, attributed to divine will, as the conservatives demand. Man is "a sociable being who needs a morality made for humanity" (*Lettre à Beaumont*, 969). This leads Rousseau to formulate his position in two contradictory thoughts. But before following his argument, we must recall where his moral reflection stands in relation to his political meditations on society and his psychological analysis of the individual.

The Third Way

The partisans of the Enlightenment in the eighteenth century believed that humanity could be cured of its ills provided it subscribed to their school of thought: by contributing to the flourishing of the arts and sciences, by making these accessible to everyone by extending the benefits of civilization we would promote the reign of prosperity and happiness on earth. Rousseau's first intervention in public debate, his *Discourse on the Sciences and the Arts*, was directly opposed to what he judged to be an illusion: No, he replied, the extension of civilization does not contribute to ameliorating the fate of humanity. The proposed remedy is no remedy at all; but that is because the malady was not correctly identified. Man is defined by his liberty, therefore by his morality, not by his knowledge or even his intelligence; so it is not by trying to extend the latter that we truly contribute to ameliorating his condition. Rousseau never stopped practicing the arts and sciences, for he was not "against" them, as his adversaries, the defenders of the Enlightenment, would have us believe; but he had another conception of man. When we are surprised today that a civilization as advanced as twentieth-century Europe could have produced the horrors of Auschwitz and Kolyma, we are behaving like disciples of Voltaire or D'Alembert, who never understood Rousseau's warning: it is not by accumulating more knowledge, nor by going more often to the theater that man becomes better, that is, more human. "We can be men without being scholars" (*Emile*, IV, p. 290).

Having swept aside the illusory solution recommended by the Encyclopedists and their friends, who in his opinion only obscure the debate, Rousseau can then face the question. First of all, what defines human misery? Is it the absence of good manners, of refinement, of culture? No. The Second Discourse, *On the Origin of Inequality*, seeks to establish a precise diagnosis. The unhappiness of men is due to the fact that they are forced to live together, and each person wants to achieve his goal at the expense of the others. Animals are satisfied with attending to their needs. Man has acquired a consciousness of the gaze of others; therefore, he cannot prevent himself from comparing himself to them and to the image of himself reflected back to him. Now, to be better than others also means that others must be worse than I am; to desire my happiness is to work for their unhappiness. Men are devoured by envy and jealousy, and each searches for his happiness to the detriment of others. Not only have others become my masters (they decide what I must do), they are also my enemies, and I must eliminate them. As Rousseau would say several years later, human unhappiness comes from the fact that "opinion, making the whole universe necessary to each man, makes all others born enemies, and insures that no one finds his good except in the ill of others" (*Lettre à Beaumont*, 937). Humanity has entered irreversibly into the social state, but this state is deplorable: this is the first conclusion he arrives at from his observation.

How could this situation be remedied? At certain moments, Rousseau tells himself that since the human condition is contradictory, since the individual's aspirations do not coincide with those of the society to which he belongs, the solution would be to opt for one of the elements to the detriment of the other. "What causes human misery is the contradiction . . . between nature and social institutions, between the man and the citizen. . . . Give him entirely to the state or leave him entirely to himself; but if you divide his heart, you tear him to pieces" (*Political Fragments*, VI, p. 41).

The Social Contract, like other political writings, analyzes the consequences of the first choice, the choice to give man entirely to society, therefore to "denature" him — but this would involve an ideal society, which makes all its inhabitants virtuous. Yet, while able to explore the logic of this choice to the end, Rousseau has not really forgotten that modern man is no longer the inhabitant of some mythical Sparta, that he no longer agrees to think of himself as a simple fragment of the social entity but considers himself whole in his own right — nor has he forgotten that the individual Jean-Jacques would be very unhappy in such a state, where the individual would have to submit entirely to the collectivity. Rousseau is not describing an ideal state so that his description might serve as a working model (which would have required a revolution, something Rousseau regarded with hostility), but so that we can take advantage of an instrument of conceptual analysis that allows us to understand and judge real states. Summarizing *The Social Contract* in *Emile*, Rousseau adds his operating instructions: this is not a project for action but a mental tool. "Our first concern was to establish the true principles of political right. Now that our foundations are laid, come and examine what men have built on them" (*Emile*, V, p. 467).

Real regimes will never conform to the schema of *The Social Contract*. But there are degrees of separation, and these will determine the individual's attitude toward institutions. "What difference does it make that the social contract has not been observed, if individual interest protected him as the general will would have done, if public violence guaranteed him against individual violence, if the evil he saw done made him love what is good, and if our institutions themselves have made him know and hate their own iniquities?" (p. 473). A given society is acceptable (without being perfect) if it allows its members to develop a critical mind — in other words, if it allows them to distinguish between ideal and real — rather than obliging them to pretend that it is paradise on earth. We can see, then, how far Rousseau's ideas on life in society are from the totalitarian program for which he is sometimes held responsible.

The "social" solution is not really a solution at all. Rousseau's personal inclinations lead him toward the second choice he has envisaged: that man should be left entirely to himself! We have seen that he explored it in detail in the autobiographical writings, but finally recognized that this way was no more practical than the other. In addition, what is strictly speaking appropriate to an individual (Jean-Jacques) could not be recommended to everyone. Whatever the choice, then, failure awaits us, and Rousseau bitterly concludes that man will never know the golden age. "Unfelt by the stupid men of earliest times, lost to the enlightened men of later times, the happy life of the golden age was always a state foreign to the human race, either because it went unrecognized when humans could have enjoyed it or because it had been lost when humans could have known it" (*Geneva Manuscript*, I, 2, p. 77). The vision of the world and history that Rousseau proposes is much more tragic than that of a primitivist: society corrupts man, but man is essentially like this because he has entered into society; we cannot avoid this paradox. Our vocation is simultaneously our curse.

Yet, all is not lost. Man is double, certainly. But rather than choose one side or the other, should we not try to reconcile them? The solution to the problem would not be to opt for one to the detriment of the other, but to allow these two characters to arrive at a better understanding — not through revolution or flight but through education, taken in the broadest sense. Rousseau best succeeds in this integration of contraries, this inclusion of the natural ideal in the social real, in *Emile*, a work that antedates the autobiographical period but that he himself considers the pinnacle of his thought. And just as the systematic treatise (*The Social Contract*) proved to be the adequate form for describing the way of the citizen, and the autobiography that of the solitary individual, a literary genre particularly suited to the evocation of the third way, *Emile* is a mixed work of fiction and reflection, at once personal and impersonal. It is the book on the formation of the ideal man (still "natural" in Rousseau's vocabulary) in the bosom of society. "Although I want to form the man of nature, the object is not, for all that, to make him a savage and to relegate him to the depths of the woods" (IV, p. 255). "There is a great difference between the natural man living in the state of nature and the natural man living in the state of society. Emile is not a savage to be relegated to the desert. He is a savage made to inhabit cities" (III, p. 205). And Rousseau, who dreams of unity, knows nonetheless how to see himself for what he is: "I am a composite being," he says of himself in the *Letter to Franquières* (264).

The solution to the human problem cannot lie in total submission to society, nor in a retreat into solitude. Everyone would agree on that, but how are we to think about going beyond this sterile alternative? The first way of man was leading him to an "all-social" state (as we say something is "all-electric"); this is the way of "socialism," we might say, understanding the word in the literal sense (or should we say "societism"?). This will also be the preference of the Partisans of scientism. The second way threatened to enclose him in the "all-individual," the way of individualism. But Rousseau also conceived of transcending this opposition by a third way that leads beyond it, even if he did not give it a particular name. Yet this is the way that deserves to be called "humanist" because it recognizes both the sociability and the autonomy of the individual. Rousseau no longer seeks here to denature man but to adapt his nature to existing society, and at the same time to bring his life closer to the ideal. "One must constantly twist and turn in order to reconcile [the rights of nature and our social laws]. One must use a great deal of art to prevent social man from being totally artificial" (*Emile*, IV, p. 317). Radical solitude is contrary, not to the state of nature, true, but to the nature of man as he really exists, that is, in society. It is possible to sublimate the sociability of men without denying it, even if everyone will not be able to follow this way. "Other men," we read in *The New Héloïse*, "seek only power and the admiration of others"; some, however, those who decide to resist this pressure, achieve "tenderness and peace" (I, 60, p. 136). The very possibility of this choice is crucial.

Rousseau imagines this third way from the beginning of his reflection on society, even if he does not always grant it as visible a place as that of the two first ways. This ideal history of humanity, as it is presented in the *Discourse on the Origin of Inequality*, actually involves more than two stages. Between the state of nature (imaginary origin) and the state of society (current reality), there is a third, intermediate stage in which man is no longer a beast and is not yet the miserable being he will become. This is, if you will, the "savage" state—the state in which humanity has known its greatest felicity. "This period of the development of human faculties, maintaining a golden mean between the indolence of the primitive state and the petulant activity of our amour-propre, must have been the happiest and most durable epoch. The more one thinks about it, the more one finds that this state was the least subject to revolutions, the best for man, and that he must have come out of it only by some fatal accident" (*Inequality*, II, 48).

The *Lettre à Beaumont* describes in similar terms this ideal "second state": "Men begin to cast their eyes on their comrades, they begin also . . . to take in ideas of suitability, justice and order; moral beauty starts to become perceptible to them and conscience acts"; men are, then, "essentially good" (936–37). This state, reconciling the truth of society with the ideal of nature, is therefore quite possible. Rousseau does not recommend a return to this "savage" state any more than he advocates a return to the state of nature; but when he searches for something concrete to replace the deplorable state of society in which we live, he thinks again of a compromise between the state of nature and the state of society, of a moderate or mixed ideal.

We must return as well to the correlative opposition between self-love and *amour-propre*. After all, if Rousseau were content to condemn *amour-propre*, identified with our sociability itself, he would not be far removed from the path taken by his predecessors, La Rochefoucauld and Pascal, or the Stoics before them. The relevant question is whether the sort of relations rooted in amour-propre—vanity and the desire to surpass others—exhausts the entire field of the social, as his predecessors sometimes suggest, basing on it their condemnation of all life on society; or whether other relations exist, equally social, but that no longer pertain to resemblance and therefore do not lead to comparison, to the desire for substitution and rivalry. Now, there too, we can confirm that Rousseau imagined this other kind of social relationship and glimpsed its effects on human identity, even if the term by which he designates it is not as common as "self-love" and "self-regard." This third feeling, midway between the two others, is "the idea of consideration" (*Inequality*, II, 170), a recognition of our humanity that has not yet degenerated into vanity and mistrust. Between the pure state of nature, in which man neither regards his comrades nor feels regarded by them, and the pure state of society, projected onto an imaginary Poland, in which everyone "regards each other" and knows he is observed, there is a middle world. Here, sociability is a basic given, but we can choose between living in the eyes of the crowd or retreating from it to our circle of friends, or under cover of anonymity.

The third way recognized by Rousseau, which may go unnoticed if we stick to the grand articulations of his doctrine, has a very particular interest: it is not radically opposed to the two others, but integrates and articulates some of their elements. And while the first two ways, each coherent in itself, lead man nonetheless to unhappiness (because he is obliged, precisely, to sacrifice part of his being), the third way alone contains a promise of happiness, since it escapes the familiar threats: a happiness that is uncertain, yet possible. This is a fact too rarely emphasized in the commentaries on Rousseau. While he is capable of exploring hypothetically the pure state of nature or the pure state of society, the individual and the social, when he seeks to formulate his opinion on the desirable fate of real humanity, he opts for the "middle way." But what exactly does he mean by this?

The Double Existence

Rousseau manages to reconcile the two opposite poles of existence by imagining two major phases in Emile's education (this constant demand for education shows once more, even in passing, that Rousseau is not a primitivist: the newborn child is far from perfect). The first phase, which Rousseau calls, as we have seen, "negative education" and which we might also label "individual education," continues from birth until "the age of reason" — here, around fifteen years old. The second phase, of social (or "positive") education, begins at this moment and ends only with our death. The goal of the first is to favor the development of the "natural man" in us; that of the second, to help us adapt to life with other human beings. In the course of the first phase, Emile will learn "all that relates to himself"; during the second, he will become familiar with "relations" and will acquire the "social virtues" (III, p. 208).

Natural man knew only relations to things, and the ideal of the citizen was equally to lead relations to men into relations to things. This will also be the principle of the first phase of education, but not the second. "So long as he knows himself only in his physical being, he ought to study himself in his relations to things. This is the job of childhood. When he begins to sense his moral being, he ought to study himself in his relations to men. This is the job of his whole life" (IV, p. 214). "The child observes things while waiting to observe men. Man ought to begin by observing his kind and then observe things if he has the time" (V, p. 454). Individual education will rest above all, then, on the physical being: it will help to exercise the senses, to perfect the organs. It will seek to make the child independent on the material level (this is the opposite of infantilization): in order to accomplish his will, he should not need "to put another's arms at the end of his own" (II, p. 84). This independence is clearly not the equivalence of self-sufficiency, the ideal of the solitary individual: this is the goal of adult life, and concerns the moral rather than the physical. This first independence corresponds to the acquisition of a first liberty, a first autonomy: the child learns to act by himself.

It must be said here that if we were to take Rousseau's statements literally, they would become untenable. Having seen a child grow up, we could not possibly believe, as Rousseau seems to do, that relations to things and relations to persons come one *after* the other, or that the child reduces the second to the first: "The child raised according to his age is alone. . . . He loves his sister as he loves his watch, and his friend as his dog" (IV, p. 219). This is empirically false, just as it is false to imagine, as Rousseau does, that one begins to become interested in others only at the age of fifteen, ignoring the rapport that binds the child, from birth, to all the persons in his surroundings (and especially to his mother). "One begins to take an interest in those surrounding us; one begins to feel that one is not made to live alone. It is thus that the heart is opened to the human affections and becomes capable of attachment" (p. 220). If we want to retrieve some meaning in Rousseau's remarks, then, we ought to extract them, once more, from the temporal dimension in which they are projected and consider the two forms of education, the two aspects of the personality, simultaneously, indeed on an atemporal plane. Rousseau's ideas would then concern not the two phases of the child's development but the two poles of our being at every moment of its evolution.

The goal of "negative" education, we might say then, is the acquisition of independence. Physical independence first, as we have seen (to be capable of doing everything oneself), which is then extended to social life. Even living in the midst of men, Emile must not submit to the dictates of the received opinions around him, but "see with his eyes, feel with his heart, that no authority govern him beyond that of his own reason" (p. 255). He must prefer the call of individual conscience and reason, of the judgment that reason is capable of formulating, to authority — whether political or familial in origin, whether exercised openly or covertly. This liberation from conventions, from stereotypes and the dictates of fashion, follows and amplifies the acquisition of physical independence (here we are still in the domain of the autonomy of the *I*).

Freedom in this strong sense (and no longer in the sense of indeterminacy) is therefore not an initial given but the — always imperfect — result of education. "Man is born free," Rousseau writes (*Social Contract*, I, 1, p. 131), but *men* are born dependent, first on the adults who ensure their survival, then on common opinion, which gives form to their existence. Negative education is a progressive liberation; men are increasingly free to the extent that they mature — until the day they begin to become the slaves of their own habits or fall back into the dependence of old age. Rousseau is much closer here to Augustine than to his adversary Pelagius, who believed in complete initial freedom. For Rousseau, liberty is acquired — like individuality, like morality as well. Therefore, we must not confuse the freedom that is a distinctive feature of the species with the progressive and conditional freedom of the individual.

The second phase — or rather the second side — of domestic education is entirely different. "Emile is not made to remain always solitary. As a member of society he ought to fulfil its duties. Since he is made to live with men, he ought to know them" (*Emile*, IV, p. 327). And this second step, social education, is by far the most important in Rousseau's eyes. "Up to now our care has only been a child's game. It takes on true importance only at present. This period, when ordinary educations end, is properly the one when ours ought to begin" (IV, p. 212). Through "negative" education, the individual achieves inner coherence; the judgment he makes on his conduct depends only on him. Here the second test intervenes, for which social education prepares him. The action must now satisfy criteria common to all beings; it can find them only in the context of relations between men (we come close, here, to the finality of the *you*).

The two sides of education correspond to the two "states" of humanity according to Rousseau (the state of nature and the state of society). With the first, we emphasize the isolated individual and his capacities; therefore, the call to reason and morality must be set aside. By contrast, however, these move to the center of the second phase. But just as the ideal of the first is not the solitary individual (it is rather the possibility for an already social individual to count on himself), the goal of the second phase of education is not to produce a citizen, in Rousseau's use of the word. The new way, Emile's, is not reached by the mechanical addition of elements derived from the first two (the ways of the citizen and of the solitary stroller). Human society is taken here in its broadest sense: no longer a single country but the whole earth. In his political writings, Rousseau had already envisaged this way of social and moral education, distinct from the civic education of the citizen: it is embodied in the character of Socrates (in the *Discourse on Political Economy*) or in the figure of Christ (*Social Contract*). Rousseau's humanism parts company here with his "socialism," but is still not an individualism; this particular individual lives necessarily in interaction with other men.

Defense of Morality

We begin to glimpse now the place of morality in Rousseau's thought. That men always know how to distinguish good from evil is part of his anthropology, as we have seen; or rather, if that capacity were not guaranteed, it would make no sense to speak of *human* beings. Morality is not only advisable; it is. Its disappearance, if it were acknowledged, would involve pathology. "The voice of conscience [synonymous with morality for Rousseau] can no more be stifled in the human heart than that of reason in the understanding; and moral insensitivity is as unnatural as madness" (*Third Dialogue*, p. 242). It is in the nature of men to know how to distinguish between good and evil; even if there were exceptions, they would only prove the rule: the existence of monsters does not destroy the identity of the species.

The first adversaries Rousseau encounters on his path are therefore the advocates of scientism, or, as he will say, the materialist philosophers, who deny this capacity to distinguish between good and evil, for they think that everything in human behavior is the inevitable effect of causal series that transcend the individual; without liberty, man is also, necessarily, amoral. "To prevent the directive of some importuning morality from coming into opposition with theirs, they undermined it at its roots by destroying all Religion, all free will, consequently all remorse" (*Third Dialogue*, p. 238).

Is Rousseau's accusation justified? To tell the truth, his humanism is not incompatible with a materialist position (and we know that Rousseau himself thought of giving his meditations the title *The Wise Man's Materialism*; cf. *Confessions*, IX, 344). The two doctrines, however, do not share the same subject. Materialism is a hypothesis about the structure of the world; humanism is an anthropology in relation to which moral and political values are established. The two become incompatible, however, from the moment that materialism shifts into scientism, and values, to the extent that they exist, are presented as the necessary consequences of human properties discovered by science. The individual will must submit to that of the group from the moment the group has had access to these discoveries.

The materialism Rousseau criticizes here, first reduced man to an egotistical and solitary being, and then declared that egotism deserves to become the law of society. What Rousseau is fighting against, then, is not materialism as such, but the description that contemporary materialists thought they were justified in making of man, and the reasoning by which they based how one ought to be in being. The position of those whom it is preferable to call the advocates of scientism amounts to debasing man to the level of inert matter, transforming the person into a thing. We would arrive at the same outcome by making purely human regulations as constraining as natural causes, which has always been their dream. "If the laws of nations could, like those of nature, have an inflexibility that no human force could ever conquer, dependence on men would then become dependence on things" (*Emile*, II, p. 85). This would nonetheless be a violence done to the real nature of men.

On the other side, morality is attacked by the individualists. To tell the truth, the same "philosophers" who imagine man submitting to implacable laws make an exception for themselves and behave personally like individualists: they believe they can freely choose the way of greatest satisfaction. This is the position taken by Diderot and Grimm: "The sole duty of man is to follow all the inclinations of his heart" (*Confessions*, IX, 435). Emile's tutor warns his disciple against any temptation to allow his behavior to be guided solely by the movements of the heart or by the intensity of experienced pleasure: "Inform me, then, at what crime a man stops when he has only the wishes of his heart for laws and knows how to resist nothing that he desires" (*Emile*, V, p. 444). If the individual thinks only of himself, "good" is merely a superfluous synonym for pleasure.

The individualists do not deny moral attitudes, but claim that every man judges as he likes: from people to people, and even from individual to individual. So Rousseau's defensive strategy changes here. It is not adequate for him to declare, as Montaigne did, that culture ultimately becomes our nature: certain values, for Rousseau, have the additional advantage of remaining in conformity with what he believes to be human nature. "Nature, we are told, is only habit. What does that mean? Are there not habits contracted only by force which never do stifle nature?" (I, p. 39). Rousseau proposes the analogy of plants, whose branches are forced to develop horizontally. Acknowledging the fact does not make this way of growing any more natural. Nature is not only a first custom. Rousseau would go so far as to say that the great moral principles are the same everywhere, and hardly influenced by practices.

His conception of the moral life in *Emile* and contemporaneous writings finds its point of departure in the Christian tradition, and not in the pagan morality of the Ancients. He does not seek to establish an art of living that would lead every individual separately to the ideal of the good life, but places himself in the perspective of benevolence, a relation that presupposes sociability. In some respects, religion is allied here with morality. "If man is made for society, the truest religion is also the most social and the most human" (*Lettre à Beaumont*, 969). Morality, liberty, and sociability always form an alliance. Rousseau does not even want to imagine that a moral conception other than the Christian one is possible. "In every country and in every sect the sum of the law is to love God above everything and one's neighbor as oneself" (*Emile*, IV, pp. 311–12).

Rousseau embraces a highly selective interpretation when he speaks of the Christian religion: what he takes from it is precisely this perspective of benevolence, an essential sociability, as well as its universalism. Rousseau takes this to be a specifically Christian contribution (which is historically inaccurate, since the Stoics already defended the "society of the human race"): "the healthy ideas of natural right and the brotherhood of all men were disseminated rather late and made such slow progress in the world that it was only Christianity that generalized them sufficiently" (*Geneva Manuscript*, I, 2, p. 81). Rousseau does not refer to the fact that this universality concerns only the relation of men to God, and is not related to the terrestrial realm (Christianity is not against slavery). At the same time, Christianity is somewhat reduced to what Rousseau calls a "Religion of Man": "Through this saintly, sublime, genuine Religion, men — children of the same God — all acknowledge one another as brothers" (*Social Contract*, IV, 8, p. 220).

For Rousseau, not only do virtue and morality exist exclusively in society, they are no more than an acknowledgment of the existence of others: they are defined by the possibility of extending the same attitude to all of humankind; justice is in league with universality. "The less the object of our care is immediately involved with us, the less the illusion of particular interest is to be feared. The more one generalizes interest, the more it becomes equitable, and the love of mankind is nothing more than the love of justice" (*Emile*, IV, p. 252). Forgetting the self is a source of wisdom for man. "The more his cares are consecrated to the happiness of others, the more they will be enlightened and wise and the less he will be deceived about what is good and bad" (p. 252). This is how the Savoyard Vicar identifies the good man and the wicked man with the altruist and the egotist. "The good man orders himself in relation to the whole, and the wicked one orders the whole in relation to himself. The latter makes himself the center of all things; the former measures his radius and keeps to the circumference" (p. 292).

And Rousseau, who entirely understands the demands that each particular state must address to its citizens, nonetheless places above these the universal principles of morality (this is a logical, not a chronological, order): "Let us first find that religion and that morality, and these will be for all men; and then, when national formulas become necessary, we shall examine their foundations, relations, proprieties, and after what belongs to man, we shall then say what belongs to the citizen" (*Lettre à Beaumont*, 969). This universal philanthropy, or justice, or morality, is not confused with the love of those close to us.

Rousseau's universalism, it must be said, is general without being abstract. All men participate in the same species; still, particular men are not replaced by the abstraction of humanity. That would be a failing of which the "philosophes" are guilty, and which amounts, in the end, to transforming every individual into a means to arrive at a concept. Rousseau dismisses "those supposed Cosmopolites who, . . . boast of loving everyone in order to have the right to love no one" (*Geneva Manuscript*, I, 2, p. 81). Let us mistrust those who, in order to defend Man, are ready to sacrifice men to him. The idea of "humanity" is acceptable only if one does not forget that it is made up of all men, taken one by one.

Rousseau has reduced the Christian religion to these two formulas, the universality of the self and the love of one's neighbor, which he calls the "essential verities of Christianity." On this basis, he can proclaim that this doctrine serves "as the basis of every good morality" (*Lettre à Beaumont*, 960), namely, his own. But he is perhaps more accurate in his terminology when he speaks of an "essential religion" (977), "common to all peoples" (975), established on the basis of "general principles common to all men" (971), with the help of this unique criterion: that this religion is addressed, rightly, to all, that it crosses all frontiers, for "the infidel is also a man." It is therefore "a universal religion which is, as it were, human and social Religion" (976). But such a religion is none other than a humanist morality.

Critique of Christian Morality

Is Rousseau's relation to Christian morality reduced to extracting what he judges to be its core? No, for at the same time he formulates several critiques, and these allow a clearer view of his own position.

First of all, Rousseau shares the Moderns' choice in favor of autonomy, against blind submission to a law handed down from elsewhere, whether from men or from God, and which was not first accepted by the individual. This is why he admits to several "doubts about revelation" (*Lettre à Beaumont*, 998), or, unlike simple believers, not having "the happiness to see in revelation the evidence they find there" (964). He wants to search for the criteria of good and evil in himself, not in a holy writ. For the same reason, Rousseau prefers to submit to the principles he finds in the Gospels rather than to the Catholic hierarchy (here we can see the traces of his Protestant education).

We may wonder whether the freedom of conscience Rousseau claims is not compromised by his simultaneous call, notably in *The Social Contract*, for a "civil religion," a set of norms that would be enforced by the state. But if we note the contents of this civil religion, the contradiction disappears. What Rousseau suggests is that the state set itself up as the guarantor of freedom of conscience (and consequently of a plurality of conceptions of the good), therefore that it punish all those opposed to it. The only intolerance concerns those who are intolerant: "There can exist Religions which attack the foundations of society, and it is necessary to begin by exterminating these Religions in order to assure the peace of the State" (*Letter to Voltaire*, 119). The doctrines that teach the hatred of men deserve to be hated. In the *Lettre à Beaumont*, after evoking the minimal dogma of "essential religion," he adds:

"If someone is dogmatically against it let him be banished from society as an enemy of its fundamental laws" (976). If someone preaches the destruction of society, it has the right and even the duty to defend itself against him. The chapter of *The Social Contract* devoted to civil religion takes up this theme again, adding to banishment the pain of death for those who have transgressed the rule of good conduct, which is surely excessive; but Rousseau is describing here the logic of the state, not the fate of the individual. He is not threatened with any punishment if he does not seek to destroy a (tolerant) society by violent (intolerable) means.

In other respects Rousseau even more clearly distinguishes himself from the Christian tradition. When Christ is asked who, more specifically, is the neighbor, he answers with the parable of the Good Samaritan. This involves two singular elements. First, he speaks of a suffering being, the despoiled and wounded traveler; then he handles the answer to the question, "Who is my neighbor?" obliquely. Jesus substitutes for it the question "Who is the neighbor of the sufferer?" (Luke 10:29–37). The axis of the relationship is therefore no longer an *I* but a *you*. In Christianity, the suffering of the individual can be interpreted as a mark of election: when I myself or my neighbors are happy, we cannot be sure that this illustrates God's will, since this happiness is also in my interest; suffering, on the other hand, which I cannot desire, is a sign of divine intervention. Rousseau participates in setting greater value on the *you*, but the suffering of others does not play a comparable role in his thought. "Pity," as it appears in his doctrine, is not charity but a feeling of belonging common to the same species. The suffering being does not have a particular status here but simply offers each person the most suitable means of identifying with others, and therefore facilitates the adolescent's education.

Rousseau even thinks that one must beware of making compassion the touchstone of all morality, for it might then degenerate into complacency and a laxness toward others (when they are wicked). Love and friendship are meant for individual beings, not for the suffering and unknown "neighbor." If we want to generalize — and for Rousseau, this is a desirable transformation — it is better to extend this benevolence to everyone, and not only to sufferers; better, therefore, to leave it up to justice, through universal principle, than to Christian charity (*agape*). "One yields to [pity] only insofar as it accords with justice. . . . For the sake of reason, for the sake of love of ourselves, we must have pity for our species still more than for our neighbor" (*Emile*, IV, p. 253). The feeling for humanity attributed to Socrates, as well as to Jesus, is closer to a sense of universal justice than to compassion for the suffering. In this Rousseau follows other philosophers of the past who preferred to act through reason rather than compassion, but who hastened to add that in the absence of a rational attitude (alas, a frequent situation), pity was nonetheless the only acceptable reaction.

Rousseau's most important twist on Christian morality is yet to come: it is found in the reflection on the nature of evil. To grasp it better, we might characterize moral conceptions according to the distance they posit between the sources of good and evil. Christian doctrine offers several responses to this interrogation. In order to constitute itself, the Church needed — surprise — to identify good with itself, evil with others (Jews, pagans, heretics); beyond its terrestrial sources, good comes from God, evil from the devil. We might say that such an interpretation approaches an "external Manicheanism": the source of evil is entirely alien to that of good and it is outside us.

At other times, however, good and evil are perceived as equally inherent in every man but they flow from opposite sources, identified as flesh and spirit, synonyms here for terrestrial and celestial; the victory of good over evil is assured by the spirit's domination over the flesh, since the flesh is of Satan and the spirit of the Lord, as Saint Paul constantly reminds us. Evil is introduced into man through original sin, the possibility of good has appeared thanks to Christ's sacrifice. We are now faced with what we might call "internal Manicheanism" (familiar to the early Manicheans): the opposition is still radical, but its two terms are inherent to each man. This is what allows the Christians to separate morality from the intersubjective framework that belongs to it: to lead a monastic life, to mortify the flesh, to refuse pleasures are virtuous acts, although they concern a solitary subject. All asceticism is foreign to the teaching of Jesus as it is presented in the Gospels, but it will be introduced into Christianity later on; the demand for a second purity indeed replaces the need for love. In this second form, Christianity is related to certain doctrines that precede it, such as Platonism, and to others that follow it, such as, on occasion, Kantian thought.

Now Rousseau, who personally experiences panic when confronted by the flesh, nonetheless rejects any form of Manicheanism (apart from a few ambiguous formulas). Evil does not flow from the body, nor of course from the spirit: virtues and vices arise from exactly the same source, which is the socialization (and therefore, as we have seen, humanization) of man. The very possibility of good and evil appears at the moment when man takes notice of the existence of other men. This is why Rousseau is not content with simply condemning our social state, which is responsible for all our faults, for it is equally the basis of our best qualities. "Good and evil flow from the same source" ("Lettre sur la virtu," 325). One of the *Political Fragments* confronts this question directly. "It is certain that their virtues and their vices, and in some way all their moral being arose from this [social] interchange. . . . Morally speaking, is society in itself, then, a good or a bad thing? The answer depends on the comparison of the good and the bad that results from it, on the weighing of the vices and virtues it has engendered in those who compose it" (*Political Fragments*, VI, pp. 37–38). At first sight, evil wins out; but we must not jump to conclusions, for in these matters counting is not enough. "The virtue of a single good man ennobles the human race more than all the crimes of the wicked can degrade it" (pp. 37–38).

It is a constant of Rousseau's anthropological thought to emphasize the ambiguity of features that define the very identity of man: the perfection of the individual is coupled with the decrepitude of the species, he says in the *Discourse on the Origin of Inequality*. Human sociability, the need that all people feel for one another, is the reason for our fall, but also the hope of our redemption: this is the profane history that Rousseau sets up in place of Christian dogma.

Having become separate from the animals by his discovery of the gaze that other men cast on him, and consequently by consciousness of self, having torn himself away from the state of nature, man has committed himself to a movement of self-transformation: he is, as Rousseau says, perfectible. Yet it is this liberty that is the common source of good and evil: the origin of the two is indeed the same. In man there is not one part that comes from God and another from the devil. "To complain about God's not preventing man from doing evil is to complain about His having given him an excellent nature, about His having put in man's actions the morality which ennobles them, about His having given him the right to virtue" (*Emile*, IV, p. 281).

We must conclude, then, that some of Rousseau's most celebrated formulas are not to be taken literally. His doctrine is often characterized in brief by saying: for Rousseau, natural man is good, society is bad. Yet neither of these propositions is accurate. In the state of nature, man does not do evil, certainly; but neither does he do good. Ignorant of other men, he does not even understand the meaning of these notions; that is why he is not entirely man. On the other hand, society opens the way for both good and evil. It is inconceivable that man should be definitively cured of the evil within him — for then he would be deprived of his humanity as well. So no one who proposes to reform society in order to make all men good and happy can legitimately claim affiliation with Rousseau, as the revolutionaries of a later generation (or more recently) have done. No society, perfect as it may be, could suppress the essential moral ambiguity of communal life. It is not the fault of this or that society if men are wicked: they are so because they are sociable beings, free and moral — in other words, because they are human.

Humanist morality is based here on humanist anthropology; and it will be no surprise to see that from this point of view, Rousseau is rather close to Montaigne. Montaigne is not unaware that "there are souls so monstrous that they could commit murder for the mere pleasure of it" (*Essays*, II, 11, 316), which does not make them entirely wicked beings but double, or ambivalent, beings; and this pleasure in evil cannot be dissociated from pleasure in good: "For in the midst of compassion we feel within us I know not what bittersweet pricking of malicious pleasure at seeing others suffer" (III, 1, 599). This pleasure has no independent source; it springs up in the very midst of our love for others. Or, according to a paradoxical formula: "Nature herself, I fear, attaches to man some instinct for inhumanity" (II, 11, 316). Human nature surprises us once again: it includes inhumanity. Where does this propensity to evil come from? From the very fact that we cannot live without others. One of the shortest essays in Montaigne's book offers an explanation in its title: "One man's profit is another man's harm" (I, 22, 77), and he recalls this inextricable situation: each man seeks profit, yet we are numerous; it is therefore impossible to be satisfied without injuring others. "Let each man sound himself within, and he will find that our private wishes are for the most part born and nourished at the expense of others" (I, 23, 77).

Man discovers good and evil only in the state of society and through society; but his discovery does not determine him one way or another, it simply offers him the possibility of *becoming* good or evil. From the moral point of view as well, man is marked by his perfectibility, that is, his indeterminacy, and the capacity to transform himself. Once more, Rousseau's humanism has nothing "naive" in it; it imagines man no better than he is, but sees him as a potentiality, as capable of good as he is of evil. This choice separates him from the Jansenists, but not from the Christian tradition. Rousseau is not unaware of this debate within it. "God, it is said, owes His creatures nothing. I believe He owes them all He promises them in giving them being. Now, to give them the idea of good and to make them feel the need for it is to promise it to them" (*Emile*, IV, p. 282). God owes us nothing: this Jansenist formula means that we should not expect God to reward us on earth in response to our efforts to be virtuous. Man is not free to save or damn himself; salvation can come only from divine grace. Rousseau judges, on the other hand, that the very possibility of distinguishing between good and evil is proof of the presence of God within us; but also that there will be no other. It is therefore incumbent upon men to act in order to approach the good. Divine recompense is nothing more than the well-being experienced through this action.

Rousseau goes on, in an equally Pelagian spirit: "They [Christian traditionalists] live as people persuaded not only that they must confess this or that particular, but that this is enough to go to paradise; and I, on the contrary, think the essence of religion consists of practice, that not only must a man be good, merciful, humane, and charitable; but that whoever is truly so believes enough to be saved" (*Lettre à Beaumont*, 962). For Rousseau, as for Pelagius, the hypothesis of original sin is no longer acceptable (the Church is right to consider them heretics in this respect). Unlike Pelagius, however, Rousseau does not think that man can become perfect: the social state has provided him, irremediably, with both vices and virtues. Man is not, at the outset, entirely bad, but neither is he good: for Rousseau, man's necessarily social existence plays the same role that original sin plays for doctrinaire Christians. Works are sufficient for salvation, no need for grace; but this salvation will never be more than partial. Man holds part of his fate in his hands; he is therefore responsible himself for the good and the evil he accomplishes — which would be impossible if he were entirely bad.

Conscience and Reason

As distinct from the individualists' art of living (by the emphasis on sociability) as from Christian morality (notably by his choice of autonomy), Rousseau's moral conception is not radically opposed to these; it

borrows elements from each and structures them in a new way. We have
seen that Rousseau imagined the existence of man as double, at once
individual and social (hence also the double education, negative and
positive); the distinction extends to the moral level. Like the individualists, Rousseau is sensitive to aesthetic demands for coherence with the
self, but he restricts its reach. Where communication with his peers is
concerned, this principle is insufficient: the good of others is not increased by my continuing harmony with myself. The demands for a
maximum intensity of experience, for internal coherence of the person,
and for a harmonious form of existence, are not illegitimate; they even
allow us to understand a great deal of the admiration we can feel for an
individual. They cease to be defensible, however, from the moment that
we refuse to recognize any limit and want to extend them to the totality
of existence.

The reason for this restriction is that these values do not acknowledge
human sociability. There would be no problem if the human being were
living alone on earth: the immanent criterion of coherence would then
be a universal criterion. But the fact is that no isolated human being
exists, and each of our acts, were it done solely for our own pleasure,
affects those close to us. The impact of my search for pleasure on each
of them and on the community must be taken into account; good exists
only in relation to others. A dividing line can then be traced, separating
the personal from the social. The act of writing verse at one o'clock in
the morning in one's room, as Baudelaire would say, lies on one side of
this barrier; the act of breaking the glazier's colorless glasses to punish
him for not contributing to the embellishment of life is on the other.
Immanent criteria must not be ignored, but they cannot reign undivided
because they turn their backs on the necessarily common existence of
men.

Rousseau endeavors to surmount the dichotomy of the universal and
the particular by the concept of conscience, which is the true capstone
of his moral theory. Conscience is a distinctive feature of men; it is the
capacity to separate good and evil and therefore the counterpart of
human liberty, without which morality has no meaning: "Infallible
judge of good and bad which makes man like unto God. . . . Without
you I sense nothing in me that raises me above the beasts" (*Emile*, IV, p.
290). Rousseau would also say that it is a part of God in man, proof
that "justice has another foundation than this life's interest" (*Third Dialogue*, p. 242). All men have a conscience, but each possesses it indi-

vidually; it exists only in the mind of the particular person, and never in abstract entities such as nation, race, or class: "There is never any disinterested love of justice in these collective bodies. Nature engraved it only in the hearts of individuals" (p. 237). By situating the measure of good and evil within each individual, Rousseau remains faithful to the Protestant tradition. It should not be thought that he lapses into becoming an arbitrary individualist: the laws of conscience are common to all, they make up part of the very definition of the species, they are the part of God in man, yet God is one. Rousseau will spell out these laws: autonomy, finality, universality.

Conscience, or the capacity for moral judgment, is to be distinguished from feeling as well as from reason. Feeling varies according to individuals and circumstances; conscience is the same in everyone, marking our common membership in the same species, since it arises from the internalization of the social fact. Man is provided with conscience because he is man; this does not mean that dehumanized men do not exist who have stifled this voice in themselves that tells them good from evil. On its side, reason is equally a capacity common to all, but it has no content and can lead us toward any purpose. Morality will not be reduced to a submission to traditions, but neither does Rousseau seek to base it on reason. "I do not draw these rules from the principles of a high philosophy, but find them written by nature with ineffaceable characters in the depth of my heart. I have only to consult myself about what I want to do. Everything I sense to be good is good; everything I sense to be bad is bad. The best of all casuists is the conscience; and it is only when one haggles with it that one has recourse to the subtleties of reasoning. . . . Too often reason deceives us. We have acquired only too much right to challenge it. But conscience never deceives us; it is man's true guide" (*Emile*, IV, p. 286).

This does not mean that conscience will never find any support from reason. Man benefits from seeing them as complementary, rather than feeling that he must choose between them. Without conscience, reason is mute: "By reason alone, independent of conscience, no natural law can be established" (p. 235). But on its side, conscience without reason is blind and can stray: "Reason alone teaches us to know good and bad. Conscience, which makes us love the former and hate the latter, although independent of reason, cannot therefore be developed without it" (I, p. 67). "To know the good is not to love it: man does not have innate knowledge of it, but as soon as his reason makes him know it, his conscience leads him to love it" (IV, p. 290; cf. also *The New Héloïse*, VI, 7, p. 561). The joint action of the two is therefore what must be sought: moral notions are "true affections of the soul enlightened by reason," an "ordered development of our primitive affections" (*Emile*, IV, p. 235). As often happens in Rousseau, this synthetic position does not appear only belatedly in his development but can be found throughout, in competition with more partial points of view. As early as 1751, he writes: "The purest soul can lose its way even on the path of goodness if mind and reason do not guide it" (*Discourse on the Virtue Most Necessary for a Hero*, p. 7).

The complementarity of conscience and reason may be presented in yet another way. In the Catholic tradition, the individual does not pose questions to his conscience: it is enough to consult the law, or its interpreter on earth, the Church, to know the right path. Common values are affirmed by an equally common representative. This structure can be found outside Catholicism as well: Hobbes wants the state and its sovereign to fix what is just and unjust for everyone; the individual must not interrogate himself but submit. In the Protestant tradition, by contrast, the mediation of the church no longer exists, and each must examine his heart of hearts to hear the voice of God. This gives him the right to contest institutions and laws. This initiative left to individuals is precisely what Hobbes dreaded, because of the possibility that it might lead directly to religious wars.

Rousseau in general follows the Calvinist choice. But he first takes care to distinguish between simple personal inclinations and the voice of conscience, which he imagines to be the same in everyone since it is inspired by God, and this allows him to specify its contents. Is it not conceivable, however, that two individual consciences might contradict each other, that the intimate convictions of the Catholic and the Protestant, of the Christian and the Muslim, of the believer and the atheist may not coincide? Rousseau does not examine the question in these terms, but it seems that this is the point where reason can intervene. Even if it is universally inspired, conscience is known to us only through the individual's expression of it. Reason, on the other hand, has common rules, known to everyone; it might therefore serve as a mediator in case of conflict between consciences. It is in this sense that the "affections of the soul" are "enlightened by reason": reason provides a framework whose universality is recognized by all men.

Duty and Delight

How do we proceed to satisfy the demands of conscience? Having postulated that the nature of man is not bad but neutral, or rather indeterminate, Rousseau can imagine a double form of the good: man achieves it either by following his own good inclinations or by surmounting his bad ones. The first way is that of goodness; it consists of submitting to (one part of) nature. The second is that of duty and virtue: here one obeys the injunctions of the will and surmounts another part of one's nature. On one side, then, the good man "yields to his inclinations in practicing justice, as the wicked yields to his in practicing iniquity. To satisfy the taste which brings us to do good is goodness but not virtue" (*Letter to Franquièrces*, 267). On the other, we have the virtuous man: "Virtue does not consist only of being just, but in being so by triumphing over one's passions, by ruling over one's own heart" (267).

Rousseau does not always judge the two terms of this alternative in the same way. We might say that in the programmatic texts, he privileges virtue, to the detriment of goodness: goodness is uncertain, for it comes to us from elsewhere; virtue, on the other hand, deserves our confidence since it is the product of our own will. "He who is only good remains so only as long as he takes pleasure in being so. Goodness is broken and perishes under the impact of human passions. The man who is only good is good only for himself" (*Emile*, V, p. 444). The virtuous man, on the other hand, acts in full knowledge, because his will is good. He is the merit of his actions. This is the aspect of Rousseau's morality that Kant systematized.

At other times, however, and in particular in the more intimate texts, Rousseau demonstrates greater sympathy for natural goodness than for voluntary virtue, or at least a regret that the second should always supplement the first. Imagining a being like himself, who would do good by inclination rather than duty, he comments: "He would be good because nature would have made him so. He would do good, because it would be sweet for him to do so. But if it were a matter of fighting his fondest desires and breaking his heart to fulfill his duty, would he do that also? I doubt it. The law of nature, or its voice at least, does not extend that far. There must be another voice that commands, and nature must be silent" (*Second Dialogue*, p. 126). When the good is contrary to my pleasure, duty must supplement nature; the best solution would be, however, to avoid being drawn into such a conflict. Rousseau is more trusting here of our instinct for goodness than of imposed virtue: "The instinct of nature is . . . certainly more secure than the law of virtue," he writes (*Second Dialogue*, p. 158). It is enough to let natural goodness speak in us; the results will be the same as, or indeed superior to, those we would have obtained through virtue.

In the *Reveries*, Rousseau commits himself so far in this direction that he leaves the humanist framework behind. He is no longer certain that his inclinations are good, but decides nonetheless to submit to them. He is now prepared to renounce any pretentions to goodness, and to be content with the happiness procured by the simple satisfaction of his desires. "In my present situation, I no longer have any other rule of conduct than in everything to follow my propensity without restraint. . . . Wisdom itself wills that in what remains within my reach I do whatever gratifies me . . . without any rule other than my fancy" (*Reveries* VII, 57). But how can one be sure that what pleases me, what satisfies my inclination, is also good for others and not only for myself? The adoption of a purely individual criterion can ensure the quality of the experience; it will tell us nothing about its virtue. Here, Rousseau has put himself "beyond good and evil."

Yet he would like to see in this attitude "great wisdom and even great virtue" (58). But nothing supports this claim. The individual can be happy surrendering to his inclinations without constraint; but those other qualifiers, wisdom and virtue, cannot be claimed for him without first changing the meaning of these words. In reality, Rousseau has renounced the search for a morality in order to devote himself to the search for an art of living. And he is not unaware that the two do not necessarily go together. In a page from *Emile*, for example, he writes bitterly: "The sight of a happy man inspires in others less love than envy" (IV, p. 221). Pity is natural to man, but envy and malicious pleasure, as Montaigne would say, are no less so; he is not sure that we would not prefer to see all men around us unhappy rather than happy. Now, if this is the case, can we still have confidence in our heart and its choices? Is it enough to declare in advance that natural inclinations are preferable to those imposed on us by opinion? Are we sure of always being able to recognize one or the other? Such a position can no longer be distinguished from that of the individualists.

Rousseau is faced here with the great dichotomy that structures the history of European moral thought, the dichotomy of happiness and virtue. We encountered it earlier, and it has served us to define the individualist arts of living; we essentially retained its implications for sociability. Now let us review it here for itself. Antique morality, which aims at harmony with nature, results in happiness. Christian morality, for which nature is tainted by sin, aspires to the good. Or perhaps we should say that each time, one of the two terms submits itself to the other and renders it to the optional limit; but the hierarchy is not the same. Virtue is victorious here, as is happiness in the system of the Ancients. We can also retrieve the opposition within each of the two traditions. Thus the message of the Stoics, simplified to an extreme and therefore approaching Christianity, would be: virtue is happiness; be virtuous and you will be happy. The message of the Epicureans and of their modern individualist and Utilitarian disciples, by contrast, is: happiness is virtue; there is no virtue but that which consists of aspiring to happiness (from this point of view, Montaigne is an Epicurean).

Rousseau knows these two paths, and he is capable of borrowing from both. He formulates the second this way: "Be just and you will be happy" (*Emile*, IV, p. 282); "to do good" is still a way of "enjoying life" (V, p. 411). But this linking is not obvious, Rousseau knows that it is not enough to be good or virtuous to be happy; simply, without it, he is certain not to be. "Virtue does not bring happiness, but it alone teaches us how to enjoy it when we have it," he writes to d'Offreville (4 October 1761, IX, 147). The first way is closer to that of the *Rêveries*: I enjoy life, therefore it is good.

Yet there is something unsatisfying when this dichotomy is presented as a choice of all or nothing. The humanist cannot find any satisfaction in two terms taken in isolation. To make the happiness of the individual an ultimate goal amounts to ignoring the common life of men. But to demand submission to duty and to virtue signifies a slight to personal autonomy. Nor is it possible to dispense with one of the two terms. To willingly renounce virtue and duty is dangerous: all our inclinations are not good; they must be controlled, taking into consideration the interest of others and not only our own. But, on the other hand, to renounce happiness, and therefore also to cherish goodness, to determine always to triumph over one's passions is no more satisfying; if it were, one would arrive at the paradoxical conclusion that only the wicked can be virtuous, since good people have nothing to overcome!

The humanist position consists, here, as it does in the relation between the natural and the artificial (and for the same reasons), not of choosing one of the terms but of going beyond the choice itself. How is this possible? A Kantian formula evokes this search for equilibrium to which Rousseau also aspires, even if he is not always conscious of it: "Epicurus wanted to give virtue a motive and he deprived it of its internal value. Zenon wanted to give virtue an internal value and he deprived it of motive. Christ alone gives it an internal value and also a motive. . . . Epicurus taught to search for happiness, without being particularly worthy of it. Zenon taught the search for dignity, without happiness in view. Christ taught the search for happiness by being worthy of it" (*Fragments*, XIX, 6838, 6894).

It is in love that the resolution of the tension between virtue and happiness, between duty and goodness, is resolved. "Love of oneself, just as friendship that is the sharing of it, has no other law than the feeling that inspires it; one does everything for one's friend as for oneself, not out of duty but out of delight," writes Rousseau (to Sophie d'Houdetot, 17 December 1757, IV, 394). Delight, which is happiness in love, in its turn results in the good. Through his interpretation of love, through this integration of nature and liberty, Rousseau can also imagine uniting good and happiness: love makes one happy, just as it produces good. In itself, pleasure is not the good, but the good can be pleasure, as it is in love. Here, man is no longer alone, and at the same time he does not go against his inclinations. One must love oneself in order to accept oneself and accept the world: this is the path explored in the *Rêveries*, and was after all the path to which Montaigne was committed. We must prefer altruism to egotism and aspire to virtue, as *Emile* teaches. But we must also know that we *need* to love others, and that their happiness ensures our own.

Humanist conceptions of love and morality are joined, here, by making the *you* the ultimate goal of the action of the *I*. But while morality is constraint, love is joy. Montaigne had already revealed the possibility that the morality of duty may be overtaken by the reign of love: "A single dominant friendship dissolves all other obligations" (*Essays* I, 28, 142). What separates these two forces is not their end but their field of action: one can love only a few individuals, one can be moral with everyone. Private life and public life each has its own principle; the two must be coordinated, not confused, made complementary, not conflictual. What separates the two forces is not their direction but their mode of existence: morality pertains to the will, love does not. That is why one must be supplemented by the other. But that is also why man is forbidden any "pride": he could never be entirely the master of his fate, since he will never be able to command his love. If human behaviors pertained entirely to the will, we might produce a new man who conforms to a preestablished project. But Rousseau is a humanist, not a scientist; he does not believe that man is infinitely malleable matter in his own hands (that it is all a function of will) or in the hands of God (that will counts for nothing). Man is double, or mixed; he needs morality *and* love.

Benevolence is neither natural nor artificial; it consists of cultivating what is already inside us. By discovering his sociability, man experiences the need for affective attachments. Love and friendship are therefore constitutive of man. Indeed, that is why there is no contradiction between the demand for authenticity and that of virtue, both of which are present in Rousseau's thought. Authentic man, who wants above all to be faithful to himself, is neither alone nor simply egotistical: to be truly oneself, one must go through others; without his attachments, man is no longer truly man. It is not Rousseau's loving or virtuous man who risks his authenticity, it is de Sade's solitary egotist. By loving, one does not sacrifice one's being, one completes it.

Yet, by loving an individual, I prefer him to others, and I want him to prefer me too: "With love and friendship are born dissentions, enmity, and hate" (*Emile*, IV, p. 215). But at the same time it is the provenance of moral action itself: "The first notions of good and bad are born of the sentiments of love and hate" (IV, p. 235). We understand why education is so important: the passions from which we are made are not in themselves either good or wicked, but they become so.

Nature and will, necessity and liberty can be reconciled. Man is an incompletely determined being, potentially good, potentially bad. Everything is possible, nothing is certain. We must not take a stand against nature, nor submit to it: we must choose within it and guide it. The inclination for good is within us, but if we do not cultivate it, it withers and dies. "The eternal laws of nature and order do exist. For the wise man, they take the place of positive law. They are written in the depth of his heart by his conscience and reason. It is to these that he ought to enslave himself in order to be free" (V, p. 473). Here, servitude and liberty find common ground.

Fragile Happiness

To do good to the other is to take him as the goal of one's action; unlike the Christians, Rousseau is not aiming at God through men, nor at any abstraction. In love, the *you* also becomes the end of the action of the *I*. Love is the accomplishment of the good, without in any way being a virtue: one does not love out of duty but out of delight. It is through love that the morality of the good and the ethic of happiness, the ideal of benevolence and the ideal of the good life, can come together.

Yet Rousseau's conception of man's felicity does not resemble that of other theoreticians of happiness and the good life. His search can never find a definitive answer. Rousseau's man (who is different from the man Rousseau) does not aspire to that wisdom which allows an acceptance of life in all its diversity; he will never say: whatever is, is good. Nor will he be content to say, like Montaigne, whose serenity he does not share, that one will never overcome one's own imperfection. He no longer has recourse, on another side, to the certainty brought by the immediate relation to God, a being infinite and infallible. The happiness of this man is limited to the strictly human sphere. For this very reason, it is always threatened.

As if to warn us against any facile optimism, Rousseau recounts, in the incomplete sequel to *Emile*, *Emile et Sophie*, that the couple separate and undergo new sufferings. But it is within *Emile* itself that Rousseau prepared us for this outcome: it is inscribed in the condition of man who, through the need he feels for others, through the dependence in which he lives, is struck by a constitutional lack. He must count on others to reach happiness, yet these others, finite beings like himself, are not worthy of trust since their own desires are diverse and shifting. "If each of us had no need of others, he would hardly think of uniting himself with them. Thus from our very infirmity is born our frail happiness" (IV, p. 221).

There is no happiness without others, says Rousseau. "Each will feel that his happiness is not at all inside him but depends on all that surrounds him," he writes in the "Lettre sur la vertu" (325). And in *Emile*: "I do not conceive how someone who needs nothing can love anything. I do not conceive how someone who loves nothing can be happy" (IV, p. 221). We are happy because we love, we love because without the other we are incomplete. But if our happiness depends exclusively on others, these others also hold the instruments of its destruction. "The disorder of our lives arises from our affections far more than from our needs" (V, p. 443). Physical and material needs are of course to be satisfied first; however, the affections are the essential elements of human life, and they depend on others. "The more [man] increases his attachments, the more he multiplies his pains" (p. 444). At an early stage, augmenting one's attachments reinforces the feeling of existing; but by making oneself so dependent on others, one is taking infinite risks. For "all that we love will escape us sooner or later, and we cling to it as if it should endure eternally" (V, p. 816). There is no happiness outside of love, but love is fragile.

So, what should we do? Should we retreat into proud solitude, as the Stoic sages advocate, in order to spare ourselves future disappointments? Detach ourselves from earthly goods, as the Church Fathers and Pascal recommend, so as to love infinitely only the sole infinite being, God? Rousseau would have loved to believe in the immortality of the soul, and sometimes he did not disdain its profane equivalent, the immortality promised by his works. But when he meditates on the ways open to ordinary men — whom, he has taught us, yield nothing to "philosophers" — he no longer acknowledges any but those accessible to everyone: attachments, friendship, love, with their inevitable freight of illusions and disappointments.

Chapter 9

The Need for Enthusiasm

*M*orality and anthropology are closely related, even when the first is not based on the second: we must know what men are in order to decide what we would like them to become. In European history, one image of man is recognized as more influential than others, so that we find it as much among conservatives as among the proponents of scientism and individualists, even if the conclusions they draw from it are different. This is the image of an essentially solitary and egotistical being, embodying the dictum "man is a wolf to man." The key word, here, will become *interest*: this is the name given to the governing motive of human conduct. The moral doctrine of Benjamin Constant is elaborated in conflict with this conception of man

If we place ourselves outside the theological context, we find that La Rochefoucauld is the first eloquent spokesman for the doctrine of interest in France; we can begin, then, by reviewing his version of it.

The Reign of Interest?

This phrase could stand as the epigraph for the whole collection of *Maxims*: "Our virtues are most often merely vices in disguise," the extract from a suppressed maxim (181 in the first edition), which specified that it was amour-propre that accomplished this cosmetic disguise. La Rochefoucauld evokes this theme throughout his book by speaking of the veils that conceal the passions (M 12), of hidden desire, of the secret, of the circuitous path taken by the will (M 54), of dissimulation

(M 62), of hypocrisy (M 218), and of the fact that "all our virtues" are in reality "simply the art of looking honest" (MW [Maxims Withdrawn by the Author] 605), "a mere phantom conjured up by our passions; we give it a decent name so that we can do what we like with impunity" (MW 606). In the last maxim of the collection, he sums up the subject of his work as "the falsity of so many sham virtues" (M 504).

We might say that here we have one of the immediate meanings of the maxims of La Rochefoucauld: to warn us that what we naively take for virtues, for acts accomplished with the best intentions, are in reality merely products of our egotism, of the aspiration to serve our interest — egotism and interest that have, however, taken the precaution of throwing a modest (and "virtuous") veil over their schemes. La Rochefoucauld's goal is to reveal our meanness to us, to make a high opinion of ourselves impossible, to "humiliate the ridiculous pride that fills [the human heart]," satisfied with the "deceptive appearance of virtue" (to Thomas Esprit, 1665). All our morality is hypocrisy: we have an *interest* in conforming to it. "We never blame vice or praise virtue except through self-interest" (MW 597). What we claim to accomplish in the name of the good, we do in reality out of egotism. "We should often blush at our noblest deeds if the world were to see all their underlying motives" (M 409).

True, in his prefatory remarks La Rochefoucauld is careful to declare that his analysis concerns only the virtues of the pagans, and not of those who cultivate the Christian religion. "The virtue of the ancient pagan philosophers, who have been so touted, was established on false foundations," he writes, justifying himself to Father Thomas Esprit. Man deceives himself and deceives others by the appearance of virtue — but only "when faith is not part of the equation," when he has not been "sustained and trained by Christianity" (6 February 1664). There will be one virtue, then, that seems to warrant La Rochefoucauld's approval, and that is humility, "the real key to the Christian virtues" (M 358). To recognize our weakness, our wickedness, our ignorance is indeed directly contrary to the interests of self-regard. But La Rochefoucauld hastens to correct himself: not only is this virtue extremely rare (MP 35), it can in turn be manipulated by its contrary, pride, becoming its best disguise: "Humility is often merely feigned submissiveness assumed in order to subject others" (M 254).

A great number of the maxims not only reconfirm this lesson but imitate, in addition, the syntactical structure of the inscription. We might formulate it this way: "*A* (a virtue) is (unveiled) often (cautionary clause) as *B* (a vice, passion)." Such examples abound, and amount to a veritable matrix, a maxim machine. "In most men love of justice is only fear of suffering injustice" (M 78). "What passes for generosity is often merely ambition in disguise" (M 246). "Loyalty as it is seen in most men is simply a device invented by *amour-propre*" (M 247), and so on.

All human behavior, then, is dictated to men by their interest. It is true that La Rochefoucauld, frightened by the unlimited extension of his explanatory principle, hastens to specify, in his "Word to the Reader" in the second edition of the *Maxims*: "The word Interest is not always meant to signify an interest in goods but most often an interest in honor or glory." This qualification makes the assertion easier to defend, but removes much of the radicalism of the initial statement: if the chief spur to human activity is not the desire for goods similar to material goods, or egotistical satisfaction, but the aspiration to glory and honors, how could we avoid taking into account other human beings who are their only possible suppliers? Man cannot be self-sufficient. When La Rochefoucauld confirms that "we never praise except out of self-interest (M 144), we must choose one of two possibilities: either the term *interest* retains its common meaning, but is then insufficient to describe all praise; or this meaning is extended to include every demand for satisfaction, and in this case its application is accurate but its generality is such that it no longer teaches us much.

Interest and Feeling

At the beginning of the nineteenth century, Benjamin Constant would try to construct an argument against the doctrine of interest. We know that in his youth, Constant considered himself a disciple of Helvetius, who, following La Rochefoucauld, made the notion of interest the cornerstone of his philosophy. And in his first doctrinal writings, for example, in the work *The Republican Constitution*, Constant insistently demands that we take interest into account. The general will is guided by common interest; this in turn arises from the combination of particular interests. Constant dislikes becoming intoxicated with big words without asking himself what particular realities they denote. For a political structure to be solid, it must correspond to the interests of the participants: "These principles have their guarantee in the interest of governors and governed, in the public spirit that is the product of that interest" (VIII, 11, 420). Throughout his life, Constant would not forget this essential motive of human action. "If interest is not the motive of all individuals, because there are individuals whose nobler nature raises them above the narrow conceptions of egotism, interest is the motive of all classes" (*Filangieri*, I, 5, 204). In his *Journal*, Constant provides numerous illustrations of this essential motive of human actions: we have only to seek beyond the declared motivations of the protagonists.

Acting out of one's interest is a trait common to all men, unlike privileges and honors; interest thus easily finds its place in a vision of the world based on the ideal of equality. To respect each person's interest is to grant each person the same dignity. This is not enough, however, to justify the *exclusive* usage of this notion in the analysis of human behavior, in the fashion of Helvetius and La Rochefoucauld. At the very beginning of the nineteenth century, years during which Constant translated Godwin, studied the work of Bentham and Utilitarian thought in general (which cites as authority the notion of "enlightened self-interest"), the references to interest as motive are regularly accompanied by reservations: interest is present in the behavior of men, but it is not sufficient to explain everything. It is from this moment that Constant's humanism parts company with their individualism. A general anthropology that has only this category at its disposal is a shaky science. That is why Constant submits those who seem to be his partisans to critical analysis (it is not important here if he was historically correct): Epicurus among the Ancients (in *Du polythéisme romaine*, VIII, 1), and among the Moderns, Helvetius himself (cf. *Religion*, preface, 579) and Bentham (in the *Principles* of 1806), that is, Utilitarianism.

First of all, we must agree on the meaning of the word. La Rochefoucauld, as we have just seen, was tempted to enlarge it to include any benefit for the subject, direct or indirect. Interest could be found, according to this usage, in the sacrifice of individual well-being to that of humanity: it is always, in a very general sense of the word, in the interest of the subject. But Rousseau had already warned against such an extension of meaning, which deprives the term of any discriminatory power. "Everyone, they say, works toward the public good for his interest; but how is it that the just work toward it to their detriment? What does it mean to be willing to die for one's interest? Of course, no one acts but for his good; but if the issue is a moral good, one will never explain by interest alone anything but the actions of the wicked" (*Emile*, IV, 599). Rousseau explains this in more detail in a contemporaneous letter. In a very general sense, no action is accomplished against the interest of the subject (against the love of self). But we must then distinguish between the interest of the merchant who is trying to obtain pecuniary advantages and the "spiritual or moral interest" that injures no one and contributes "to our absolute well-being" (to Offreville, 4 October 1761, IX, 144).

Constant is in complete agreement: we can no longer speak of "interest" if my interest brings advantage to others. The only real "interest" is that which directly serves my egotism, without being mediated by the idea of duty or the person of a strange beneficiary. "Interest well understood? A miserable system, based on an equivocal absurdity, leaving passion necessarily to judge this interest, and putting on the same level and condemning in the same name of calculation the strictest egotism and the most sublime devotion!" (*Religion*, I, 3, 73). It is better, then, to renounce such a disconcerting use of the words *interest* and *utility*.

Constant's critiques of the attempt to explain everything by interest are of two sorts: either moral or factual. If we propose that interest alone governs men, we would be obliged to renounce all morality (*Principes*, II, 7, 64), yet the image that we contrive of ourselves influences our behavior: he who believes he is immoral becomes so. But if the only reasons to reject the doctrine lie in the undesirable consequences of its adoption, we would not have truly left the doctrine behind, since we would have judged the principle by the measure of its utility. Constant therefore advances a second sort of reason for rejecting the absolute reign of interest: because it does not allow us to explain a great part of human behavior, namely, the faculty of the human soul "to be subjugated, dominated, exalted, independently and even against its best interest" (*Religion*, Preface, I, xxvi). Constant's usual examples illustrating this faculty are religious feelings, love, enthusiasm, and devotion (we shall return to this). Interest is here dismissed in the name of what man is, not what he should be.

The theory of exclusive, dominant interest is false, but this is not why it is so rarely held. It even had a powerful incarnation in recent history, namely, Napoleon himself. The emperor's practical philosophy, according to Constant, was reduced to this principle. Napoleon was "self-interest personified" (*The Spirit of Conquest and Usurpation*, app. 2, p. 161). "He did not regard men as moral beings, but as things" (*Les Cent jours*, II, 1, 206). "The conviction that the human race is devoted only to its interest, obeys only force, deserves only contempt" characterizes, according to Constant, the spirit of Napoleon (I, 6, 130). It is on this conception of man that his politics is based: "If there is only interest in the heart of man, tyranny need only frighten or seduce him in order to dominate him." But the responsibility for this fatal doctrine does not lie only with Napoleon. It was already practiced and promulgated in the course of the eighteenth century by the absolute monarchy, adept at a "savage" Epicureanism. It was also professed by the materialist thinkers of the Enlightenment, who gravely asserted "that man had no motive but his interest." Yet the facts teach a different lesson: the tyranny of Napoleon was encouraged by the people themselves, who love to submit to strongmen. The multitude "hastened to solicit from him their enslavement" (*Conquest*, 162), and Constant did not forget that for twelve years he saw "only begging hands that aspired to chains" (*Les Cent jours*, 303). Do we see here the simple manifestation of "interest"?

The poverty of this theory led, in the end, to the fall of Napoleon. Simultaneously, this very fall illustrates the falseness of the theory. "In order to know men, it is not sufficient to despise them," Constant says forcefully (*Conquest*, I, 14, p. 80), challenging a major current of modern Western thought. The truth wins out, even if it takes its time. We glimpse here in outline the role reserved for writers and thinkers, the role of criticizing and improving the common representations of man and society. The Napoleonic tyranny was at least partially due to the success of philosophical theories that reduced man to a being subject to the reign of interest.

Constant, for his part, does not endorse the image of an entirely egocentric man. For how shall we explain a human being's disinterested actions? In one of his more philosophical texts, Constant relates it to the superiority of ideas over sensations: every man is prepared to sacrifice present sensation to "the hope of future sensation, that is, to an idea" (*Perfectibilité*, 584). As soon as we are unsatisfied with the present moment, we bring into play considerations of our dependence on other men and the world, which is no longer reduced to egotistical interest alone. In sum, the only consistent version of the doctrine of interest would be a reduction of man to pure consumer of immediate pleasures; yet such a reduction is manifestly false. Man has a consciousness of himself and his belonging to time, hence of his finitude. If we did not have to die, we might be tempted to lead a life in the name of interest alone, in order to accumulate and preserve the maximum benefits; but such is not the case. "Death, which interrupts his calculations, which makes these successes useless; death, which seizes power in order to hurl him into the gulf naked and disarmed, is an eloquent and necessary ally of all the feelings that bring us out of this world" (*Religion*, II, 4, 117). The consciousness of death makes the undivided reign of interest impossible.

In other words, explaining human behavior by the exclusive principle of interest is insufficient because it implies that every individual is strictly limited to himself. Now, every person expands outside himself, in time as well as in space: in time, for unlike the other animals, man can imagine his death and therefore the life of the universe without him; in space, too, for other human beings are part of him, and this fact is equally present in his consciousness. This is why a humanist morality is necessary, and not only an individualist art of living.

In an earlier time, valorizing individual interest was liberating and announced the advent of modernity. Taking account of each person's interest was preferable to the submission of the whole society to an immutable hierarchy, to the profit of those who wielded authority. These rulers ignored the interests of their subjects and consoled them by distributing honors among them. The sovereignty of the people also meant that the people acted in their own interest. But within modernity itself, several doctrines collided: that of the exclusive dominance of interest and that of interest moderated by enthusiasm. In the humanist perspective, enthusiasm carries a greater value than interest.

Decentered Man

We have already seen the place Constant reserved for sociability, and his refusal to accept the internal self as the center of each individual. But if this center is not inside him, where is it? The center is moving, Constant would respond: it is situated sometimes internally, sometimes externally. The main thing is that no man is systematically limited to the here and now, to his needs and his biological instincts. "Man has always been pursued by the thought that he is not here below only in order to take pleasure, and that to be born, to propagate, and to expire do not form his unique destination" (*Religion*, II, 2, 109). The man who has managed to satisfy all his interests is not yet fulfilled; he is summoned by something outside him. "There exists in us, then, a tendency that is in contradiction with our apparent goal and with all the faculties that help us to advance toward that goal. These faculties, all adapted to our usage, correspond between them to serve us, are directed toward our greatest utility, and take us for the unique center. The tendency that we have just described pushes us, by contrast, outside ourselves, imprints us with a movement whose goal is not our utility at all, and seems to bear us toward an unknown, invisible center, in no way analogous to our usual life and daily interests" (I, 1, 49).

To the egocentrism of current actions is opposed what we might call the "allocentrism" of these rarer but in no way exceptional acts. The two are equally natural. "The nature that has given man love of himself for his personal preservation has also given him sympathy, generosity, pity, so that he will not sacrifice his peers" (*Filangieri*, IV, 6, 401). Here, Constant is following in the footsteps of Rousseau.

We can try to define the contents of this "mysterious disposition" by observing the examples Constant provides (this enumeration already figures in the *Principes de politique* of 1806, but will be completed and elaborated in 1824). "All these passions have . . . something mysterious, contradictory," he writes. "Love, that exclusive preference for an object which we could have long passed by, and which so many others resemble; the need for glory, that thirst for a fame that must endure after us; the pleasure that we find in devotion, a pleasure contrary to the usual instinct of our nature; melancholy, that free-floating sadness, in the midst of which is a pleasure that eludes analysis" (*Religion*, I, 1, 49–50). Sociability, the basis of humanist morality, therefore makes up part of this allocentric disposition characteristic of the species. To this is added a certain ecstasy before the vastness of nature, which seizes us "in the silence of the night, at the ocean's edge, in rural solitude," as well as "tenderness and enthusiasm" (48–49). Constant situates within this field the subject under examination in this book, namely, religious feeling, defined as a response to our "drive toward the unknown, toward the infinite" (50), "the need man feels to communicate with nature that surrounds him, and the unknown forces that seem to him to animate this nature" (II, 1, 99). Constant is the only one of the great French humanists to reserve such a central place for religion; but his subject of reflection is never the nature of the gods, only the religious feelings of men.

What all these examples have in common is, first of all, the evident irrationality of our acts, the absence of any immediate utility (they do not pertain to the logic of interest). More positively, they are also characterized (except for melancholy, which is particularly enigmatic: why is this a pleasure? Rousseau already observed this: "Melancholy is the friend of delight" [*Emile*, IV, p. 229]) by their "allocentrism": the nature of God, the beloved being to whom one is devoted, the great ideals as well as the sources of glory have in common the fact that they are situated outside the subject, that they transcend him instead of remaining immanent in him. He who does not feel this need to surpass himself is not a human being: "the need for enthusiasm is ubiquitous" (*Religion*, XV, 1, 565). Lastly, a functional characteristic: though all our other acts and actions could help but could not be set up as ultimate goals, these "passions" can define the term, therefore also the meaning of an existence; they are no longer means but ends (I, 1, 49).

One must not be lured by reassuring chimeras and embrace "naive" humanism: men are not moved by this need for enthusiasm *instead* of by their interests; all Constant is saying is that the principle of interest cannot account entirely for human behavior. This is, indeed, why man is "a double and enigmatic being," and sometimes finds himself "displaced on this earth" (50). In every situation, then, "the chief question is to know whether feeling or interest predominates" (II, 2, 110).

One could imagine that besides these two great motives of human actions there is a third, which would be reason, reflection, intelligence. Surely, some of our actions are the pure product of this third motive? No, Constant replies, for reason is endlessly supple and can serve all masters; it is an instrument, not a force. "Logic furnishes insoluble syllogisms for and against all propositions" (I, 3, 592). Reason does not deserve any particular praise: whatever your objective, it can muster appropriate arguments. The mind is "the vilest of instruments when it is separated from conscience," Constant will say, in a spirit close to Rousseau (I, 4, 63); "in the name of infallible reason, Christians were thrown to the wild beasts, and Jews sent to the bonfires" (I, 3, 592). On the other hand, it is impossible to massacre individuals in the name of their happiness. Only two "systems" exist, Constant concludes. "One assigns us interest as a guide, and well-being as our goal. The other proposes perfection as our goal, and as a guide intimate feeling, the abnegation of ourselves and the faculty of sacrifice" (preface, 33).

What is the balance of power between these two aspects of the human being? Here, too, we must not delude ourselves. Most of the time, interest holds sway; disinterested feeling reigns only "during those brief hours that bear little resemblance to the rest of our existence" (I, 1, 49). Even love, which is familiar to everyone, and which holds in check our tendency to make "each of us his own center and his own proper goal," affects only a momentary reversal (X, 10, 432). Most men stifle this feeling: this is the bitter conclusion Constant comes to "at sixty years of age." Only a few succeed in maintaining it. "Men seem divided by nature into two classes: those whose intelligence raises them above their interests and their personal relations, and those who are locked into this sphere" (*Souvenirs historiques*, 80). Never mind. The main thing is not to know what part of the population is animated by an ideal of justice and love, but to know that this ideal is inextinguishable. "There will always remain some of those men for whom justice is a passion, the defence of the weak a need. Nature has willed this continuity: no-one has ever been able to break it; no-one will ever be able to do so" (*Conquest*, II, 17, pp. 139–40).

The opposition between "enthusiasm" and "interest" allows Constant to be specific about his opposition to contemporary Utilitarianism, and therefore to clarify the relation between humanists and individualists. Bentham's Utilitarianism is not a simple egotism; it does not imply that each person is content to seek what is in his own interest; but it submits the judgment of good and evil to the community's decision concerning what is of greatest utility. Constant immediately perceives the dangers inherent in this. The individual would have no more rights, but only the advantages granted to him to the extent that these contribute to the common good. Now, these advantages are fragile. If my physical immunity, for example, is protected only because it is useful to society, one day society may see things differently. Likewise, if an action is advantageous to one society but harmful to another, that does not make it right. From this we can conclude that neither individual happiness nor that of the community can, without further qualification, become the ultimate goals of the moral life: individual happiness cannot because it may harm other individuals, that of the community cannot because it may require the sacrifice of individual happiness or that of another community.

The idea that men know justice, devotion, and love allows us to think about morality from another angle. "The definition of morality," writes Constant, is that it "indicates to men how they can be happy, by making their peers happy" (*Additions*, 525). This indication of the means to find happiness is what separates Constant from the Utilitarians. The happiness of others is necessary to our own; neither the individual nor the community can be happy all alone. Society itself is not a simple aggregate of individuals similar to one another; we need one another in order to live happily.

In granting his sympathies to "enthusiasm" over "interest," by restricting the meaning of this last term to material and egotistical interest, by separating himself from the Utilitarians, Constant is faithful to Rousseau but also challenges a prior tradition that wanted to find in interest — the rational demand of each human being — a remedy against damage done by the passions, against the uncontrollable desire for glory and honors, an outmoded remnant of the feudal code. Machiavelli, Hobbes, and Spinoza thought that interests could serve as a rampart against the dire consequences of the passions. Montesquieu equally subscribes to this vision. He writes: "And, happily, men are in a situation such that, though their passions inspire in them the thought of being wicked, they nevertheless have an interest in not being so" (*The Spirit of the Laws*, XXI, 20 p. 390).

Constant might have hesitated to follow Rousseau, here, rather than Montesquieu, all the more since the damages that most often come to his mind are the excesses of the Terror, and are explained much less effectively as the blind submission to egotistical interest, as a headlong search for utility, than as a by-product of the passions. Robespierre was one of those men for whom "justice is a passion, the defense of the weak a need"; we know the macabre outcome of this politics guided by feeling and enthusiasm, rather than the search for each person's interest. Revolutionaries of all eras will let themselves be guided by a higher ideal, rather than following the interests of their fellow citizens. Isn't this preference responsible for the bloody trail left by revolutions in the modern history of peoples?

To confront this objection, a distinction must be made between two forms of "sentiment" or "enthusiasm," which, however, are both opposed to interest in the strict sense of the word. Constant does not formulate the distinction in abstract terms, but he uses it currently when he turns toward examples. We can surmount our own interests either in the name of an abstract cause or in order to care for individuals other than ourselves. When these two forms of self-transcendence enter into conflict, Constant opts for the second. He adheres entirely to the choice of Mme de Staël, who, he recalls, had her political preferences but was prepared to aid royalists and revolutionaries alike if by chance they were threatened and persecuted. "The view of a suffering being reminded her that there was in the world something much more sacred for her than the success of a cause or the triumph of an opinion. . . . The banishment of all opinions found in her more zeal for protecting them in their misfortune than they had met in her for resisting them while they held sway" (*Mme de Staël*, 212–13). And it is in similar terms, akin to the Christian definition of the neighbor, that he praises his friend Julie Talma. "She hated the party in opposition to hers, but she zealously and perseveringly devoted herself to the defense of every individual she saw oppressed. . . . In the midst of political storms, while all were victims in succession, we saw her often lend all the succor of her activity and courage to persecuted men of opposite sides at the same time" (*Lettre sur Julie*, 187).

We recognize here the finality of the *you* as a fundamental humanist value. Love, devotion, and tenderness for individuals do not belong to the same series as values in whose name one enlists the guillotine. The suffering and oppression of others more easily engages these sentiments, but they are not alone in so doing. Constant's "need for enthusiasm" requires simply that we are prepared to sacrifice our own interests, perhaps even our life, not that of others. Morality, for Constant, resides in a capacity to renounce the preference for the self, not in the pursuit of noble goals; the "power of sacrifice," as he calls it, is the "power-mother of all virtue" (*Mme de Staël*, 222).

Morality and Religion

Two tendencies confront each other, then, within every human being: his interest, on the one hand, his "sentiment" on the other (his egotism and his "allocentrism"). This last can in turn take two forms, even leaving aside the engagement in favor of abstract causes: this site external to the individual may or may not be embodied in another human being— on one side, love, devotion, desire for glory; on the other, nature and the divine. These two varieties are currently called moral sentiment and religious sentiment. The feelings themselves both lead man outside himself and combine harmoniously. This is not always the case, however, with moral sentiment and positive religions. What are the relations between the two? The examination of this question is one of Constant's

chief motivations in his work on religion, to which he gives this revealing, provisional title: "Relations of Religion to Morality among the Peoples of Antiquity" (*Journal*, 6 September 1804).

Morality in this general sense of the word, meaning the transcendence
of personal interest, is a pure embodiment of the feeling Constant is
speaking of; it is also universal, a characteristic of the human race. "The
relations of human societies being the same everywhere, moral law,
which is the theory of these relations, is also everywhere the same"
(*Religion*, XII, 11, 510). Which does not mean that individuals are
equally moral, but that they approach this ideal more or less: morality
"is revealed to all minds," but only "to the extent that they are enlightened" (XII, 121; 513). However, unlike sentiment, positive religions or
religious forms are infinitely variable, and they can be as much the
product of this sentiment as of interest. One can, in effect, use religion
in an attempt to contact the infinite, as much as to ask for God's help in
one's current affairs (therefore magic, purely utilitarian, is a religion
stripped of religious feeling).

Religion, we might say, oscillates between disinterestedness and interest, between morality and politics. One of its two chief forms, which
requires the presence of a caste that serves it exclusively — the "priestly
religions," in Constant's terminology — is much more inclined to a compromise with politics than the other kind, religion without priestly vocation, which Constant prefers for this reason. From this point of view,
Protestantism is superior to Catholicism. The first conclusion of this
examination, then, is negative: religion cannot serve as the basis of morality, and it should be as isolated as possible from political authority.
The second conclusion is positive: though religion cannot be the foundation for morality, morality will be the measure of how we evaluate
particular religions: each of them comes closer to religious feeling the
less interested in and farther removed it is from political power. "Morality becomes, then, a kind of touchstone, a proof to which religious
notions are submitted" (XII, 2, 469). The ways of God are not impenetrable; they are subject to principles of justice.

Such a reinterpretation of the religious phenomenon allows us to understand the place Constant envisaged for religions within a democracy.
His ideal is that of a secular state in which the central power would
guarantee each person the right to practice the religion of his own
choice. Rather than having to choose among religions, why not wel-
come them all, taking care only that they are contained within the pri-

vate sphere of individuals and so do not lead to new religious wars? "This multiplicity of sects, so appalling to us, is what is most salutary for religion" (*Principles of Politics*, XVIII, p. 285). This religious pluralism (which is clearly not a return to polytheism) not only conforms to the liberal politics of separation between private and public, it is equally favorable to the perfecting of religion itself and its action on society. "Divide the torrent, or, better said, allow it to divide itself into a thousand streams. They will fertilize the ground that the torrent would have devastated" (*Religion*, XV, 4, 577). The same model could be applied to different conceptions of the good. Constant has his (humanist) morality, but others are conservatives who privilege conformity to norms; still others are individualists and care only for personal realization. Should the state choose? Certainly not. The free search for the good and the true is here the only value of the state: pluralism, not humanism, must be its credo. The state must be vigilant, however, in making sure that no group shall seize political power or violently oppress the others: intolerance cannot be tolerated.

This first articulation of the two notions, in which morality appears as a purified religion, does not yet say it all. To be moral is, above all, to be capable of preferring the other to oneself. By imagining the extreme case, one ought to say, then: to be moral is to be capable of sacrificing oneself, of finding higher values than one's own life. But how shall we prefer something to our own life if we think that it is the only one that we have? "What is there beyond life, for one who sees only nothingness beyond?" (*Religion*, I, 4, 62). If this life is all I have, why risk it, why not try to enjoy it to the greatest extent possible? If God is dead, is everything permitted? "If life is, at bottom, only a bizarre apparition, without past or future, and so short that it scarcely seems real, what good is it to immolate oneself for principles whose application is at the least only a remote possibility? Better to profit from every hour, uncertain as we are of the hour that follows, to become intoxicated with each pleasure while pleasure is possible" (62).

"Morality needs time," Constant asserts (*Conquest*, I, 5, p. 59), that is, a reference to life after death. Ancient peoples availed themselves of means other than religion to arrive at morality: they believed in the value of glory, which resides not in us but outside us, including in future generations. This is why Achilles, the ancient hero, could prefer glorious death to a long, uneventful life. But men in the modern period, the era of individuals, the era of the quotidian, have renounced the pursuit of glory and are content with their private pleasures. We must not delude ourselves on this point: "What we lack, and what we must lack: conviction, enthusiasm, and the power to sacrifice interest to opinion" (*Religion*, preface, 580). Constant wonders, then, if morality thus deprived of its foundation may not disappear.

Constant's argument may seem a little forced here, carried away as he is by his apologia for religious feeling in the face of the proponents of scientism, and forgetting the paths suggested by other pages he has written himself. Does the sole possible basis for moving beyond the self lie in faith in immortality, and therefore religion? He himself reminded us that we all know another, much more familiar, form of surpassing that characterizes our life at any given moment, not in time but in space — which the *other* represents for every *I*. Constant writes: "The idea of sacrifice . . . is inseparable from all lively and deep affection. Love takes pleasure in immolating to the being it prefers all that otherwise it holds most dear" (II, 2, 107). And when, at the beginning of his book on religion, Constant evokes other forms of the "allocentric" disposition, he enumerates, after religious feeling: "love, enthusiasm, sympathy, devotion" (preface, 31). But if love and other authentic emotions illustrate daily the capacity for sacrifice, what need do we have of immortality? Rather than relying on life after death, can't we rely on those who exist outside us and who are yet part of us, whose happiness produces our own? Even if we have only one life, and this must end definitively with our death, we could conclude, we are not condemned to construct this life as a supreme value, since there is continuity between interior and exterior: sociability replaces immortality. This is the greatness of man but also his misery, for others, like ourselves, are fallible.

Morality and Truth

What is the place of morality in the human world? Constant proposes to distinguish between two complementary perspectives that cannot be reduced to each other. The first is that of the objective world; the second, that of the human subject who lives in it. The second is not simply a way leading to the first, in the way that fruitless attempts lead to success; it has its own separate ideal. The first perspective is that of science (Constant says: of philosophy), and its goal is truth. The second is that of morality (and thus historically of religion), which aspires not to truth but to good. The choice between the two depends on our objective.

Here is their description projected onto the history of religions, in which polytheism embraces the first, Christianity the second (as it happens, this is very close to the opposition between the Ancients and the Moderns, with which the present investigation began). "In the ancient belief system [polytheism], which philosophy had subjugated, man was lowered to the rank of imperceptible atom in the immensity of this universe. The new form [Christianity] restored his place at the center of a world that was created only for him: he is at once God's work and His goal. The philosophical notion is perhaps truer, but the other is so full of warmth and life; and from a certain point of view, it also has its truth, one that is higher and more sublime. If we place greatness in what really constitutes it, there is more greatness in a proud thought, in a profound emotion, in an act of devotion, than in the entire mechanism of the celestial spheres" (*Religion*, I, 5, 66). In truth, man is merely an atom lost in the universe; but the human world is not (simply) that of objective truth; it is also the world of warmth and greatness. Morality and science need not submit to each other; and if we take the strictly human perspective, morality possesses a higher value.

In one of his first publications, when he was around thirty years old, Constant had already encountered this problem by way of a political argument. He insisted on the necessity of introducing what he called intermediate principles between abstract postulates and particular facts; and he illustrated this need with the critique of a Kantian thesis. "The moral principle, for example, that says that truth is a duty, if it were understood in an absolute and isolated manner, would make all society impossible. We have proof of this in the very direct consequences that a German philosopher has drawn from this principle, a thinker who goes so far as to claim that lying would be a crime, even to murderers who would ask whether the friend they are pursuing is not hidden in your house" (*Réactions politiques*, VIII, 136). The absurdity of the consequence leads Constant to situate the general principle in an appropriate frame; this is where Constant's humanism parts company with the moral rationalism of Kant. To tell the truth can be an obligation only within the boundaries of a society where individuals cooperate among themselves. The murderers and their victim do not form a society; they are rather like two countries at war: no obligation has any more currency here. "To tell the truth is therefore a duty only toward those who have the right to truth. Yet no man has the right to truth that injures another" (137). The principle of society wins out over the principle of truth; the requirement of friendship authorizes the lie.

Aware of Constant's argument, Kant felt stung to the quick and replied, the same year (1797), with a monograph entitled *On a Claimed Right to Lie Out of Humanity*. What especially disturbed Kant was the use Constant made of each person's immediate experience; for Kant, principles flow from reason, and have nothing to do with the possible observation of particular suffering (here, the death of the persecuted). Kant is not interested in the practical consequences of acts: to lie is, in itself, contrary to the principles of the good, whatever the circumstances. The hierarchy of values embraced by Constant is different: the goal is to do no harm to another, which can often be served by veracity (for instance, in all contractual relations), at other times by lying (as when faced with murderers). Love of one's neighbor must win out, according to Constant, over the love of truth. The starting point for the moral act is the *you*, not the *I*. Anything rather than cause another's suffering: this can make suicide virtuous as well. "He who feels that under torture he would betray friendship, would denounce other unfortunates, would violate secrets confided to his care, fulfills a duty by taking his own life" (*Religion*, XIII, 4, 535). All other principles give way before this one. This does not mean that we can all be heroes, but we can share the same ideal.

Once more, Constant displays his attachment to a humanist postulate that I have called the finality of the *you*. The refusal to imagine that the other's well-being may be subjugated to any superior objective, even universal moral duty, shows us Constant using a Kantian principle against Kant himself. Constant is led to this by his infallible sense of the concrete: rather than thinking of the happiness of humanity, he is thinking of the happiness of men taken one by one. The other will always be an end not a means, not even the means to make moral law triumphant. For the same reason, Constant criticizes William Godwin, who would like the whole of human relationships to be subject to justice, and who does not understand that love, a stranger to justice, is at the same time superior to it. "It is not by stifling the sweetest affections that we will bring happiness to the human race" (*De Godwin*, 565).

The relations between two individuals do not fall under the objective perspective of science, nor do they aspire to truth, but rather obey the demands of friendship. To be sure, the suffering of others must not dictate all my behavior, for it can be true or feigned or both, endured or chosen or both, making a third person suffer or not—who can also become an *other* (a *you*). The general postulate must be qualified (as Constant would say) by an "intermediate principle." Nonetheless, in my conduct toward the other, I allow myself to be guided by the principle of good, not truth. Julie Talma, Constant's best friend, is dying before his eyes. Should he tell her so? "I wondered if the truth were not a duty; but what would have been the result of a truth that Julie feared to hear?" (*Lettre sur Julie*, 198). Love, friendship, affection win out over duty. Germaine de Staël, with whom he was living, has an interest incompatible with his own. Must he spell it out? "I say nothing that is not true, but I do not tell the whole truth" (to Rosalie Constant, 23 July 1803). He is perhaps deceiving himself in the choice he makes; yet he does not renounce his principle. "You would say that there is duplicity in my conduct; but with a passionate person, duplicity that spares pain seems to me worth more than candor that would do more harm" (to the Comtesse de Nassau, 13 July 1809). When it comes to passion, truth is not a priority. "I am the most honest man in the world, except in love," Constant writes in his *Journal* (13 April 1805).

In the private world, the obligation to tell the truth plays only a subaltern role. Even in the public world, telling the truth is not the main thing, but being able to seek it. Like Montaigne, Constant might proclaim: truth itself is suited to the gods alone; we men are born to quest after the truth. He devotes a section of his *Principles of Politics* of 1806 to this question. Upholding error is, to be sure, fatal to the public spirit. But the imposition of a truth already established is no less so. Truth is indispensable where the objective world is concerned; but the benefits of truth might be annulled by its mode of social existence, the obligation inflicted by authority. The absence of truth is harmful; but blind submission is no less so. If we are committed to seeking the truth rather than only submitting ourselves to it, we also accept the "natural route" to it: "Reasoning, comparison, examination" (XIV, 3, 310). The effect of the method wins out, here, over its result. That is why Constant can conclude: "Free error is worth more than imposed truth" (*Filangieri*, IV, 6, 408). A truth commanded is sterile, free inquiry is fertile ground; and for Constant, the real virtue of liberty consists precisely in that it allows the examination of all opinions, the pursuit of all arguments. Hence this paradox: "If one had to choose between persecution and protection, persecution would be better for enlightenment" (*Principles of Politics*, XIV, 4, 316).

Constant does not say: everyone believes in his own truth, and so much the better. But: the free confrontation of opinions, heated and contradictory debate, critical and respectful dialogue with the adversary are a higher social value than the adherence to a dogmatically constituted truth, whether it be divine revelation or an axiom imposed by the state. "The truth is especially precious because of the activity that is inspired by man's need to discover it" (*De M. Dunoyer*, 561). Debate, which is only the means to it, here becomes the goal. This inscription of truth in the social world clearly does not mean that one renounces the possibility of truth. The search for truth, not the consolation by an agreeable lie, remains the horizon of all knowledge. But this objective vision of the world, in which men and the knowing subject himself take part, does not annul the specificity of the intersubjective relationship. In his own moral world, if there were an ultimate conflict between truth and humanity, Constant would choose humanity.

Epilogue

The Humanist Wager

*K*nowledge of the past satisfies, first of all, a basic human need to understand and organize the world, to give meaning to the chaos of events happening in quick succession. We surely know, even if we do not always think about it, that we are formed from this past; to make it intelligible is also to begin to know ourselves. In the light of the past, the present is transformed: we cease to take the actors' self-justifying or self-glorifying interpretation of their acts, and read them instead in perspective. Words lend themselves to all uses, therefore we cannot trust the descriptions offered by our contemporaries. By confronting the past—though it seems an indirect route— we can gain access more easily and more directly to the world around us. To understand the thought of yesterday allows us to change the thought of today, which in turn influences future acts. To act directly on the will of men is difficult, and useless besides: it is not their will that goes astray (men always desire their good), but their judgment (they seek good where it is not). To clarify judgment is one way to act on their will, and it is here that history can help. The ideas of the past, constructed by the historian, are actions in the present: to think differently allows us to change our way of acting. In this case, saying is doing.

Where are we in this regard today, at the beginning of the twenty-first century, the beginning of the new millennium? What does the study of a small segment of European thought teach us about Europe's past and present?

In the course of the "long nineteenth century" (1789–1914), this part of the world accepted the passage to modernity. That passage, as Tocqueville describes it, from the aristocratic age to the democratic age, from a

226

preorganized and hierarchical universe and society to a situation in which one can claim allegiance to the principle of equality and cherish the choices of one's own will. The thought of the philosophers of the preceding centuries entered this world on the political and institutional levels. But this transformation generated many new sufferings, for which the remedy was sought in several attempts to challenge the great choices of modernity — attempts that in turn dominated the "brief twentieth century" (1914–89).

On the ideological level, these attempts inspired two distinct intellectual families, one conservative, the other scientistic. The conservatives claim affiliation with the old society; in practice, they are content with a compromise between old and modern forms. Like everyone, they accept the benefits of modern medicine, send their children to school, and take part in elections (situations in which one exercises one's wishes and choice), instead of simply accepting what is given by God and nature. In politics, the conservatives favor authoritarian regimes, but without going so far as to eliminate all personal autonomy: they respect the separation of private and public, and encourage initiative in economic matters, which has proven to be an inexhaustible source of wealth. They are allied with the Church, without seeking to institute true theocratic states. To eradicate freedom of conscience would be too onerous an enterprise. They claim affiliation with nationalism, therefore a preference for the collective to the detriment of the individual, but without demanding the unconditional sacrifice of the individual on the altar of the nation. This conservative attempt at restoration enjoyed a certain success, midcentury, in Southern Europe (from Portugal to Greece). Since then, it has given way to more openly democratic forms of government.

Authoritarian regimes often refer to the past; totalitarian regimes to the future. But that is not the only difference. The defenders of totalitarianism also claim a rigorous knowledge of the world, for they postulate that human beings are entirely determined by impersonal and implacable laws; this is why the intellectual family of scientism takes an interest in them. Certain knowledge, the reason for their contempt for traditions, makes them prefer recourse to expeditious, even violent methods to arrive at their goals. The Nazis in Germany participated in the conservative ideal, but they parted company with other members of the family by this appeal to science, as well as by recourse to revolutionary and violent means in order to transform the world. In this they join the other version of scientistic utopia, communism, which claims to retain certain ideals of modernity while betraying them by their methods. The universality of humankind is negated through pitiless class warfare, resulting in the physical elimination of class enemies. The freedom of the subject to choose his fate, the appeal to universal reason, are negated by submission to the collective will, itself confiscated by a party composed of professional militants and in practice subjected to the goodwill of a few individuals. This revolutionary utopianism, although claiming affiliation with science, has nothing scientific about it in reality: it is a perversion of determinism, first making it absolute, then claiming to derive values from it.

Once again, and even more seriously, the cure was clearly worse than the disease. After spawning countless victims, it was abandoned: in the case of German Nazism rather quickly, thanks to its military defeat; much more slowly, because it was better camouflaged behind a generous facade, in the case of Russian communism. Scientistic utopianism, like theocracy, maintains power today only outside of Europe; within it, these ideologies continue to inspire extremist groups, which can harm democracy in the short run but cannot reverse it.

The brief twentieth century, on the political level, appears to be a parenthesis, one of remedies attempted and challenged; the twenty-first, from this point of view, reconnects with the nineteenth. It inherits that century's adherence to the democratic project, but also certain maladies: nationalism and xenophobia have reawakened, even if the colonial spirit in its traditional forms is dead; material inequities, hence social tensions, are exacerbated as well. Other dangers are new, in particular the threats to nature: having privileged the chosen to the detriment of the *given*, men, like the sorcerer's apprentice, have endangered their own lives by destroying natural resources. Were there other weapons to be found in the ideological arsenal of the past that could combat these ills?

To renounce reforming the present in the name of the distant past or an indefinite future does not mean, in fact, that we are renouncing all action in the present, but that we would want to base this action on principles compatible with it, in this case on democratic principles. Two new options present themselves here, which we can observe in action around us: on the one hand, the reinforcement of individualism, in the narrow sense, and on the other the practice of a technical, nonutopian scientism.

We sometimes call any movement of modernity individualism because of the new place it grants to the autonomy of the individual. But in the narrow sense, individualists are those who assert the rights of the personal will without worrying about the inherently social life of men.

Autonomy, which signifies a law assumed by the subject, recognizes society; independence, the expression of desires and personal wills, is what the individualist cherishes. May 1968, in which a plethora of political projects flourished that were to rule the life of the community, was also marked, paradoxically, by a great (symbolic) victory of individualism that brandished this motto: Prohibited to prohibit! No prohibition, therefore no law, therefore no constraint on the individual on behalf of society.

Individualism does not always take such frivolous forms; we can see it at work in the most varied aspects of contemporary society. Towns and villages, complex and hierarchical places of habitation, are increasingly replaced by the suburban dwelling, in which houses line up one after the other, or by cities of housing developments, interchangeable lodgings. Each person is alone in her car — as she is also, paradoxically, in public transport, where she is condemned to anonymity. Even as I write, a movement is being spawned in the public housing projects outside of Paris, that consists of attacking public buses, one of the last links between these neighborhoods and the rest of the city. The new forms of communication and information do not necessarily facilitate human interaction: everyone is seated alone in front of his computer screen, and even when several of us are watching the same program together on television, our gazes remain parallel and have no chance to meet. Certain people take refuge in religion, but they are not always in contact since each person can choose his own, drawing from the vast repertory of centuries and civilizations. Children do not yet grow up all alone but often stay with only a single parent, or alternate between the two.

This increasing solitude, this social autism does not lead, as we might have expected, to a greater differentiation between individuals — quite the contrary. Montaigne had already understood that, taken in isolation, men resemble each other; it is their constellations that are unique, unparalleled. Liberty is illusory when behaviors take the same forms and seek to conform to the same images.

The scientism that leaves traces in democratic societies is very different from what we see in totalitarianism: here, there is no revolutionary project, no violent submission of the individual, therefore no terror. However, here as there, people believe they are observing immutable laws at work in society, and they are inclined to guide their actions by those laws. Politics then becomes a domain on which we consult experts, and the only debate is over the choice of means, not ends. We are entering into the reign of instrumental thought, in which every problem must find a purely technical solution. This perspective deeply influences the organization of life in society. Not only does the "technician" (in general, collective and anonymous) enjoy great prestige, but in addition, the possibility of doing something becomes sufficient reason to do it: *capability* becomes *wish*, which is transformed in turn into *duty*. Technocracy and bureaucracy are sanctified, procedures and regulations become intangibles.

Probably nothing illustrates this reign of instrumental thought in democratic societies better than the role played by economic practices. This is not a question of pitting one conception of the economy against another but rather the category itself, which has reached exorbitant dimensions. One often has the impression that economic prosperity has become the sole measure and the sole aim of these societies, subordinating any political objective. Social positions are immediately translated into terms of consumer capacity, which condemns their actors to passivity. Yet this exclusive domination of the economic is illusory. Behind the demands for higher salaries are often hidden demands for greater social recognition, for more respect, for a more dignified communal life. All human needs do not lend themselves to measurement by money. Consumer society pushes us to forget this obvious fact.

In utopian scientism, particular human beings, instead of being final ends, are transformed into means for achieving an objective that transcends them, namely, the ideal state. In technical scientism, the instruments of human well-being — effectiveness, production, consumption — are transformed in turn into final ends; but as a result, men become the instruments of instruments, slaves of their own tools. Now, if the final end is economic effectiveness, the door is open to increasing constraint on individuals. The oppression here is not violent, as in the totalitarian state; it is indirect and diffuse, but as a result it is more difficult to circumscribe and reject.

Technical scientism is dominated by these two apparently incompatible principles: everything is determined (life submits to rigorous laws, science must still progress in order to know them in their entirety); anything is possible (we can achieve any objective we like). This last aspect of our societies generates in turn the growing need to seek judicial responsibility for all misfortune. I no longer want to admit that uncontrollable forces might have caused my house to be flooded, that climatic disturbances might have made my roof collapse, that an avalanche has carried away my son. Since everything can be controlled, a human being must be responsible for this disaster, someone I can take to court. I no longer allow illness to strike me at random: the fault must lie with the society that provoked it, or the doctors who did not want to cure it. One of them must pay.

Moreover, the possibilities of influencing humanity's fate have certainly grown in the past decades in a spectacular way: the *chosen* plays a larger part, while that of the *given* diminishes. The totalitarian masters dreamed of forging new men, free of their congenital weaknesses, but they had only very basic means at their disposal: indoctrination, torture, concentration camps. The technicians of democratic societies are on the way to mastering the genetic code of living species; they will then be capable of producing new specimens of those species. If they wished, they could eliminate our hereditary defects by modifying our genes; eventually, they will be able to cause a mutation of the human race itself. For the first time in its history, humanity will be capable of making itself conform to its own wishes.

The criticisms of individualistic and technocratic democracy are not new; they have often been the starting point for conservative or totalitarian projects. But are we really limited to these alternatives? Is there nothing in the democratic tradition itself that allows us to combat its drift? I believe there is. That is its humanist core, which was constituted at the same time and in the same spirit as the project of modern democracy. To have a better grasp of this neohumanist project, it is instructive to study humanism in the process of its inception, between the sixteenth and nineteenth centuries. The pioneers' vigor of thought contrasts advantageously with the watered down secondary school versions to which we have become accustomed, and which no longer manage to capture our attention. This is why my book has been dedicated to the study of the French humanist tradition, from Montaigne to Tocqueville, including Descartes, Montesquieu, Rousseau, and Constant.

Humanism is, to begin with, a conception of man, an anthropology. Its content is not very rich. It is limited to three traits: the belonging of all men, and of them alone, to the same biological species; their sociability, that is, not only their mutual dependence for purposes of nourishment and reproduction, but also for becoming conscious and speaking beings; finally, their relative indeterminacy, therefore the possibility of engaging in different choices constitutive of their collective or biographical history, choices responsible for their cultural or individual identity. These traits — this "human nature," if you will — are not valorized in themselves; but when humanists add to this minimal anthropology a morality and a politics, they opt for values that would be in conformity with this "nature," rather than being purely artificial products of an arbitrary will. Here, nature and liberty are no longer at odds. This is the case with the universality of the *they*, the finality of the *you*, and the autonomy of the *I*. The three pillars of humanist morality are, in effect, the recognition of equal dignity for all members of the species; the elevation of the particular human being other than me as the ultimate goal of my action; finally, the preference for the act freely chosen over one performed under constraint.

None of these values is reducible to another; they can even, on occasion, conflict. But what characterizes the humanist doctrine is indeed their interaction, and not the simple presence of one or the other. The praise of liberty, the choice of sovereignty figure equally in other doctrines, individualistic or scientistic; but in humanism they are limited by the finality of the *you* and the universality of the *they*: I prefer to exercise my personal freedom rather than to be satisfied with obeying, but only if this exercise does not harm another (the freedom of my fist stops at the cheek of my neighbor, said John Stuart Mill, in a spirit shared by the humanists). I want my state to be independent, but that does not give it the right to make other states submit to it. Autonomy is a liberty contained by fraternity and equality. *You* and *they* are not equivalent either. As citizens, all members of a society are interchangeable, their relations governed by justice based on equality. As individuals, the same persons are absolutely irreducible, and what counts is their difference, not their equality; the relations that bind them together require preferences, affections, love. This plurality of values explains in turn why there are several ways of being antihumanist: Bonald or Taine deny (for different reasons) the autonomy of the *I*; Pascal rejects, in the end, the finality of the *you*; Joseph Gobineau, Ernest Renan, and Baudelaire are opposed to the universality of the *they*.

The humanists do not "believe" in man, nor do they sing his praises. They know, first of all, that men cannot do everything, that they are limited by their own plurality, since the desires of some only rarely coincide with those of others. They do not choose their history and their culture; nor their physical being, whose limits are quickly reached. They know, above all, that men are not necessarily good, that they are even capable of the worst. The ills they have mutually inflicted on one another in the twentieth century are present in memory and prevent us from crediting any hypothesis that presupposes human goodness. To be honest, these proofs were never lacking. But it is precisely in living through the horrors of the war and the camps that modern humanists, men like Primo Levi, Romain Gary, and Vasili Grossman, have made their choice and confirmed their faith in the human capacity *also* to act freely, *also* to do good. Modern humanism, far from ignoring Auschwitz and Kolyma, take them as a starting point. It is neither proud nor naive.

If one adheres both to the ideal of indeterminacy and that of shared values, a path exists that can link the two together; we call it education. Men are not good but can become so: that is the most general meaning of this process, of which scholarly instruction is merely a small part. In the modern Western world, and that is another novelty, most children are no longer "givens" (born by accident); as a general rule, they are chosen. As a result, greater responsibility lies with all those who can influence the transformation of the child into a free and interdependent adult: her family first, but also school, indeed society as a whole. For it is not only a matter of ensuring the child's survival, or of facilitating his success, but of allowing him to discover the highest joys. For this, certain traits must be cultivated, others marginalized, rather than approving all just because they are there.

Humanism does not define a politics with any precision; diverse, indeed contradictory choices, can be compatible with humanist principles (thus the distinction between "liberals" and "republicans": collective autonomy can challenge individual autonomy). Yet, adherence to its values guides the choice of governments, as it does the attitude of the governed. The demand for equality has operated since the foundation of democratic regimes and continues to do so in our day, yet it is not the only political value. To this passive and minimal humanism is added an active, much more ambitious humanism. To make human individuals the finality of our institutions, of our political and economic decisions, might cause a peaceful revolution. To believe in the inherent sociability of individuals implies that one redefines the ends of society. To privilege the autonomy of the *I* does not mean only to ensure her right to vote so that she might choose her rulers, but also to combat overcautious conformity. The state and its institutions have their own logic, which pushes them to grow and find reinforcement until they become ends in themselves; it is incumbent upon each citizen to resist these tendencies, since the state and institutions should be in his service. Resignation to the claimed fatality of social or economic "laws," on the other hand, contradicts humanist principles.

Humanism is not at all opposed to technology as such, but it is opposed to technology that ceases to be a means and becomes an end in itself. Shall we not rejoice, from a humanist perspective, that physically oppressive work may be eliminated, that men and women may be replaced by machines that will perform the most onerous tasks? Shall we not approve the possibility for people to live in greater comfort, to meet more easily, to learn more and more effectively? Yet all these advantages brought by technology cease to be advantages when the servant becomes a master preoccupied uniquely with its own interests. And this is not only true of machines. It is enough to observe our most indispensable institutions, the hospital, the school, the court, to perceive that what should serve man can reduce him in turn to the role of instrument.

An objection: but the autonomy of the *I* is the infinite dispersal of individual wills; the finality of the *you* the retreat into private life alone; the universality of the *they* the substitution of the cold rule of the state for the warmth of local communities. Now, these drifts are not inevitable. Autonomy is not the rejection of common law but the participation in its establishment. Love of those dear to us is not a substitute for political commitment, it completes it and can, in addition, provide it with values. The imperfection of the love object does not prevent the perfection of love, said Descartes; we must remember that the love of a humble human being can be more precious than solemn declarations on the well-being of humanity. Humanism asserts that we must serve human beings one by one, not in abstract categories. To conclude, the legal and humanitarian sphere of universality does not exhaust the public world, nor prevent the maintenance of communities of origin or interest.

Contrary to what Bonald would suggest, the dike can find its source in the torrent — or, to use Rousseau's more appropriate metaphor, the remedy can be found in the illness. The humanists assert that men do not have to pay a price for the freedom they have recently acquired: they are not obliged to renounce either common values, social relations, or the integrity of the self. The pact in whose name the devil claimed his due never really existed. But the chosen must be enlisted in the aid of the given. These values are not automatic; they must be assumed by a deliberate act. Voluntary associations, the choice of friendship and love, can conpensate for the weakened relations of kinship and neighborhood. The self is, of course, multiple; this does not prevent one from acting as a responsible subject. The others are everywhere—inside him, around him, and even in the values he cherishes; it is thanks to them that he can face the threats of the devil. Far from being hell, the *others* represent a chance to escape from it.

Humanist doctrine does not, however, address all human needs. It says nothing about the basics of survival: to be fed, to be warm, to be without fear for tomorrow or for one's closest relations. It does not teach us the best economic mechanisms of the moment; it does not tell us whether the market should decide everything or whether the state should also have its say. It is allied with love but does not speak of what gives daily experience its flavor and is found at the source of so many of our pleasures: the intensity of the moment, sexual pleasure, ecstasy. Humanism teaches us nothing about our deep need to understand the world and live in harmony with it, which can lead us equally to science or to the disinterested contemplation of nature. It does not tell us whether to be religious or not. Humanist thought is content to guide the analysis and action of the world of human interchange; but within this world all others are situated.

The democratic regime has affinities with humanist thought, as authoritarian regimes have with conservatism, totalitarian regimes with utopian scientism, and anarchy with individualism. But these affinities do not become imperative demands, and the characteristic feature of democracy is to tolerate a plurality of doctrines, provided none of them is identified with political power or provokes the subjection and death of others. Without this mode of existence, doctrine becomes official dogma and would contradict and annul its meaning—the affirmation of autonomy. The democratic, secular state does not choose among conceptions of the good, provided that these do not contradict its ultimate principles; within this framework, which is vast, it leaves the field open to ideological debate. The adherents of the other families of modern thought are not necessarily brutal and wicked; they grasp and emphasize aspects of human experience that the humanists judge marginal, but this judgment can also be mistaken: the free examination of the world must always be pursued. The work of the great humanists themselves becomes the theater of these conflicts, and this is how their thought progresses: their work is not simply the exposition of a doctrine.

The humanist enterprise could never bring itself to a halt. It rejects the dream of a paradise on earth, which would establish a definitive order. It envisages men in their current imperfection and does not imagine that this state of things can change; it accepts, with Montaigne, the idea that their garden remains forever imperfect. It knows that the desire for autonomy is countered by the pleasure of voluntary servitude; that the joy felt in making the other the end of my action is overshadowed and hampered by the need to transform him into an instrument of my own satisfaction; that universal respect easily gives way to a preference for "our people" over "others." Sisyphus's stone never stops tumbling down, or another just beside him — but the fate of Sisyphus is not a curse; it is simply the human condition, which can never be definitive or perfect. Or rather, which consists, as in an alchemical operation, of converting the relative into the absolute, of building something solid out of the most fragile materials.

Rather than a science or a dogma, humanist thought proposes a practical choice: a wager. Men are free, it says; they are capable of the best and the worst. Better to wager that they are capable of acting willfully, loving purely, and treating one another as equals than the contrary. Man can surpass himself; this is what makes him human. "You must wager. This is not voluntary: you are launched." Not to wager is to make the opposite wager; and in this case there is nothing to gain. But unlike Pascal, the humanists do not demand an act of faith in God; they are content to spur us to know and make an appeal to the will. In this respect they follow the Christian humanists, who earlier refused resignation. "What good is man," Erasmus exclaimed at the beginning of the sixteenth century, "if God acts on him as the potter acts on the clay?" Erasmus believed that no being came to earth without justification, without "final cause," and saw the existence of man, an imperfectly determined being, therefore endowed with freedom, as proof that God was not content to offer men grace but allowed them to seek salvation by means of their own works. If everything is played out in advance, what good is man? The humanists of the French tradition do not necessarily believe in final causes, but they judge it useful to act as if this way were really open to men. It is true that, unlike Pascal, they do not promise those who wager "an eternity of life and happiness," but only a fragile and fleeting felicity.

God owes us nothing; neither does Providence or nature. Human happiness is always in suspension. We can, however, prefer the imperfect garden of humankind to any other realm, not as a blind alley, but because this is what allows us to live in truth.

Bibliography

BIBLIOGRAPHICAL NOTE

In the present volume, I used many of my previous publications, namely: "Droit naturel et formes de gouvernement dans *l'Esprit des lois*," *Esprit* 75, 3 (1983): 35–48; "La comédie humaine selon La Rochefoucauld," *Poétique* 14, 53 (1983): 37–47; "L'Être et l'Autre: Montaigne," *Yale French Studies* 64 (1983): 113–44; "Benjamin Constant, politique et amour," *Poétique* 14, 56 (1983): 485–510; *Frêle bonheur, essai sur Rousseau* (Paris: Hachette, 1985); "Rousseau: La troisième voie," *La revue Tocqueville* 17, 2 (1996): 151–64; "The Gaze and the Fray," *New Literary History* 27, 1 (1996): 95–106; "The Labor of Love," *Partisan Review* 3 (1997): 375–83; *Benjamin Constant: La Passion démocratique* (Paris: Hachette, 1997). I am grateful to Hachette for the authorization to reprint parts of those texts.

CLASSICAL WORKS

Augustine. *Confessions.* Translated by F. J. Sheed. Indianapolis, Ind.: Hackett Publishing, 1992.

Baudelaire, Charles. *The Complete Verse.* Translated by Francis Scarfe. London: Anvil Press, 1986.

———. *Œuvres complètes.* Paris: Gallimard-Pleiade, 1975–76.

Boetie, Etienne De La. *Discours de la servitude volontaire.* Paris: Bossard, 1922.

Constant, Benjamin. *Additions.* In *Principes de politique applicables a tous les gouvernments.* Geneva: Droz, 1980.

———. *Adolphe, the Red Note-Book.* Translated by Carl Wildman. Indianapolis, Ind.: Bobbs-Merrill, 1959.

———. *Cecile.* In *Œuvres.* Paris: Gallimarde-Pleiade, 1979.

———. Charriere, Isabelle (letters to). In *Œuvres complète,* by Isabelle Charrière, vols. 3 and 4. Amsterdam: G. A. Van Oorschot, 1981–82.

———. *Constitution républicaine* (*Fragments d'un ouvrage abandonné sur la possibilité d'une constitution républicaine dans un grand pays*). Paris: Aubier, 1991.

———. *Correspondence*. Paris: Gallimard, 1955.

———. *De Godwin*. In *Ecrits politiques*. Paris: Gallimard-Folio, 1997.

———. *De la force du gouvernment actuel de la France* . . . Paris: Flammarian-Champs, 1988.

———. *De la perfectibilité*. In *Ecrits politiques*. Paris: Gallimard-Folio, 1997.

———. *De la religion considerée dans sa source, ses formes, and ses développements*. Arles: Actes Sud, 1999.

———. *Des réactions politiques*. In *De la force du gouvernment actuel de la France* . . . Paris: Flammarian-Champs, 1988.

———. *De Mme de Staël*. In *Portraits, Mémoires, Souvenirs*. Paris: Champion, 1992.

———. *Ecrits politiques*. Paris: Gallimard-Folio, 1997.

———. *Filangièri*. Commentary in *Oeuvres*, by G. Filangièri, vol. 3. Paris, 1840.

———. Gerando, Annette de (letters to). In *Lettres, 1807–1830*, by Benjamin Constant and Mme Racamier. Paris: Champion, 1931.

———. *Histoire abregée le l'égalité*. In *Oeuvres complète*, vol. 3. Tubingen: M. Niemeyer, 1993.

———. *Journal*. In *Œuvres*. Paris: Gallimarde-Pléiade, 1979.

———. *Les Cent jours*. In *Œuvres complète*, vol. 14. Tubingen: M. Niemeyer, 1993.

———. *Lettre sur Julie*. In *Portraits, Mémoires, Souvenirs*. Paris: Champion, 1992.

———. *The Liberty of the Ancients Compared with that of the Moderns*. In *Political Writings*, ed. Biancamaria Fontana. Cambridge: Cambridge University Press, 1988.

———. *Littérature du 18e siècle*. In *Œuvres complète*, vol. 3. Tubingen: M. Niemeyer, 1993.

———. *Ma Vie (La cahier rouge)*. In *Œuvres*. Paris: Gallimarde-Pleiade, 1979.

———. Nassau, Mme de (letters to). In *Lettres de Benjamin Constant à sa famille, 1775–1830*. Paris: Stock, 1931.

———. *Political Writings*. Edited by Biancamaria Fontana. Cambridge: Cambridge University Press, 1988.

———. *Principles of Politics Applicable to All Representative Governments*. In *Political Writings*, ed. Biancamaria Fontana. Cambridge: Cambridge University Press, 1988.

———. *The Spirit of Conquest and Usurpation and Their Relations to European Civilization*. In *Political Writings*, ed. Biancamaria Fontana. Cambridge: Cambridge University Press, 1988.

Constant, Benjamin, and Rosalie Constant. *Correspondence*. Paris: Gallimard, 1955.

Bibliography

Constant, Benjamin, and Mme Racamier. *Lettres, 1807–1830*, Paris: Chamion, 1931.

Descartes, René. *Cogitationes privatae*. In *Œuvres*, vol. 10. Paris: Vrin, 1966.

———. *Philosophical Writings*. Translated by John Cottingham, Robert Stoothoff, and Dugald Murdoch. Cambridge: Cambridge University Press, 1985.

Erasmus of Rotterdam. *La Diatribe sur le libre arbitre*. In *Œuvres*. Paris: LGF, 1991.

Euripides. *The Suppliant Women*. Vol. 3. Edited and translated by David Kovacs. Cambridge: Harvard University Press, Loeb Classical Library, 1998.

Hobbes, Thomas. *On the Citizen*. Translated by Richard Tuck and Michael Silverthorne. Cambridge: Cambridge University Press, 1998.

———. *Opera philosophica*. Edited by William Molesworth. Volume 3. London 1841. Reprint. Aalen Verlag Scientia, Darmstadt, 1966.

Hugo, Victor. *Poésie. Œuvres*, vol. 2. Paris: Imprimerie nationale, 1909.

Kant, Immanuel. *Fondements de la métaphysique des moeurs. Œuevres philosophique*, vol. 2. Paris: Gallimard-Pléiade, 1985.

———. *Fragments, Gessammelte Schriflen*. Vol. 19. Berlin, 1934.

———. *Théorie et pratique, sur un pretender droit de mentor de humanité. Œuvres philosophique*, vol. 3. Paris: Gallimard-Pléiade, 1986.

La Rochefoucauld, François De. Correspondence. In *Œuvres complètes*. Paris: Gallimard-Pléiade, 1964.

———. *Maxims*. Translated by Leonard Tancock. London: Penguin, 1959.

Mallarmé, Stéphane. Correspondence. *Œuvres complètes*. Paris: Gallimard-Pléiade, 1983.

Mill, John Stuart. *Three Essays*. Oxford: Oxford University Press, 1985.

———. *Utilitarianism*. Oxford: Oxford University Press, 1998.

Montaigne, Michel de. *The Complete Works: Essays, Travel Journal, Letters*. Translated by Donald M. Frame. Stanford, Calif.: Stanford University Press, 1958.

Montesquieu, Charles de. *Lettres persanes*. In *Œuvres complète*. Paris: Seuil, 1964.

———. *Mes Pensées*. In *Œuvres complète*. Paris: Seuil, 1964.

———. *The Spirit of the Laws*. Translated by Anne M. Cohler, Basia Carolyn Miller, and Harold Samuel Stone. Cambridge: Cambridge University Press, 1989.

———. *Traité des devoirs*. In *Œuvres complète*. Paris: Seuil, 1964.

Nicole, Pierre. *Les Visionnaires*. Paris, 1668.

Pascal, Blaise. *Pensées*. Translated by A. J. Krailsheimer (according to the Louis Lafuma edition). London: Penguin Books, 1995. [The French edition (Garnier, 1966) contains also *Pascal's Life* by his sister Gilberte.]

Pascal, Gilberte. *Pascal's Life*. In *Pensées*, ed. Louis Lafuma. Paris: Garnier.

Pico della Mirandola, Giovanni. *De la dignité de l'homme*. Paris: Combas, Ed. De l'Éclat, 1993.

Bibliography

Plato. *Œuvres complètes*. Paris: Gallimard-Pléide, 1950.

Plutarch. *Sur les délais de la justice divine*. In *Œuvres morales*, vol. 7. Paris: Les Belles Lettres, 1974.

Porphyrus. *Isagogè*. Paris: Vrin, 1947.

Renan, Ernest. *Œuvres complètes*. Paris: Calmann-Lévy, 1947–61.

Rousseau, Jean-Jacque. *Botany Writings*. Translated by Charles E. Butterworth, Alexandra Cook, and Terence E Marshall. In vol. 8 of *The Collected Writings*, edited by Roger D. Masters, and Christopher Kelly. Hanover, N.H.: University Press of New England, 1990–.

———. *The Collected Writings*. Edited by Roger D. Masters and Christopher Kelly. Hanover, N.H.: University Press of New England, 1990–.

———. *The Confessions*. Translated by Christopher Kelly. In vol. 5 of *The Collected Writings*, edited by Roger D. Masters and Christopher Kelly. Hanover, N.H.: University Press of New England, 1990–.

———. *Discourse on the Origins of Inequality*. Translated by Judith R. Bush, Christopher Kelly, Roger D. Masters, and Terence Marshall. In vol. 3 of *The Collected Writings*, edited by Roger D. Masters and Christopher Kelly. Hanover, N.H.: University Press of New England, 1990–.

———. *Discourse on Political Economy*. Translated by Judith R. Bush, Christopher Kelly, Roger D. Masters, and Terence Marshall. In vol. 3 of *The Collected Writings*, edited by Roger D. Masters and Christopher Kelly. Hanover, N.H.: University Press of New England, 1990–.

———. *Discourse on the Sciences and the Arts and Polemics*. Translated by Judith R. Bush, Christopher Kelly, and Roger D. Masters. In vol. 2 of *The Collected Writings*, edited by Roger D. Masters and Christopher Kelly. Hanover, N.H.: University Press of New England, 1990–.

———. *Discourse on the Virtue Most Necessary for a Hero*. Translated by Judith R. Bush, Christopher Kelly, and Roger D. Masters. In vol. 4 of *The Collected Writings*, edited by Roger D. Masters and Christopher Kelly. Hanover, N.H.: University Press of New England, 1990–.

———. *Emile, or On Education*. Translated by Allen Bloom. New York: Basic Books, 1979.

———. *Essay on the Origins of Language*. Translated by John T. Scott. In vol. 7 of *The Collected Writings*, edited by Roger D. Masters and Christopher Kelly. Hanover, N.H.: University Press of New England, 1990–.

———. *The Geneva Manuscript*. Translated by Judith R. Bush, Christopher Kelly, and Roger D. Masters. In vol. 4 of *The Collected Writings*, edited by Roger D. Masters and Christopher Kelly. Hanover, N.H.: University Press of New England, 1990–.

———. *Julie, or the New Héloïse*. Translated by Philip Stewart and Jean Vaché. In vol. 6 of *The Collected Writings*, edited by Roger D. Masters and Christopher Kelly. Hanover, N.H.: University Press of New England, 1990–.

———. *Letter to Franquières*. Translated by Charles E. Butterworth, Alexandra Cook, and Terence E Marshall. In vol. 8 of *The Collected Writings*, edited by Roger D. Masters, and Christopher Kelly. Hanover, N.H.: University Press of New England, 1990–.

———. *Letter to Malesherbes*. Translated by Christopher Kelly. In vol. 5 of *The Collected Writings*, edited by Roger D. Masters and Christopher Kelly. Hanover, N.H.: University Press of New England, 1990–.

———. *Letter to Mr. Philopolis*. Translated by Judith R. Bush, Christopher Kelly, Roger D. Masters, and Terence Marshall. In vol. 3 of *The Collected Writings*, edited by Roger D. Masters and Christopher Kelly. Hanover, N.H.: University Press of New England, 1990–.

———. *Letter to Voltaire*. Translated by Judith R. Bush, Christopher Kelly, Roger D. Masters, and Terence Marshall. In vol. 3 of *The Collected Writings*, edited by Roger D. Masters and Christopher Kelly. Hanover, N.H.: University Press of New England, 1990–.

———. *Political Fragments*. Translated by Judith R. Bush, Christopher Kelly, and Roger D. Masters. In vol. 4 of *The Collected Writings*, edited by Roger D. Masters and Christopher Kelly. Hanover, N.H.: University Press of New England, 1990–.

———. *The Reveries of the Solitary Walker*. Translated by Charles E. Butterworth, Alexandra Cook, and Terence E Marshall. In vol. 8 of *The Collected Writings*, edited by Roger D. Masters, and Christopher Kelly. Hanover, N.H.: University Press of New England, 1990–.

———. *Rousseau, Judge of Jean-Jacques*. Translated by Judith R. Bush, Christopher Kelly, and Roger D. Masters. In vol. 1 of *The Collected Writings*, edited by Roger D. Masters and Christopher Kelly. Hanover, N.H.: University Press of New England, 1990–.

———. *The Social Contract*. Translated by Judith R. Bush, Christopher Kelly, and Roger D. Masters. In vol. 4 of *The Collected Writings*, edited by Roger D. Masters and Christopher Kelly. Hanover, N.H.: University Press of New England, 1990–.

———. *Writings Related to Music*. Translated by John T. Scott. In vol. 7 of *The Collected Writings*, edited by Roger D. Masters and Christopher Kelly. Hanover, N.H.: University Press of New England, 1990–.

(Unless otherwise specified, the following works are from *Œuvres complète*. Paris: Gallimard-Pléiade, 1955–95.)

Rousseau, Jean-Jacques. *L'Art du jouir*. Vol. 1.

———. *Correspondence complète*. Oxford: Voltaire Foundation, 1965–95.

———. *Ebauches des confessions*. Vol. 1.

———. *Ecrits sur l'abbé de Saint-Pierre*. Vol. 3.

———. *Lettre à Beaumont*. Vol. 4.

———. *Lettre à d'Alembert*. Vol. 5.

————. *Lettre à Franquiere*. Vol. 4.

————. *Lettres écrites de la montagne*. Vol. 3.

————. *Lettres morales*. Vol. 4.

————. "Lettre sur la vertu, l'individu et la societe." *Annales de la societe Jean-Jacque Rousseau* 41 (1997): 313–27.

————. *Mon portrait*. Vol. 1.

————. *Pygmalion*. Vol. 2.

————. *Preface a Narcisse*. Vol. 2.

————. *Rêveries*. Vol. 1.

Sade, D. A. F. De. *La Philosophie dans le boudoir*. Vol. 25 of *Œuvres complètes*. Paris: J.-J. Pauvert, 1968.

Sales, François de. *Correspondence: Les Lettres d'amitié spirituelle*. Paris: Desclée de Brouwer, 1980.

Seneca, *Lettres à Lucilius*. Vol. 2. Paris: Les Belles Lettres, 1947.

Taine, Hippolyte. *Derniers essais de critique et d'histoire*. Paris, 1894.

Tocqueville, Alexis de. *Democracy in America*. Everyman's Library, 1994.

————. *The Old Regime and the Revolution*. Translated by Alan S. Kahan. Chicago: University of Chicago Press, 1998.

————. *Œuvres complètes*. Vol. II. Paris: Gallimard, 1953.

Thèophile de Viau. *Œuvres poétiques*. Paris: Minard, 1951.

COMMENTARIES

Alquié, F. *La découverte métaphysique de l'homme chez Descartes*. Paris: PUF, 1966.

Bady, R. *L'Homme et son "institution."* Paris: Les Belles Lettres, 1964.

Bénichou, P. *Le Sacre de l'écrivain*. Paris: Corti, 1973.

————. *Le Temps des prophètes*. Paris: Gallimard, 1977.

Brown, P. *La Vie de saint Augustin*. Paris: Seuil, 1971.

Brunschvicg, L. *Descartes, Pascal lecteurs de Montaigne*. Neuchâtel, La Baconnière, 1942.

Bullock, A. *The Humanist Tradition in the West*. New York: W. W. Norton, 1985.

Cassirer, E. *The Individual and the Cosmos in Renaissance Philosophy*. New York: Harper, 1963.

Compagnon, A. *Nous, Michel de Montaigne*. Paris: Seuil, 1980.

Comte-Sponville, A. *Petit Traitè des grandes vertus*. Paris: PUF, 1995.

————. *Valeur et vérité*. Paris: PUF, 1994.

Comte-Sponville, A., with L. Ferry. *La Sagesse des Modernes*. Paris: Laffont, 1998.

Conche, M. *Montaigne et la philosophie*. Treffort: Ed. Du Mégare, 1987.

Dumont, L. *Essais sur l'individualisme*. Paris: Seuil, 1983.

Ellul, J. *La Technique ou l'enjeu du siècle*. Paris: A. Colin, 1954.

Ferrari, J. *Les Sources françaises de la philosophie de Kant*. Paris: Klincksieck, 1980.

Ferry, L. *L'Homme-Dieu*. Paris: Grasset, 1996.

Festugière, P. *La Saintetè*. Paris: PUF, 1942.

Figgis, J. N. *Studies in Political Thought from Gerson to Grotius*. New York: Harper, 1960.

Friedrich, H. *Montaigne*. Paris: Gallimard, 1968.

Furet, F. *La Révolution française*. Paris: Hachette, 1997.

———. *Le Passé d'une illusion*. Paris: Laffont, 1995.

Goldschmidt, V. *Anthropologie et politique: Les Principes du système de Rousseau*. Paris: Vrin, 1974.

Gouhier, H. *L'Antihumanisme du XVIIIe siècle*. Paris: Vrin, 1987.

Grimal, P. *Les Erreurs de la liberté*, Paris: Les Belles Lettres, 1989.

Hirshman, A. *Les Passions et les Intérêts*. Paris: PUF, 1980.

Holmes, S. *The Anatomy of Antiliberalism*. Cambridge: Harvard University Press, 1993.

Kolakowski, L. *God Owes Us Nothing: A Brief Remark on Pascal's Religion and on the Spirit of Jansenism*. Chicago: University of Chicago Press, 1995.

Kristeller, P. O. *Renaissance Concepts of Man*. New York: Harper and Row, 1972.

Lagarde, G. de *La Naissance de l'esprit laïque au déclin du Moyen Age*. Paris: Droz, 1946.

Larmore, Ch. *The Morals of Modernity*. New York: Cambridge University Press, 1996.

Lefort, Cl. *L'Invention démocratique*. Paris: Fayard, 1981.

Lévinas, E. *Entre nous*. Paris: Grasset, 1991.

Manent, P. *La Cité de l'homme*. Paris: Fayard, 1994.

Masson, P.-M. *The Discovery of the Individual, 1050–1200*. Toronto: Toronto University Press, 1987.

Mesure, S., and A. Renaut. *La Guerre des dieux*. Paris: Grasset, 1996.

Philonenko, A. *J.-J. Rousseau et la pensée du malheur*. Paris: Vrin, 1984.

Quinton, A. *The Politics of Imperfection*. London: Faber and Faber, 1978.

Renaut, A. *The Era of the Individual: A Contribution to a History of Subjectivity*. Princeton: Princeton University Press, 1997.

Rigolot, F. *Métamorphoses de Montaigne*. Paris: PUF, 1988.

Robin, L. *La Morale antique*. Paris: Alcan, 1938.

Romilly, J. de *La Grèce antique et la découverte de la liberté*. Paris: Éditions de Fallois, 1989.

Schneewind, J. B. *The Invention of Autonomy*. Cambridge: Cambridge University Press, 1978.

Sidgwick, H. *Outlines of the History of Ethics*. Boston: Beacon Press, 1960.

Skinner, Q. *The Foundations of Modern Political Thought*. Cambridge: Cambridge University Press, 1978.

Taylor, Ch. *La Liberté des Modernes*. Paris: PUF, 1997.

Todorov, T. *Nous et les autres* [On Human Diversity]. Paris: Seuil, 1989.

Troeltsch, E. *Protestantisme et Modernité*. Paris: Gallimard, 1991.

———. *The Social Teachings of the Christian Churches*. New York: Harper, 1960.

Villey, M. *Seize Essais*. Paris: Dalloz, 1969.

Vlastos, G. *Platonic Studies*. Princeton: Princeton University Press, 1973.

Voelke, A. J. *Les Rapports avec autrui dans la philosophie grecque*. Paris: Vrin, 1961.

Index

active vs. contemplative life, 109–14, 163
Adolphe (Constant), 91–93, 106
aestheticism, 29, 174–77. *See also* beauty
agape (love-charity), 119, 128–30, 135, 163–64, 192
American Revolution, 3
Ancients. *See* Greeks
anthropology, 30–31, 40, 207
Aristotle: on friendship, 122, 130, 163; on the imperfection of the human condition, 169; on the incompleteness of mankind, 89; on love, 116, 128; and Montesquieu, 82; on sociability, 86–87
Arminius, 43
art of living, 162–65
asceticism, 193
atheism, 36
atomism. *See* individualism
attachment, 88–90, 129, 131, 205–6
Augustine, Saint, 21, 37, 128, 132
Augustinians, 62
Aurevilly, Barbey d', 177
autobiographies, modern, 147, 154
autonomy, 3, 47–79; vs. biological constraints, 41; and civil liberty, 88; conservatism on, 227; Constant on, 44, 71–79; definition of, 47; Descartes on, 55–61, 66, 67, 69, 72, 76; and equality, 232; and fraternity, 232; in humanist doctrine, 31, 33, 71; and

individualism, 80, 165, 228–29; of individuals, 139, 159; La Rochefoucauld on, 69, 70–71; vs. law, 54; liberty as, 31; and love, 136–38; Montaigne on, 48–54, 67, 69, 72, 76; Montesquieu on, 61–66; Pascal on, 69; Pico della Mirandola on, 51–53; Rousseau on, 41, 66–71; scientism on, 33; and sociability, 127; and the state, 233–34; Tocqueville on, 77. *See also* freedom; free will vs. determinism; liberty; will

Bacon, Francis, 37
Baudelaire, Charles, 174–77, 197, 232
beauty, 174–77, 175. *See also* aestheticism
Bénichou, Paul, 174
Bentham, Jeremy, 210
Bérulle, Pierre de, 38
biological determinism, 21–22
Bonald, Viscount Louis de, 10, 12–17, 24, 25, 234; on autonomy, 232; Constant on, 44; influence of, 16; on morality without religion, 14–15; on rights of man vs. rights of God, 15; *théorie du pouvoir politique et religieux,* 12–13, 14–15; on values, 161
Burke, Edmund, 15

Calvin, John, 12, 13, 14, 21
Calvinism, 60

Index

Campin, Robert, 147
Cartesianism. *See* Descartes, René
Catholicism, 199, 219
causality, 21–22, 62–64
Cellini, Benvenuto, 147
Charrière, Isabelle de, 92
Christianity: *agape* (love-charity), 119,
  128–30, 135, 163–64, 192; asceticism
  in, 193; on attachments, 88; on determinism vs. free will, 21; on good and
  evil, 193–96; on grace vs. freedom,
  43–44; on happiness vs. virtue, 202;
  humanism in, 43, 236–37; on human
  nature, inherent weakness of, 26; and
  Kantian thought, 193; on mankind as
  evil, 37; and morality vs. politics, 77–
  78; on original sin, 14, 196; vs.
  paganism, 208; and Platonism, 193;
  vs. polytheism, 222; Rousseau on,
  189, 190–96; on solitude, 111; and
  spiritual power, 174; on values, 161,
  162–65
Church. *See* Christianity; Protestantism;
  religion
Cicero, 98, 130, 163, 171
civilization, 178–79
civil religion, 191–92
commerce, human, 90–93
communication, 103, 109
communism, 161–62, 227–28
community, 13–14, 95–96
Conche, Marcel, 144
Condorcet, Marquis de, 10, 23
confession, 148–49
Confessions (Rousseau), 150–51
conscience vs. reason, 196–99, 204
conservatism, 11–16; on autonomy, 227;
  definition of, 4, 12; and democracy,
  31–32; on freedom, 20; vs. humanism, 33, 38–39, 45; on individualism
  vs. community, 13–14, 227; on
  knowledge, 35–36; modernity of, 11–
  12, 227; moral, 14; political, 14; and
  revolutionaries, 24–25; vs. scientism,
  44; on tradition, 15, 38; on values,
  39, 161

Constant, Benjamin, 7, 10, 25; *Adolphe,*
  91–93, 106; on autonomy, 44, 71–79;
  on Bonald, 44; on civil disobedience,
  78; on conservatism vs. scientism, 44;
  on death, 213; on decentered man,
  213–18; *De la religion,* 44; on egotism, 91–92; on free will vs. determinism, 71–72; on the French
  Revolution, 73; on the gaze of mutual
  recognition, 92–93; on Godwin, 223;
  on grace vs. freedom, 44; on independence, 105–6, 109; on interest, 209–
  13, 215–18; and Kant, 222–23; on
  legitimacy of government/law, 74–77;
  on the liberty of the Ancients vs.
  Moderns, 67, 75–76, 107–8; on love,
  123–24, 135, 138; on morality, definition of, 216–17; on morality and religion, 218–21; on morality and truth,
  221–25; on nature as the basis of
  law, 41; political activism of, 78–79;
  on the political vs. personal sphere,
  116; on religious feeling, 215–16; on
  Rousseau, 73–74; on sociability of
  mankind, 33, 90–93; on solitude, 94,
  106, 108; on the state of nature, 90–
  91; on totalitarianism, 78; on Utilitarianism, 216–17; on vanity, 92–93
contemplative vs. active life, 109–14,
  163
custom, 143–45, 188–89

Darwin, Charles, 23
death, 117, 213
decentered man, 213–18
Defoe, Daniel: *Robinson Crusoe,* 70
De la dignité de l'homme (Pico della
  Mirandola), 51–53
De la religion (Constant), 44
democracy: and conservatism, 31–32;
  and economics, 230; Euripides on, 67;
  and freedom, 2–3, 18–19; and humanism, 31–32, 231, 235–36; and individualism, 31; liberal/republican
  aspects of, 77; plurality within, 235–
  36; and religion, 219–20; Rousseau

on, 67; and scientism, 25, 31, 32, 229–31; Tocqueville on, 17–19
Descartes, René: on autonomy, 55–61, 66, 67, 69, 72, 76; Bonald on, 12–13; on friendship, 132; on individualism and community, 95–96; on knowledge, 57; on laws, submission to, 55; on love, 133; on mankind as master of nature, 37; on memory, 56; and Montaigne, 55–56, 57; on perfection and God, 89–90; on reason vs. tradition, 58–59; on solitude, 112–13; on theology vs. philosophy, 57
determinism, 20–22, 62–63. *See also* free will vs. determinism
devil's pacts, 1–3, 46
Diderot, Denis, 27–28, 99, 114, 188

education: humanism on, 38–39; and indeterminacy vs. shared values, 233; Montesquieu on, 64; Rousseau on, 38, 70, 184–87
egotism: and humanism, 42; and individualism, 26–27, 28; La Rochefoucauld on, 208; and love, 121; vs. sociability, 91–92. *See also* interest
Emile (Rousseau), 181–82
Encyclopedists, 27, 179
Enlightenment humanism. *See* humanism
enthusiasm, 213, 216–18
Epictetus, 98
Epicureanism, 202, 212
Epicurus, 28, 165, 203, 210
equality, 16–17, 31, 232
Erasmus of Rotterdam, 43, 44, 60, 62, 236
eros (love-desire), 119–24, 127
Esprit, Jacques, 172
Essays (Montaigne), 53, 146–48
ethics. *See* morality; morality, humanist; values
Euripides, 67
evil, 193–96
Eyck, Jan van, 147

Faust, Johann, 1–2
Ficino, Marsilio, 37

Francis, Saint (of Salesia), 128–29
fraternity, 31, 232
freedom: conservatism on, 20; and democracy, 2–3, 18–19; and fidelity, 126–27; grace, 43–44; vs. grace, 60; and individualism, 3–4, 26, 28; and love, 136–38; and morality, 85, 86; and necessity, 34, 44; political, 67; of reason, 2; as rejection of God, society, and self, 3–5; and socialism, 24. *See also* autonomy; free will vs. determinism; liberty; will
free will vs. determinism, 21–22; Constant on, 71–72; humanism on, 33–35; Montesquieu on, 62–65, 72; Saint Paul on, 21, 62
French Revolution, 3, 31, 73
friendship: Aristotle on, 122, 130, 163; Descartes on, 132; and the excellence of the individual, 163; Montaigne on, 48, 122, 125, 130, 132, 134–35, 155, 167; Rousseau on, 123

Galileo, 55–56
Gary, Romain, 233
gaze of mutual recognition, 86–88, 92–93
gentility, 169–74
German national socialism, 161, 227–28
glory, 94–95, 110–11
Gobineau, Joseph, 232
Goldschmidt, Victor, 25
good and evil, 193–96
Good Samaritan parable, 192
Greeks: on happiness vs. virtue, 202; humanism of, 43; vs. Moderns, 67, 75–76, 96–97, 107–9; on values, 162–63, 164–65
Grimm, 188
Grossman, Vasili, 233
Grotius, Hugo, 68, 85

habit, 143–45, 188–89
happiness, 169, 201–3, 205–6, 216–17
hedonism, 28
Héloïse, 129–30
Helvetius, 27–28, 44, 209, 210

Hobbes, Thomas, 65, 76; on conscience, 199; on freedom vs. grace, 60; on interest, 217; Montesquieu on, 81; on the state of nature, 80–81; on values, as chosen, 39, 42
Hugo, Victor, 174
Huguenots, 155
humanism, 29–36; active vs. passive, 32, 138, 160–61, 233–34; anthropological traits of, 231–32; and anthropology, morality, and politics, 30–31, 40; vs. atheism, 36; and autonomy, 31, 33 (*see also* autonomy); Christian, 236–37; vs. conservatism, 33, 38–39, 45; definition of, 4, 5, 6, 29–30; and democracy, 31–32, 231, 235–36; on education, 38–39; and egotism, 42; and equality/universality, 31; on free will vs. determinism, 33–35; on good vs. evil in mankind, 37–38; in history, 42–46; on imperfection, 236; incoherence/plurality of, 44–46; vs. individualism, 33, 38–39, 45; on knowledge, 35–36; and liberty, 32; limits of, 235; and love, 135–38; modern, 233; and morality, 32; on multiplicity of mankind, 34–35; naive perversions of, 38–39; and others, 235; political, 32; and politics, 233–34; prideful perversions of, 36–38; and religion, 36; vs. scientism, 33, 35, 38–39, 45; and self-consciousness, 32; and technology, 234; and universalism, 42; on values, as artificial but nonarbitrary, 39–40; the wager of, 236–37
humanitarian sphere of relations, 116, 119
humility, 208

idealism vs. realism, 148, 168–69
imperfection: Aristotle on, 169; humanism on, 236; and love, 132–35; Montaigne on, 38, 205, 236
independence, 105–9
individualism, 25–29; and aestheticism, 29; and autonomy, 80, 165, 228–29; and community, 13–14, 95–96; defini-

tion of, 4, 5, 26; and democracy, 31; Descartes on, 95–96; dissemination of, 29; on education, 38; and freedom, 3–4, 26, 28; on happiness vs. virtue, 202; vs. humanism, 33, 38–39, 45; on morality, 188–89; Rousseau on, 97, 150; and sadism, 28; and the self, disappearance of, 19–20; on sociability, 165; and solitude/egotism, 26–27, 28, 94–97; Tocqueville on, 17–18, 19–20, 29; and utilitarianism, 28–29; on values, 39, 162–65. *See also* individuals
individuals, 139–59; autonomy of, 139, 159 (*see also* autonomy; freedom); changeability of, 142–45; as ends, 127–32, 138, 145–49, 155–56; and the human condition, 154–59; Montaigne on, 229; Plato on, 133; plurality of, 140–42, 145, 159; resemblance among, 229; self and others, knowledge of, 153–54; uniqueness of, 116–19, 149–52, 159, 232; universality of, 157–59
interdependence, 80–93; attachment, 88–90; the gaze of mutual recognition, 86–88, 92–93; human commerce, 90–93; sociability, 82–86; the social nature of mankind, 80–82
interest, 209–25; Constant on, 209–13, 215–18; and death, 213; and decentered man, 213–18; definitions of, 210–11; vs. enthusiasm, 213, 216–18; Hobbes on, 217; La Rochefoucauld on, 207–9, 210; Montesquieu on, 217; and morality, 216–25; and religious feeling, 215–16; Rousseau on, 210–11, 217; and Utilitarianism, 216–17. *See also* egotism

Jansenism, 21, 37–38, 43, 173, 196
jealousy, 179
Jesuits, 21, 43

Kant, Immanuel, 30, 200; on autonomy, 47; and Christianity, 193; and Constant, 222–23; on dignity, 47; on happiness vs. virtue, 203; on the social contract, 84 knowledge: Descartes on, 57; humanism on, 35–36; of the past, 226; of self and others, 153–54; vs. wisdom, 60

La Boétie, Etienne de, 125, 130, 132, 134–35, 155–56
Lamartine, Alphonse de, 174
La Rochefoucauld, François De, 26–27; on autonomy, 69, 70–71; on convenience/conformity, 171–72; on egotism, 208; gentility in, 169–74; on humility, 208; on interest, 207–9, 210; on love, 132, 133; on pagan vs. Christian morality, 208; on self and others, 153; on truth, 170–71
legitimacy of government/law, 65–66, 68–69, 72, 73–77, 78
Lessing, Gotthold, 169
Levi, Primo, 233
Levinas, Emmanuel, 136
liberty: of the Ancients vs. Moderns, 67, 75–76, 107–9; as autonomy, 31; and humanism, 32, 232; Rousseau on, 186, 189; Tocqueville on, 16, 18–19, 41–42, 137. *See also* autonomy; freedom; free will vs. determinism; will
Locke, John, 76
love, 115–38; Aristotle on, 116, 128; Saint Augustine on, 128, 132; and autonomy/freedom, 136–38; Christian, 119, 128–30, 135, 163–64, 192; Constant on, 123–24, 135, 138; and death, 117; definition of, 115; Descartes on, 133; Saint Francis on, 128–29; and happiness, 205–6; Héloïse on, 129–30; and humanism, 135–38; of the imperfect, 132–35; and the individual as an end, 127–32, 138; and the individual's uniqueness, 116–19; La Rochefoucauld on, 132, 133; love-desire, 119–24, 127; love-joy, 119, 124–27, 131–32; Montaigne on, 120, 123, 125, 126, 130–31, 203; Saint Paul on, 128, 163–64; Plato on, 122, 127–28, 129, 130; Rousseau on, 118, 120–21, 122–23, 125–26, 132–34, 136, 203–5; self-love

vs. amour-propre, 82–83, 183; vs. sexuality, 118
Luther, Martin, 12, 14, 21, 43, 44

Machiavelli, Niccolò, 77, 217
Maistre, Joseph de, 14, 16
Mallarmé, Stéphane, 177
Malthus, Thomas, 91
Manicheanism, 193–94
Marx, Karl, 23
materialism, 27, 187–88, 212
memory, 50, 56
Mephistopheles, 1
Michelet, Jules, 174
Mill, John Stuart, 165, 232
modernity, 9–10, 226–27
Molina, 43
Montaigne, Michel de: on autonomy, 48–54, 67, 69, 72, 76; on confession, 148–49; on the contemplative life, 112; on custom/habit, 143–45, 188–89; and Descartes, 55–56, 57; on education, 38; on envy and malicious pleasure, 201; *Essays*, 53, 146–48; on friendship, 48, 122, 125, 130, 132, 134–35, 155, 167; on good and evil, 195; on good as a product of human, not God's, will, 53–54; on grace vs. freedom, 44; on happiness, 169; on the human condition, 154–59; humanism of, 42–43; on humanists vs. theologians, 6; on human life as unfinished/imperfect, 6; on idealism vs. realism, 168–69; on imperfection, 38, 205, 236; on individuals, as ends, 145–49, 155–56; on individuals, changeability of, 142–45; on individuals, plurality of, 140–42, 145; on individuals, resemblance among, 229; on individuals, universality of, 157–59; on knowledge, 36; on living in the present, 167; on love, 120, 123, 125, 126, 130–31, 203; on love of family, 48–49; on memory, 50; on morality vs. politics, 77; on nature vs. culture, 53; nominalism of, 141, 148; on reason, 50–52; Rousseau on, 151; on scholastic knowl-

Montaigne, Michel de (*cont.*)
edge, 50; on self-knowledge, 167; on
sociability, 109, 110, 112; on solitude,
94, 95, 98, 109–11; on truth, 169, 224;
on wisdom, 166–69
Montesquieu, Charles de: and Aristotle,
82; on autonomy, 61–66; on education,
38, 64; on evil as learned, 38; on the
flexibility of mankind, 34; on free will
vs. determinism, 62–65, 72; on Hobbes,
81; on interest, 217; on legitimacy of
government/law, 65–66, 68, 74–75, 78;
on man's purpose, 62; on moral vs.
physical causes, 63–64; on the natural
state of men, 81–82; on a scale of beings, 40–41; on sociability of mankind,
33; *The Spirit of the Laws,* 61
morality: and anthropology, 30–31, 40,
207; definition of, 160, 216–17, 219;
and freedom, 85, 86; and humanism,
32; individualism on, 188–89; pagan vs.
Christian, 208; vs. politics, 14, 77–78;
and religion, 13, 14–15, 189, 218–21;
vs. truth, 221–25. *See also* morality, humanist; values
morality, humanist, 178–206; vs. Christian
morality, 189, 190–96; and conscience
vs. reason, 196–99, 204; on duty and
natural goodness, 200–204; and education, 184–87; on good and evil, 193–96;
on happiness and love of others, 205–6;
on happiness vs. virtue, 201–3, 205; on
independence, 185–86; on liberty, 232;
and love, 203–5; pillars of, 232; vs.
scientism/materialism, 187–88

Napoleon I, emperor of France, 108, 211–12
nationalism, 228
Nazism (national socialism), 161, 227–28
necessity, 34, 44
Nicole, Pierre, 129
noble savage, 37
nominalism, 141, 148

Occam, William of, 26, 33, 43, 148
original sin, 196

Panetius, 170
Pascal, Blaise: antihumanism of, 232; on
attachments, 88–89, 129, 131; on autonomy, 69; on false virtues, 173; on individualism, 27; and the Jesuits, 21; on
theater, 173
Pascal, Gilberte, 90
past, knowledge of, 226
Paul, Saint: on free will vs. determinism,
21, 62; on good and evil, 193; on love,
128, 163–64
Pelagians, 62
Pelagius, 21, 36–37, 43, 89, 186, 196
personal sphere of relations, 116–17, 138
philanthropy, 119
philia (love-joy), 119, 124–27, 131–32
Philonenko, A., 102
philosophy vs. theology, 57
Pico della Mirandola, Giovanni, 142; *De
la dignité de l'homme,* 51–53
Plato, 52; on beauty, 133, 175; on individuals, 133; on love, 122, 127–28, 129,
130
Platonism, 111, 193
Plutarch, 53
political sphere of relations, 116–17, 138
polytheism, 222
Porphyrus, 158–59
Prometheas, 52
Protestantism, 37–38, 43, 199, 219
Proust, Marcel, 177
psychic determinism, 21–22

realism vs. idealism, 148, 168–69
reason: vs. conscience, 196–99, 204; freedom of, 2; Montaigne on, 50–52; vs.
tradition, 15, 58–60
recognition, gaze of, 86–88, 92–93
religion: Bonald on, 12–13; and democracy, 219–20; and humanism, 36; and
morality, 13, 14–15, 189, 218–21; religious feeling, 215–16. *See also specific
religions*
Renaissance, 77
Renan, Ernest, 176, 232
Robespierre, Maximilien, 217

Robinson Crusoe (Defoe), 70
Rogolot, François, 155
Rousseau, Jean-Jacques, 7, 79, 234; on
 Ancients vs. Moderns, 96–97; on attachments, 88, 90, 205–6; on authenticity, 204; on autonomy, 41, 66–71;
 Bonald on, 13; on Christian morality,
 189, 190–96; on Christians vs. philosophers, 44–45; on civilization, 178–79;
 on civil liberty, 88; on civil religion,
 191–92; Confessions, 150–51; on conformity, 19; on conscience vs. reason,
 196–99, 204; on consideration, 183–
 84; Constant on, 73–74; on democracy,
 67; and Diderot, 99, 114; on duty and
 natural goodness, 200–204; on education, 38, 70, 184–87; Emile, 181–82;
 on the Encyclopedists, 179; on friendship, 123; on the gaze of mutual recognition, 87–88, 92; on the general will
 and legitimacy of government/law, 68–
 69, 72, 73–74, 78; on the golden age,
 unattainability of, 181; on happiness
 and love of others, 205–6; on happiness
 vs. virtue, 201–2, 205; on independence, 185–86; on individualism, 13,
 97, 150; on individuals, 132, 149–52;
 on interest, 210–11, 217; on jealousy as
 source of misery, 179; on knowledge vs.
 wisdom, 60; on language, 86; on liberty,
 186, 189; on love, 118, 120–21, 122–
 23, 125–26, 132–34, 136, 203–5; on
 man vs. animals, 66–67; on Montaigne,
 151; on morality and society, 85, 86; on
 morality vs. politics, 77–78; on nature
 as habit, 189; on political freedom, 67;
 on the savage state, 182–83; on
 scientism/materialism, 187–88; on self
 and others, knowledge of, 153–54; self-
 judgment as man of nature, 101–4; on
 self-love vs. amour-propre, 82–83, 183;
 on sensitivity, 90; on sociability, 33,
 182, 189; on the social contract, 84; on
 solitude, 94, 97–101, 103, 104–5, 113–
 14, 181–82; on state of nature vs. state
 of society, 82, 83–86, 92, 100–101,

179–84; on tolerance, 191–92; universalism of, 190; on vanity, 87; on wisdom, 201

Sablé, Mme de, 172
Sade, D. A. F. De, 10, 27–28, 37, 204
Saint-Pierre, Bernardin de, 98–99
Saint-Simon, Claude de, 24–25
Sartre, Jean-Paul, 34
Satan's pacts, 1–3, 46
savage state, 182–83
scientism, 20–25; and autonomy, 33; vs.
 conservatism, 44; definition of, 4–5, 20;
 and democracy, 25, 31, 32, 229–31; on
 education, 38; on freedom, 22; on
 group will, 23; vs. humanism, 33, 35,
 38–39, 45, 187–88; on knowledge, 35–
 36; on knowledge of cause/effect, 22;
 modernity of, 20; technical, 230–31;
 and totalitarianism, 23–24, 161–62,
 227–28; as universalistic, 22; and utopianism, 24, 37, 63, 227–28, 230; on
 values, 23, 39, 161–62
self-consciousness, 32
self-interest. See egotism; interest
Seneca, 112
sensitivity, 90
sexuality, 118
Sieyès, Emmanuel Joseph Comte, 73
sociability, 82–86; Aristotle on, 86–87;
 and autonomy, 127; Constant on, 33,
 90–93; and decentered man, 214; vs.
 egotism, 91–92; individualism on, 165;
 Montaigne on, 109, 110, 112; Rousseau
 on, 182, 189; and society's ends, 233;
 and solitude, 109, 110, 112
social contract, 84
Social Darwinism, 161
social determinism, 21–22
socialism vs. freedom, 24
social nature of mankind, 80–82
Socrates, 157, 163, 193
solidarity, 118–19
solitude, 94–114; and the active vs. contemplative life, 109–14; and Christian
 thought, 111; and communication, 103,

solitude *(cont.)*
109; Constant on, 94, 106, 108; Descartes on, 112–13; and glory, 94–95, 110–11; and independence, 105–9; and individualism, 26–27, 28, 94–97; and the liberty of the Ancients vs. Moderns, 107–9; Montaigne on, 94, 95, 98, 109–11; and Platonism, 111; Rousseau on, 94, 97–101, 103, 104–5, 113–14, 181–82; and sociability, 109, 110, 112; and the state of nature, 100–101; and Stoicism, 98–99, 111
Sophists, 39
Spinoza, Baruch, 217
The Spirit of the Laws (Montesquieu), 61
Staël, Germaine de, 108, 124, 217–18
state of nature: Constant on, 90–91; Hobbes on, 80–81; Rousseau on, 82, 83–86, 92, 100–101, 101–4; and solitude, 100–101; vs. state of society, 82, 83–86, 92, 179–84
Stoicism, 26; on gentility, 173; on happiness vs. virtue, 202; on living in conformity with nature, 170; and solitude, 98–99, 111

Taine, Hippolyte, 21, 161, 232
Talma, Julie, 218
technology, 234. *See also* scientism
theology vs. philosophy, 57
Thèophile de Viau, 165
théorie du pouvoir politique et religieux (Bonald), 12–13, 14–15
Tocqueville, Alexis de, 16–20; on autonomy, 77; on conservatism vs. scientism, 44; on democracy, 17–19; on equality, 16–17; on free will vs. determinism, 35; on individualism, 17–18, 19–20, 29; on liberty, 16, 18–19, 41–42, 137; on materialism, 18, 19; on modernity, passage to, 226–27; on reason vs. tradition, 59–60; on well-being, pursuit of, 16–17, 18

tolerance, 191–92
totalitarianism, 23–24, 78, 161–62, 227–28
tradition, 15, 38, 58–60
truth, 169, 170–71, 224

universalism/universality, 31, 42, 190. *See also* equality
Usbek, 81
Utilitarianism, 28–29, 202, 216–17
utopianism, 24, 37, 63, 227–28, 230

values, 160–77; aestheticism, 174–77; the art of living, 162–65; Christian, 161, 162–65, 189, 190–96; conservatism on, 39, 161; and education, 233; and excellence, 163, 164; gentility, 169–74; Greek, 162–63, 164–65; and indeterminacy, 233; individualism on, 39, 162–65; La Rochefoucauld on, 169–74; living in the present, 167; loss of, 160; Montaigne on, 166–69; natural vs. artificial, 39–42; scientism on, 23, 39, 161–62; self-evidence of, 40; truth, 169, 170–71; wisdom, 166–69. *See also* morality; morality, humanist
vanity, 87, 92–93
Ventadour, Bernard de, 135
voluntary servitude, 155

Wilde, Oscar, 177
will: general, and legitimacy of government/law, Rousseau on, 68–69, 72, 73–74, 78; good as a product of human will, not God's, 53–54; supremacy of, vs. authority of religion/natural order, 9–10. *See also* freedom; free will vs. determinism
wisdom, 166–69, 201

xenophobia, 228